Business Studies Dictionary

M Steer

D1617766

Pitman

PITMAN PUBLISHING LIMITED
128 Long Acre, London WC2E 9AN

A Longman Group Company

© Pitman Publishing Limited 1985

First published in Great Britain 1985

British Library Cataloguing in Publication Data
Steer, M.
    Business studies dictionary.
    1. Business—Dictionaries
    I. Title
    338.6'03'21   HF1001

    ISBN 0-273-02413-2

Phototypeset in 9/11pt Palatino by 🅰 Tek-Art, Croydon, Surrey.
Printed and bound in Great Britain at The Bath Press, Avon.

Preface

The aim of this *Business Studies Dictionary* is to provide a comprehensive reference companion for students of Business Studies at intermediate and advanced levels.

Full coverage is given to all terms likely to be met at A level. B/TEC National and higher, RSA, LCCI and similar level examinations.

Topics covered include

Abbreviations (these appear at the end of the book)
Accounts
Advertising
Banking
British Constitution (functions of the Cabinet, legislature and judiciary)
Business organisation
Business organisations
City of London markets and institutions
Commercial services
Communications
Consumer protection
Economics
Employment and employer/employee legislation
European Economic Community (The Common Market)
Government organisations and services relating to commerce and industry
Industrial relations
Information technology
Insurance
International trade and its documentation
Law (in relation to British business)
Limited companies and company law
Marketing
Methods of payment
Physical distribution
Retailing
Stock Exchange
Transport
Warehousing
Wholesaling

Acknowledgements

The author and publisher wish to thank Kathy Cotton for her invaluable help in checking the entries and providing additional material.

A

Absorption Costing A costing system whereby *all* overhead costs—both fixed and variable—are apportioned first to cost centres and then to products. The costs are thus directly traceable and chargeable to such products and can act as a valuable guide to pricing policy.

Accelerator An economic concept that explains why investment demand fluctuates to a greater degree than demand for consumption goods. An increase in demand for a consumption good will raise the demand (the derived demand) for the factor of production, perhaps a machine, that makes it. But this derived demand will rise even faster than the demand for the product. This is because demand for investment goods is composed of a replacement and an expansion element.

In order to produce 1,000 articles a year a firm has installed 10 machines, each with a capacity of 100 articles per year, and with the understanding that one machine wears out and is replaced annually. The firm has an annual replacement demand for *one* machine. If demand rises so that the firm can sell 1,200 articles a year it might choose to install two extra machines to produce the output required. The firm's total demand for new equipment would now be *three* machines, one for replacement and two for expansion.

Acceptance credit Amount for which a bank will undertake payment in settlement of an international trade deal.

Acceptance of Bills of Exchange **A Bill of Exchange** is said to be 'accepted' when it is signed by the debtor, who promises to pay the amount shown when the debt falls due.

Accepting houses The Accepting Houses Committee is an association of 17 **merchant banks**. The accepting of **Bills of Exchange** drawn on London is still one of their main functions.

Accident insurance All insurance not covered by marine, fire or life assurance. This can be—

Insurance of liability This covers employer's liability for accidents at work; accidents which occur at public functions (the organiser will pay for insurance cover against such eventualities), and liability for accidental personal injury to or accidental damage to the property of third parties.

Insurance of property which covers a wide range of risks, including burglary and vandalism.

Motor vehicle owner's comprehensive policy which may cover damage to the car as a result of an accident, theft, fire, injury to the insured, and third party risks. (The first party is the insured, the second party is the insurer; third party may be other persons affected by the contract—passengers, pedestrians, cyclists, etc). Car insurance is compulsory before using a vehicle on the road.

Personal accident insurance covering personal injury. Short-term policies may be purchased to cover rail or aircraft journeys for persons travelling on their own, or for parties or groups.

A fidelity guarantee which can be taken out by firms to protect against dishonesty of employees,—for example, moneys embezzled from clients may be restored, but usually only after the employee has been charged in the courts.

Accommodation bill See **Bill of Exchange**

Account (Stock Exchange) There are 25 Account periods each year, usually each lasts for two weeks, but at Christmas and Easter they are longer. At the end of each Account 'bargains' cease and a new dealing period commences at once.

At the end of each period a very confused situation exists as to

2

who actually owns shares. The first seven working days of every period are spent in clearing and settling the accounts. During the first week speculators can make arrangements to carry bargains over to the new Account period. The following continuation facilities are available:

Contango is a payment made by '**bulls**' who wish to defer their purchase of shares because the rise they hoped for in prices has not come about.

Backwardation is a sum of money paid by a seller of stock for the privilege of postponing delivery of the stock until the next Account or any other future date.

Transfers are completed on Settlement Day in the second week of the account, when payments are made and stock delivered.

See also **Making-up Day, Ticket Day**

Account day On this day all bargains effected during the previous Account period are settled—normally this is the second Monday following the end of the Account, ie, the sixth working day of the new Account.

Account sales This is easier to understand if it is regarded as an account *of* a sale—it is a detailed statement of a transaction and is sent by an agent to his principal giving details of the goods sold on his behalf. It includes charges for freight, dock dues, **marine insurance**, and also the commission charged by the agent and expenses incurred by him in selling the goods. The final figure is the net proceeds of the sale.

Sometimes there is an additional *Del Credere* Commission shown; this is an extra charge by the agent for guaranteeing, and becoming responsible for, payment of the account on behalf of his principal.

Accounts An account is a statement of moneys received and paid with calculation of the balance. The accounts show the exact cost of the goods or services offered, what overheads are involved, and the exact revenue of the business.

A study of the accounts is essential to the formulation of a sound business policy for the future.

All **limited companies** are required by law to keep proper books of account, to record their transactions with regard to the purchase and sale of goods, the receipt and payment of moneys, and the assets and liabilities of the company. They must also prepare annually for the **shareholders** a **profit and loss account** and **balance sheet**; a copy of the balance sheet must be sent to the Registrar of Companies with the statutory annual return.

Accountability (in business) In general the principle of accountability is that those who conduct an enterprise should be accountable to those who provide the means which enabled the enterprise to be set up.

Acid test ratio The critical test of a firm's ability to meet its immediate commitments. The formula for calculation is:

$$\text{Acid test ratio} = \frac{\text{Liquid assets}}{\text{Current liabilities}}$$

Liquid assets would include cash, debtors (excluding bad debts). Current liabilities would include creditors and any amounts due but unpaid. A ratio of at least 1:1 is generally required. If not and the firm cannot cover current liabilities, then additional cash must be obtained. The term may also be referred to as the *quick* or *liquid ratio*.

Activity sampling A technique widely used within O & M. In order to establish the actual time taken to perform clerical tasks periodic observations are made of the activities under investigation. Observation times are calculated using random number tables and the overall length of the exercise is designed to capture information throughout a complete job cycle. The information gained is used as an aid to planning improved clerical methods.

Actuary An expert in life assurance who estimates premiums from statistical analysis of probabilities in the mortality, sickness and retirement fields.

Ad valorem duty This duty is charged 'according to value', so

4

that an *ad valorem* duty is one varying with the declared value of the goods; it is usually calculated as a percentage. See also **specific duty**.

Ad Valorem Stamp Duty   Government duties on Stock Exchange contracts are charged according to the value of the stocks and shares involved in the transaction.

Adjudication order   An order of the **Bankruptcy** Court, adjudging a debtor to be a bankrupt, and transferring his property to the **Official Receiver**, or a trustee appointed for the purpose.

Administration   The functions concerned with management of a business, or organising and conducting public affairs.

Administrative law   This is defined by Sir Ivor Jennings as 'the law relating to the Administration. It determines the organisation, power and duties of administrative authorities.' The activities of government departments, local authorities and public corporations require lawyers to be familiar with administrative processes likely to affect the rights and obligations of their clients. Broadly speaking it may be said that Parliament makes laws (the legislative function), government departments, local authorities and public corporations carry out the laws passed by Parliament (the executive function), and the Courts adjudicate disputes according to those laws (the judicial function).

Advertising   The means by which firms or individuals make known to the market what they have to sell, or what they want to buy. There are many reasons for advertising but these fall broadly into two categories: informative advertising—announcing a new or modified product or service, and persuasive advertising to show the merits and claims of a particular product as superior to the competition.

Media advertising—also known as above-the-line advertising—refers to the five traditional media of press, television, radio, cinema and outdoor (posters). This is mostly handled by advertising agencies who receive commission on the purchase of space, air time and sites. There is an increasing trend nowadays for firms to employ below-the-line advertising techniques, often handled by their own in-company advertising department. Six principal media come under this heading—direct mail, point-of-sale, sales promotion and merchandising, exhibitions and sales literature.

Advertising agency Besides undertaking market research for companies wishing to advertise, the advertising agent will create, produce and distribute advertisements using whatever media are suitable.

Advertising media The main fields of advertising are: the daily press, radio and television, the cinema, point of sale displays, hoardings, postal advertising, sample advertising, and telephone selling.

Advertising Standards Authority (ASA) This has been set up to improve the quality of informative advertising, to maintain standards within the industry, and to control dishonest and undesirable advertisements.

It supervises a code of advertising practice which is a detailed document setting out general principles to which advertisers and advertising agents should adhere. It is a voluntary code, but much more detailed in its requirements than the **Trade Descriptions Act**. There is provision for complaints made by the public about advertisements to be investigated, and for the authority to make recommendations where appropriate.

Advisory, Conciliation and Arbitration Service (ACAS) Established by the **Employment Protection Act 1975** the duties of ACAS are:
1 to offer conciliation and advisory services in an industrial dispute,
2 to provide conciliation services in any complaint about the working of **industrial tribunals**,
3 to refer matters which require arbitration, after advice and

conciliation services have been offered, to the Central Arbitration Committee,

4   to conduct enquiries into industrial relations in any particular industry or organisation,

5   to publish advisory material, guidance on 'codes of practice', and generally promote good industrial relations.

After-sales service   This is an essential service which must be offered by the retailer who sells consumer durables (washing machines, television sets, etc). These often carry a guarantee for a specified period, during which time the manufacturer is obliged to repair them free of charge.

Against all risks (aar)   Insurance against complete loss or any particular loss or injury that may be suffered in marine transit. This is the same as WPA (with particular average); in contrast an FPA policy (Free of Particular Average) covers only against total loss. 'Average' in this case means 'the expense or loss to owners arising from damage at sea to the ship or cargo'.

Agent   An agent is one who is authorised by another to act for him and in his name, the person who authorises him being called the principal. The two most common types of mercantile agent are brokers and factors. A **broker** merely sells the goods for his principal and arranges delivery, but never actually has the goods in his possession; he charges brokerage for his services. The **factor** actually has the goods in his possession, sells and delivers them to the buyer, and renders an account, less his commission, to his principal. Factors are particularly useful in the export trade.

   See also **commission agent, freight forwarding agent, insurance broker, overseas agent, auctioneer, del credere agent.**

Aggregate Money Demand (AMD)   Total demand by the public for entrepreneurial goods.

Agricultural co-operatives   These are formed by groups of farmers or growers who between them finance the purchase of

7

processing plant and distribution centres; profits are shared by the owners.

Aids to trade   Commerce is a comprehensive term covering all the operations involved directly or indirectly in the purchase or sale of merchandise or services. Trade is that section of commerce involved in buying and selling; the aids to trade are the commercial services necessary for trading to take place,—banking and finance, communications (including advertising), insurance, transport and warehousing.

Air charter party   This is a written agreement between the owner(s) of an aircraft and the merchant or other organisation wishing to transport goods or passengers by air. It gives details of the aircraft, the flight, and the price to be charged. The Baltair 1962 Air Charter Party originates from the **Air Freight Market** of the **Baltic Exchange**.

Air Consignment Note   Also known as the *air waybill*. This takes the place of the **Bill of Lading** which is used in sea freight consignments.

Three parts of the Air Consignment Note are recognised by law. The first marked 'for the carrier' must be signed by the consignor and kept by the carrier; the second copy marked 'for the consignee' must be signed by the consignor and by the carrier and sent to the consignee; the third part marked 'for the consignor' is signed by the carrier and handed to the consignor when the goods are accepted for shipment.

The consignee must present his copies of the Air Consignment Note, insurance policy and the invoice, before the goods can be claimed when they are landed.

Air freight market   The Baltic Air Freight Market of the **Baltic Exchange** operates very similarly to the **Freight Market** where those in search of a vessel to carry cargo are put in touch with those who have shipping space available. The Baltic Air Freight Market finds aircraft for cargoes and cargoes for aircraft, and deals with the 'tramp' aircraft who will fly anywhere with a cargo to make a profit.

Aligned documents Export documentation has been made simpler by the introduction by SITPRO (Simplification of International Trade Procedures Board) of the 'aligned series' of export documents—a complete set of documents of the same standard size with the same information in the same position. A master sheet records all the information required; where certain details are not required on a document these parts are blanked off.

The 'aligned series' enabled the reprographics industry to develop systems which can produce sets of export documents more quickly. Among these is the Rank Xerox Automatic Overlay Device.

Documents required for carriage by sea and air are
Bill of lading/sea waybill, air consignment note/air waybill, Commercial **invoice, Certificate of origin, Certificate of insurance, Standard Shipping Note**

SITPRO Postpacks, developed in co-operation with the **Post Office** and **HM Customs and Excise**, allow single-typing completion of all necessary documentation for exportation by parcels post.

Allonge (Bill of Exchange) A slip of paper annexed to a Bill of Exchange to give room for more endorsements.

Amalgamation The union of two or more firms into one concern in order to achieve an improved return on the firm's resources.

Amortisation The provision for the paying off of a debt usually by means of a sinking fund.

Annual abstract of statistics (Government publication) This covers hundreds of aspects of national activity. Among many entries of interest to the business world are statistics concerning production, energy, iron and steel, industrial materials, building and construction, and manufactured goods.

Annual General Meeting (AGM)   The Annual General Meeting of a **limited company** is a statutory meeting which must be held once a year in addition to any other general meeting. Notice of the meeting must be sent to all **shareholders**.

The Annual Report and Accounts, and the declaration of dividends are presented to shareholders at this meeting.

Societies and clubs hold AGM's, to which all members are invited, and at which the election of a committee takes place.

Annual Percentage Rate (APR)   **Hire-purchase** interest rates are often shown in such a way that they mislead consumers. It must be remembered that a flat rate quoted on the amount borrowed to purchase goods means that the rate is applied to the full amount borrowed over the whole period of the repayments. In fact, every time a repayment is made the amount owing is reduced and, strictly speaking, the interest payable on the remainder of the money owing should also be reduced. A true APR shows the amount of interest paid when this fact is not taken into consideration, and the APR is therefore a higher figure than the percentage rate quoted.

Under the 1974 Consumer Credit Act any interest quoted by the seller must be the true annual percentage rate, calculated to an agreed formula.

Annual Report and Accounts   The **Companies Acts** of 1948 and 1967 required public limited liability companies to publish—

The **profit and loss account**—a true and fair view of the financial position of the company.

The **balance sheet** showing **share capital** and the **reserves**, any **liabilities** and provisions such as loans and taxation, and the fixed and current assets.

The directors' report.

The Companies Act 1981 covers certain exemptions—a company with not more than 50 employees, a **turnover** which does not exceed £1.4 million and a **balance sheet** of not more than £700,000 may file an abbreviated form of accounts and is not required to submit a **profit and loss account**.

Apportionment The method of fairly dividing overheads between the cost centres of a business.

Arbitrage Buying **securities** in one country and selling them in another, with the object of making a profit.

Arbitration The referring of a dispute to an independent body for hearing and decision, when the parties involved have failed to agree a settlement.
See **industrial tribunals** and **advisory, conciliation and arbitration service** (ACAS)

Arbitrator A senior member of the **Baltic Exchange** who assists in the settlement of marine disputes. The London Maritime Arbitrators Association was set up in 1960 to encourage international arbitration in London.

Articles of Association An important document drawn up on the formation of a company. It regulates the internal administration; details the classes of shares to be issued; the rights of shareholders and the qualifications required of directors; sets out the rules relating to company meetings and accounting; details provision for winding up the company. *See* **Floating a company**.

Assets All the property and possessions owned by a business, including all debts due to the business.
Fixed assets are items acquired for use in a business over a prolonged period. Examples are plant and machinery, land and buildings, furniture and fittings, motor vehicles, trade marks, goodwill.
Current or circulating assets are acquired by a business for disposal in the course of trade and will quickly be renewed again. These are stock, sundry debtors, cash in hand and cash at the bank. 'Bills receivable' are sometimes shown as a current asset. These are **Bills of Exchange** which have not yet reached the date for payment.
Liquid assets are those which are available in cash or near cash form—the total of cash, bank moneys and debtors together form the liquid capital of a business.

11

Assurance *See* **life assurance**

Attitude survey A study designed to determine people's attitudes to or beliefs about specific factors. Because attitudes are relatively enduring in nature they have a particular interest for marketing strategists.

Auction sales Auction sales occur where the commodity cannot be standardised, and has to be sampled to decide its quality. One example is the London Tea Auctions at the Tea Trade Centre, where brokers representing growers from all over the world auction their lots to the highest bidders.

Auctioneer The auctioneer is an agent for a seller; he is authorised by licence to sell goods by public auction.

Audit An audit is the checking of accounts by reference to witnesses and **vouchers.**
Internal check This is applied to entries at the time they are being prepared; it is a **bookkeeping** arrangement which minimises the possibility of errors and fraud. Whenever possible no one person carries out all the jobs or prepares all the records connected with a particular activity.
Internal audit This is additional to the internal check and is performed by officials of the business; it is a physical check of the entries *after* they have been made.
External audit This is an examination of the accounts made by a person or persons from *outside* the organisation, usually a professional auditor who acts for and is appointed by the owners or shareholders.

In the case of **public limited companies** a company must appoint an auditor or auditors at its **Annual General Meeting** to hold office until the next AGM. The auditors have right of access at all times to the company's books, accounts and vouchers.

They must report to the members on the accounts examined by them.

Autarchy Self-sufficiency.

Authorised capital   The **nominal capital**. This is the maximum amount of money a company is allowed to raise by the issue of **shares**.

Automatic teller   A computerised cash dispenser that offers bank customers instant cash withdrawal facilities. The latest machines have the ability to give information on balances and handle requests for statements and cheque books. A few also take deposits.

Autonomous corporation   A corporation with legal status conferred on it by Act of Parliament, which is not subject to day-to-day parliamentary control by the House of Commons question time procedure. The Port of London Authority is one example of such a corporation.

Average adjuster   Average adjusters and ships' valuers assist in preparing and settling marine insurance matters.

Average clause   If a policyholder is under-insured (ie has insured his interest for a sum less than its actual value), his compensation will be paid in the same relative proportion as his insurance bears to the true value of his interest. This means that if he pays premiums for an insurance which is (say) three-quarters of the true value, the compensation he receives will be three-quarters of the amount required to compensate him completely for his loss.

Average rate of return   The ratio of **profit** (after **depreciation**) to **capital** outlay.

Average stock   The average stock figure is obtained by adding the opening stock figure to the closing stock figure and dividing by two.

To find the average stock held during a year the average should be taken of the stock held at the end of each month (ie, the annual total divided by 12).

The value of stock can be taken at cost price or selling price, but consistency in the use of one or other value must be maintained.

13

B

Backwardation   This is a sum of money paid by a *seller* of **stock** for the privilege of postponing delivery of the stock until the next Account or any other future day. See **contango**

Bad debts   When debtors cannot pay their debts, the debts are said to be irrecoverable. Bad debts must be written off the books by the end of the trading period as they represent actual losses, and must be charged against **profits** in the **profit and loss account**. **Debt factoring** is one method of minimising the harmful effects of bad debts on a business.

Balance   The sum required to make the two sides of an account equal, hence the surplus or the sum due on an account. A bank statement shows the customer whether he has a credit balance or is overdrawn.

Balance of payments   The balance of payments is the difference between imported goods *plus* payment for services bought from abroad, set against exported goods *plus* payment for UK services abroad which are paid for in this country.

Balance of trade   The excess of imports over exports, or exports over imports is called the balance of trade,—this is the figure for 'visibles'—ie, trade in **goods.**

Balance sheet   This is a summary of the **assets** (what the business owns) and **liabilities** (what the business owes) of an organisation, and sets out the financial position of an undertaking at a given point in time. These facts must satisfy two conditions—

There must be sufficient detail to enable a correct judgment to be formed.

They must be brief enough to make rapid assessment possible. *The Companies Act 1967* requires a balance sheet to present—

share capital and **reserves**, liabilities and provisions for loans and taxation, fixed **assets**, current **assets**, current **liabilities**.

Companies are required by law to publish their final accounts at least once a year. This takes the form of a published **profit and loss account** and **balance sheet**.

Balanced portfolio   A **portfolio** is a collection of securities held by one investor or institution. A portfolio is said to be 'balanced' if it contains securities of different types,—some 'gilt-edged', some sound industrial shares ('blue chips'), some debentures, and some risky, but sometimes very profitable, shares in finance companies.

Ballot   A method of voting used as an alternative to a show of hands, and which protects an individual member's right to secrecy.

Baltair 1962 Air Charter Party   See **air charter party**

Baltic Exchange   This is properly 'The Baltic Mercantile and Shipping Exchange'—the basis of the operations there being the verbal contract.

The three main activities of the Baltic Exchange are—

the **Freight Market** where cargoes are arranged for ships and ships for cargoes, the **Air Freight Market**, the **Grain Futures Market** and the Oil and Oilseeds Market

The Baltic Exchange also earns large sums by the sale and purchase of ships, and by acting as agents for dry-dock and ship repair specialists and for bunkering (the provision of fuel—nowadays oil—for ocean-going vessels). Senior members of the exchange act as arbitrators in international maritime disputes, and average adjusters and ships' valuers are available for assistance in marine insurance matters.

Bank bill/banker's acceptance   See **Bill of Exchange**

Bank certificate   A certificate issued by a bank for **audit** purposes, certifying the amount of a company's **balance** in the bank's books at a certain date.

Bank clearing   See **clearing system of the banks**

Bank credit   There are two requirements for a sound credit policy in banking—

that depositors shall be content to leave funds on deposit without making sudden demands,

that borrowers are credit-worthy.

Bank credit can be given in the following ways—

Banker's credit cards (Access, Barclaycard, etc)   Holders of such cards (who need not have a bank account) are allowed credit at establishments showing the relevant sign. The card holder is given a personal credit limit.

Bank loan   These can be made to current account-holders for a specific reason and for an agreed length of time. Interest is paid on the loan, repayment of which may be made by instalments or by a lump sum. **Collateral security** may be asked for by the bank for the duration of the loan.

Bank overdraft   Permission for current account-holders to overdraw on their accounts may be granted by the bank. This permits the drawing on an account of a sum in excess of one's credit at the bank, interest being charged on the day-to-day balance of the overdraft. **Collateral security** may be asked for by the bank.

Bank draft/banker's draft   This is a method of payment through the banks or Girobank. It is, in effect, a cheque drawn on the bank itself.

It is used if businesses are uncertain of the credit-worthiness of persons or firms who owe them money. They may then insist on payment being by means of a banker's draft, rather than by the normal cheque. This means that the firm which owes the money will pay their bank the amount they owe, and the bank will then make out a cheque drawn on itself and made payable to the creditor. This type of cheque is known as a banker's draft.

Bank loan   See **bank credit**

Bank of England   The Bank of England was chartered by Act of Parliament in 1694 to enable William III to carry on the war with France. The original charter was renewed several times, until in 1844 the Bank Charter Act was passed which split the organisation into two departments—the Bank(ing) and Issue Departments.
The Bank(ing) Department deals with banking operations as they affect the Government, commercial banks, the money market, and a few firms and individuals who have accounts with the Bank of England.
The Issue Department issues banknotes as required by the public, within the limits set by the gold reserves + a **fiduciary issue** which has no gold backing but is backed by Government-held securities.
   Each week the Bank of England issues a bank return which is separated into two parts also—
The Bank(ing) Department's return is really a balance sheet, showing assets and liabilities of the Bank of England at the date shown,
The Issue Department's return is concerned solely with the issue of Bank of England banknotes.
   The Bank of England was nationalised in 1946.
Bank overdraft   See **bank credit**

Bank rate   The official rate charged by the Bank of England for discounting first-class **Bills of Exchange**; it influences the rates of interest charged by all banks for the loan of money, and the rate of interest allowed on deposits.

Bank reconciliation statement   The bank balance shown in the cash book of a firm does not very often agree with the figure shown on a bank statement of the same date. This is quite normal, but it can conceal an error. It is therefore the practice in most firms to arrange to receive daily bank statements which are checked each morning with the balance in the cash book.

Bank return (Banking Department's Return) See **Bank of England**

Banker's bank Name given to the **Bank of England** as the depository for the working balances of commercial banks.

Banker's clearing house See **clearing system of the banks**

Banker's credit cards See **credit cards**

Banking A bank is an institution which collects surplus funds from the general public, safeguards them, makes them available to the owner when required, and lends money (at interest) to those who need it and who can provide security.
The functions of banking can therefore be summarised as follows—
collecting of money from the public
safeguarding such money
transferring money by means of cheques, credit-transfers, etc.
discounting **Bills of Exchange**
facilitating foreign trade
lending money to individuals or as institutional investors
   Banks earn a living by lending the money deposited with them to earn interest, and also by charging customers for their services.
   We have in the United Kingdom three 'tiers' of banking—
the **Bank of England,** the **discount market** and the **merchant banks,** the **clearing banks**

Banking act 1979 By this Act the term 'bank' is now restricted to institutions offering a full banking service, and who have been registered as 'banks' by the Bank of England.

Bank(ing) department See **Bank of England**

Banknotes (OED) In England and Wales the issue of banknotes is the monopoly of the **Bank of England**. These notes are, by law, a valid means of clearing debts; they are, like coin, **legal tender**.

Bankruptcy   If a sole trader's or a partnership's losses are serious, the business becomes insolvent and cannot pay its way,— it becomes bankrupt. (Companies are said to go into liquidation, and are dealt with by a procedure known as 'winding up'). An insolvent business is put into the hands of the **official receiver** who instigates a public examination of the firm's finances and business affairs. If it seems that debts cannot be paid the owner(s) will be declared bankrupt, the business and stock sold and creditors paid as much as possible.

Sole traders and most partnerships have unlimited liability and the personal effects of the owner(s) of such businesses can be sold to help pay off the debts.

Banks' Ombudsman   If a bank customer is in dispute with his bank, the banks' Ombudsman may be asked to settle matters.

The advantage of the scheme, is that the participating banks are bound by the Ombudsman's decision, and he will have powers to make awards up to £50,000; if the customer disagrees with the Ombudsman's findings he is still free to pursue a remedy through the courts.

Services covered will include all personal banking including complaints about cash dispenser machines and bank charges. The main exclusion is that customers will not be able to challenge a bank's decision to reject a loan application.

The Ombudsman is expected to be appointed in the autumn of 1985.

Bargain   Any **Stock Exchange** transaction; despite its name no special price is implied.

Barriers to entry   See **perfect competition**

Barter   Barter is the exchange of goods for goods, goods for services, or services for services.

Base rate   A rate of interest set by an individual bank to which the interest rates on most of its loans are linked.

Basic human needs   The three basic human needs are food, clothing and shelter.

Batch controls   A procedure for collecting documents for processing into sets of a predetermined quantity. The documents are counted, and one or more columns totalled, and the figures entered on a *batch control slip*. The totals arrived at after processing are checked against the batch control slip to ensure that nothing has been omitted and no errors made.

Batch production   The manufacture of a product in large or small batches or lots. Each operation is carried out on the whole batch before the next operation is started. It is a production method extensively used in the engineering industry or whenever a limited quantity of one type of product is authorised for manufacture at one time.

Bear   Speculator who sells shares, commodities or currencies in the hope of buying back at a lower price before he is due to deliver. A 'bear market' is a falling market.

'Bearer' cheque   A cheque payable to a 'bearer' requires no endorsement, and entitles anyone in possession of the cheque to present it for payment.

Bearer securities   Stocks and shares for which no register of ownership is kept by the company concerned.

Beneficial owner   The ultimate owner of a security, regardless of the name in which it is legally registered.

Bid   1   Indicates what a buyer is prepared to pay for shares.
2   An approach made by one company wishing to purchase the entire share capital of another company.

Bill of Exchange   The legal definition of a Bill of Exchange is that it is 'an unconditional order in writing addressed by one person to another, signed by the person giving it, requiring the person to whom it is addressed to pay on demand, or at a fixed or determinable future time, a sum certain in money to, or to the order of, a specified person or to the bearer'. It is, in effect, a promise to pay a debt to a creditor on a set date (usually in 90 days' time). A Bill of Exchange is said to be accepted when it is signed by the debtor, who promises to pay the amount shown when the debt falls due. The signed Bill is a legally binding document and banks will accept such Bills and pay the holders for them, knowing that on a certain date the money can be collected. The bank's charge for this service is known as a discount, and the service is known as 'discounting Bills of Exchange'.

A Bill of Exchange is a negotiable instrument and can therefore be passed into the possession of another person – not necessarily a bank. When this is done the Bill should be endorsed (signed on the back) by the holder before it is passed on. If a Bill is endorsed so often that there is no room for any further names, a piece of paper—an 'allonge'—may be pasted on the Bill to allow for further signatures.

A Bill of Exchange is not an alternative to a bank loan or overdraft. It is a method of payment whereby the seller receives early payment and the buyer enjoys 90 days' credit, during which time the transaction will normally have been completed.

An Accommodation Bill is one that has been issued without value having been received; it is used to advance a sum of *money* to the payee.

Bank Bills have been signed or endorsed by a reputable bank.

Foreign Bills are either drawn in Great Britain and payable in some other country, or vice versa.

Inland Bills are both drawn and payable in Great Britain.

Trade Bills are used in commercial transactions.

A Documentary Bill of Exchange is used in international transactions; it is sent to an accepting bank with the shipping documents, without which the importer cannot claim the goods when they are landed. This Bill contains a clause to the effect that documents are to be surrendered to the importer only against payment (D/P), or in some instances against acceptance (D/A) of the Bill of Exchange.

Bill of lading   This is an official detailed receipt given by the master of a vessel to the consignor, by which he makes himself responsible for safe delivery of the goods. (See also **sea waybill** and **common short form b/l**). A ship's manifest is the total of all the bills of lading for one particular voyage.

Bill of materials   A detailed specification listing every component used in the manufacture and assembly of a product. It is important to the work of many of the production team: to the production planner in scheduling work through the factory; to the materials controller for requisitioning stocks to meet production needs; and to the accountants for calculating the materials' cost for a product.

Bill-broking   Bill-broking is a means of dealing in money,— taking it from those who have a surplus and distributing it to those who need it—by using the Bill of Exchange.

The 12 firms who are members of the London Discount Market Association specialise in bill-broking. To keep the profit margin to a minimum no expensive paper work is involved, and almost all the deals are by word of mouth.

Bill-brokers borrow money from banks, commercial firms and institutional investors. This money can be—

'Call money' which is repayable on demand, 'Short-notice' money which is usually repayable in a few days, (commercial firms wishing to lend surplus money can leave it 'at seven days' notice' to earn higher rate of interest). Institutional investors may 'run risks' with short-term investments.

With this borrowed money *bill-brokers lend to*

The Government—by discounting **Treasury Bills**, the commercial banks—by discounting or rediscounting **Bills of Exchange** if the banks cannot afford to keep them until maturity, commercial firms, by discounting **Commercial Bills**.

There is a constant movement of bills between the **discount houses** and the banks, depending on where there are surpluses of money.

Local authority bonds and **certificates of deposit** are also dealt with by the **discount houses**.

Bill-leak   Banker's acceptance held outside the banking system.

Billingsgate Market   The London fish market which has recently moved to new premises in the West India Dock Road.

Block discounting   See **finance houses association**

Blue chip   Term for the most highly regarded industrial shares.

Board of directors   See **directors, board of**

Bond **1** 'An agreement or engagement binding on him who makes it.' The Stock Exchange motto 'my word is my bond' uses the word in this sense.
2 The owners of bonded warehouses give a *bond* to the authorities promising not to release goods from the warehouse until the duty has been paid and a customs officer present at the payment. Goods in such warehouses are said to be 'in bond'.
3 A security issued by a government, nationalised corporation or a company which carries a fixed rate of interest to the holder. *Company bonds* are called **debentures.**

Bonded warehouse   A bonded warehouse is a warehouse owned by a company or private individual, but under the control of the Customs and Excise officers of the United Kingdom, where goods which are subject either to Customs or Excise Duties may be stored pending payment of duty; such goods are said to be 'bonded' or 'in bond'.

The owner or occupier of such a warehouse enters into a 'bond' with the **Customs and Excise** authorities undertaking that no goods in them shall be removed for home consumption until the duty has been paid. When the whole or part of the goods in the warehouse are sold duty is then paid on the quantity withdrawn from 'bond'. This service relieves the importer of the obligation of paying a large amount of duty at one time.

Preparation for sale, but not manufacturing, can eventually be carried out in a bonded warehouse before duty is paid; among these activities are the bottling of wines and spirits, blending and packaging of tea and coffee, and the packing of tobacco.

Bond washing   The **Inland Revenue** defines this as the practice whereby income on fixed interest securities, basically gilts, is converted into **capital**. It then becomes chargeable to **Capital Gains Tax**, a far more lenient tax than **Income Tax**, especially for higher tax-payers. In February 1985 the Chancellor of the Exchequer decided to outlaw 'bond washing',—a 'laundering' technique which cost the Exchequer £300 million a year in lost revenue—the legislation to come into effect in February 1986. By blocking the loophole which enables income to be changed into capital the Revenue brings the income streams on gilts into line with equities.

Bonus   **1**   Annual profit credited to certain life assurance policies, or discretionary payment which may be made on a matured contract.
2   Extra company **dividend** sometimes paid on exceptional profits.

Bonus share   A prosperous company may, if authorised by its **Articles of Association**, make an issue of bonus **shares** to its **shareholders**. The company capitalises its profits by using some of the profits to increase its **share capital**; the amount of the increase covers the issue of bonus **shares** which are offered to its present **shareholders** in proportion to their holdings. (Known also as **scrip issue**).

Bookkeeping   A systematic method of recording the transactions of a business in books of account.

Bought Ledger   Also called the Purchases Ledger; this contains all the personal accounts of creditors.

Bought note   This is a contract note sent by a buyer to a seller stating the terms and conditions of a purchase arranged orally, or a note sent by an agent to his principal giving full conditions of a purchase of goods on his behalf.

Bradford Wool Exchange   A highly-organised market where wool 'tops' and 'noils' are bought and sold.

Branding   A 'branded' article is one where the trade name or brand has been registered in some official way, and where the manufacturer has created and preserved a 'brand image' by advertising.
   Many large retailers buy 'own brand' goods from manufacturers. The manufacturer will package the goods for the retailer who often sells them more cheaply than goods bearing the manufacturer's own **trade mark**.

Break-even analysis   A technique concerned with finding the point at which revenues and costs coincide, i.e. neither a profit nor a loss is made.

Break-even point   This is reached when the total costs of a firm equal the total sales revenue.

Breaking bulk   This is buying in large quantities and breaking down into smaller quantities before resale.

Bridging loan   Money borrowed (usually from a bank) pending the sale of an asset. Often necessary in housing transactions.

British Government Stock   This forms a part of the 'gilt-edged' market of the **Stock Exchange**, and is issued by the government with the primary object of providing long-term funds for government expenditure.

25

British insurance market   Lloyds Corporation (Lloyds of London) is the centre of the British insurance market, which includes many very large insurance companies.

A business requiring insurance can approach one of the large companies (or its agent) direct. Alternatively he may obtain insurance cover through an **insurance broker**, who will secure the most competitive rate from a member of **Lloyds** or a company specialising in the type of insurance required.

British Overseas Trade Board (BOTB)   The Board consists of representatives of industry and commerce and of the **Confederation of British Industry**, the **Trades Union Congress**, and the Departments of Trade and Industry, the **Export Credits Guarantee Department** and the Foreign and Commonwealth Office. (See also **export services provided by BOTB**).

British Standards Institution   This organisation lays down minimum standards in the manufacture of consumer goods; the BSI 'kite-mark' sign indicates that goods are of the quality required by the BSI specification.

Though the BSI has no authority to enforce its recommendations, it has considerable influence. For instance, the Government now compels manufacturers of electrical goods and motor cycle crash helmets to produce such goods to BSI specifications.

British Technology Group   This is a public corporation ultimately reporting to the Department of Trade and Industry. BTG is the name under which the **National Research Development Corporation** and the **National Enterprise Board** have been co-operating since 1981 following the government's decision to combine the two organisations.

BTG's objective is to promote the development of new technology into commercial products particularly where the technology originates from public-sector sources such as universities, polytechnics, research councils and Government research establishments.

Under the BTG corporate plan it will concentrate its future

efforts on technology transfer, helping British industry to exploit technology from UK public sector sources. These activities will be a continuation and extension of NRDC's role in promoting the development and exploitation of inventions.

British Weeks A British Week is a promotion of British consumer and consumer durable goods at the point of sale in a selected location overseas, and is organised and financed by the Department of Trade with the British National Export Council.

Two major British Weeks are held annually, supplemented by several minor British Weeks. Their aim is to achieve an interest in all things British, especially trade with Britain, the organisation being backed by widespread advertising.

Broker Broker is the most commonly used term for dealers on the commodity markets.
See **import brokers, insurance brokers**

Brokerage The commission paid to a broker on the business done by him.

Budget A budget is a statement of the probable revenue and expenditure for the ensuing year, based on a prepared plan which fixes standards of materials, wages and expense costs to be incurred during that period.
Budgetary control is the name given to a general scheme whereby every effort is made to ensure that the performance of a business conforms to the figures predicted in the budget of the business.

Budget Day is held on a Tuesday in March/April each year when the Chancellor of the Exchequer presents to Parliament the Government's plan for raising the money needed in the coming year,—the fiscal programme. See **economy, control of.**

Budget account 1 A budget account with a clearing bank or the Girobank will enable a bank customer to spread his payments more evenly. For instance, all household expenses (mortgage payments, gas, electricity, telephone, holidays, etc) may be

27

totalled for the year, and the total divided by 12. Each month this figure is taken out of the current account of the householder and placed in a budget account which has a separate chequebook. The householder can draw on this account up to three times the monthly figure.

2   Budget accounts are also schemes operated by shops for the benefit of regular customers. By paying a stipulated amount each month by **standing order** the customer is able to obtain credit up to a stated number of multiples of the amount paid. As the debt is reduced monthly the customer is always able to obtain credit on further goods up to the limit of his individual credit; it is a system of *revolving credit*.

Building society   This organisation offers facilities to savers who receive interest, and uses the money deposited to provide mortgages for the purchase of property; mortgagors pay interest on the money they borrow.

Building societies do not make a profit,—the money received from savers and the interest they receive from investment as **institutional investors** is balanced against the money they lend to house buyers.

Bulk cargoes   Bulk cargoes of one primary commodity only are usually handled by the **commodity markets** whose middlemen finance, transport and warehouse the goods.

Bulk carriers   Large bulk carriers are used for transporting iron ore, coal and oil. A system of charges, known as '**worldscale**', is used when chartering these large vessels.

Bulk transactions   The principle of bulk transactions holds that there are general advantages in dealing in large quantities. Firstly, most suppliers are prepared to offer discounts on large quantities; secondly, the transport costs of large movements are generally less, especially when very large crude carriers or container ships are used; thirdly, the documentation of large orders is very much the same as that for small orders.

Bull   One who has bought a security in the hope of selling it at a higher price.

Bull market   One in which **bulls** prosper; a rising market.

Bullion markets   The price of gold is dictated by supply and demand, which at any particular time varies from one world centre to another. In London the price is 'fixed' by the five merchant bankers who form the *London Gold Bullion Market*, and who meet twice daily in the Rothschild offices for the ritual 'gold-fixing'. Buying and selling prices are normally expressed in US dollars per fine ounce.
The Silver Bullion Market operates in much the same way as the Gold Market but has only three members; there is only one 'fixing' a day, and quotations are made in both sterling and dollars.

Bunkering   The fuelling of ships.

Bureaucracy   Refers to the nature of authority and communications in industrial organisations and particular work settings. It is characterised by limited spheres of authority in which responsibilities clearly relate to organisational position. Communication patterns follow the hierarchical nature of the organisation.

Business Expansion Scheme   This is a new tax incentive scheme, both for proprietors of a business who are looking for outside investors to provide new **capital**, or for investors looking for an unquoted **company** in which to invest. Like its predecessor the Business Start-up Scheme, it can substantially reduce the cost to an investor of his investment (so increasing the profit), and also greatly enhances the ability of the unquoted company to attract new **equity**.

Business units   An organisation engaged in business is a business unit. The type of unit it is can be determined by identifying who provided the **capital** (the owner or owners), and who receives the profits.

Business units

The United Kingdom has a 'mixed economy' which means that some organisations are privately owned, and some are publicly owned and run by the Government and local authorities.

The following is a list of the different types of business unit:

Private Sector
Sole trader, partnership, Private Limited Company, Public Limited Company, holding companies.
Non-profitmaking Units (in the **private sector**)
Co-operative societies, friendly societies, many different clubs and societies, and agricultural and productive co-operatives.

Public Sector
Central Government Departments, public corporations, local government (County Councils and District Councils).

C

Cabinet The executive is one of the three divisions of the government, the others being the legislature and the judiciary. The Cabinet is the focal point of the executive which formulates government policy. Once policies become law they are put into effect by Central Government departments such as the Department of Trade and Industry, the Department of Energy, the Department of Employment, etc.

Cabinet ministers are the body of men chosen from the political party in power to fill the highest executive offices in the state. They direct the government and are collectively responsible to **Parliament** for every act of the Crown.

Call The amount due to be paid to a company by the purchaser of nil-paid or partly-paid shares.

Call money Bill-brokers are prepared to borrow money from any source and repay as required. Money which is borrowed and repayable on demand is known as 'call money.'

Call option An option to buy **shares** at a future date at an agreed price, whatever happens to the market.

Capital Together with labour and land, capital is one of the three factors of production; it is wealth set aside to produce further wealth. A firm's capital represents its total financial resources.

Sources of capital The primary source of capital is savings—either voluntary savings or by way of taxation—which are invested in businesses. There are many private individuals who are investors, but the funds of the large institutional investors provide the greater part of the investment funds available.

Authorised capital The amount of share capital a **limited company** is authorised to raise. By the Companies Act 1980 the minimum capital required for a **public limited company** is £50,000.

Called-up capital The amount the company actually receives from the shareholders, who may not be required to pay the full face value of their shares on allotment.

Capital employed The sum of the assets the firm is using, whether borrowed or not—the fixed **assets** + working **capital**.

Capital owned This is calculated by deducting the firm's **liabilities** from its assets. The surplus represents the **capital** owned by the firm at the date calculated.

Circulating capital (sometimes called *floating capital*) The flow of money through an organisation—ie, the current **assets**—provides the resources to use the fixed assets to the best advantage. Circulating assets are used only once in production; they comprise stock, cash and amounts owed to the firm.

Fixed capital This consists of material goods used for the production of further goods—premises, plant, machinery; they are used many times to make a profit.

Issued capital The amount of share capital which the directors decide to issue to the public. The amount they do issue, and which is actually paid for is the *issued* or *paid-up capital*.

Liquid capital That part of the **assets** of a business which can be easily transferred into cash or near cash; the total of cash, bank moneys, and debtors.

Loan capital What a company has borrowed, either on **mortgage** or by issue of debentures.

Minimum capital 1 By law a (Public) **Limited Company** must have an authorised capital of at least £50,000.

2 The minimum amount of capital which is declared by the directors of a new company to be necessary for the company to commence business. If the minimum amount is not subscribed the

amount already collected must be returned to those who subscribed it.

Nominal capital   The authorised or share capital. The amount of capital the company is authorised to raise by the sale of shares.

Share capital   The total amount of capital subscribed by the shareholders.

Social capital   Taxes and rates are enforced 'savings' which finance the building of roads, bridges, hospitals, schools, etc. which collectively form the 'social capital' of a nation.

Trading capital   The total of the fixed and circulating capital of a business is sometimes referred to as the trading capital.

Working capital   Amount of capital needed to carry on a business from day to day. It is calculated by deducting current **liabilities** from current assets. (Amounts owed to creditors are the current liabilities; stock, cash in hand, cash at the bank, and the amounts owed by the debtors form the current assets).

Capital account (Balance of Payments)   This is made up of long-term transactions,—private long-term investments, long-term Government loans, and transactions with overseas monetary authorities such as the **International Monetary Fund** (IMF).

The current account of the **balance of payments** in international trade is the balance between British imports and exports (visibles and invisibles).

Capital assets   Most businesses own certain equipment—premises, machinery, furniture, etc. These are capital assets and are used to increase the production of goods and services.

Capital expenditure   The acquisition of fixed **assets** such as plant or equipment which will be used over a long period of time.

Capital Gains Tax   When individuals sell an asset such as securities, works of art, or land, they are deemed to be trading and consequently pay Capital Gains Tax on any profit or gain made.

Capital gearing   The ratio between a company's different sources of finance—ie, between a company's **equity** (ordinary **shares** and dividend capital) and its permanent loan capital (**preference shares** and **debentures**). When deciding which source of finance to use, the cost of the sources and the company's expected yield will influence the balance between the different sources.

Capital goods   Goods which are produced for other producers to use in a further stage of production. Also called **producer goods**.

Capital market   When an individual saves money he places it for safe keeping with a bank, building society, insurance company, unit or investment trust, and all pension schemes collect vast amounts of savings from members. These 'collecting' organisations are institutional investors who invest the money in profitable ways, either in other industrial concerns which have a need for capital investment, or by lending it to other borrowers, such as the government, whose income is inadequate to meet the current requirements. The capital market exists to bring the two sides together.

Capital owned   See **capital** (types of)

Capital reserves   Reserves created by some extraordinary activity of a company, such as those created by revaluation of property.

Capital Transfer Tax   A tax applied to all gifts over a fixed sum, the tax varying according to the sum transferred.

Capitalisation of reserves   This is the process by which a company changes reserves of money into **capital** by a *bonus issue* (see **bonus shares**), thus recognising the fact that the reserves concerned are no longer available as possible **dividend**.

Captain's protest   In the case of claims in marine insurance this is a sworn statement by the captain of the vessel which gives particulars of the loss and the cause of it.

Cargo insurance The existence of an insurance policy in conjunction with **bill of lading** is absolutely vital in the import and export trade.

Cargo policies refer to the insurance of goods moving into or out of a country.

Floating policies give cover for a specified sum, and eliminate the necessity of insuring each cargo separately. When the amount is spent the floating policy is renewed.

Open-cover agreements are at a prearranged rate for any consignment up to a certain limit notified to the **underwriter** for a particular vessel, on a particular voyage. The policies are issued after notification.

Cargo liners These are vessels which carry mainly cargo but which have a few cabins for passengers. They usually keep to definite routes and schedules.

Carriage forward This means that the cost of carriage is borne by the buyer.

Carriage paid This means that the cost of carriage is borne by the seller.

Carriers Local carriers operate on a fixed route in a local area.
Universal carriers will accept goods for any destination.
See also **common carrier**

Cartel A combination of firms formed for the sake of greater economies; unlike a trust it is not usually regarded as a permanent arrangement.

Cash Cash is usually understood to mean 'ready money', or money in a bank, but has also come to denote banknotes, cheques, and other documents containing an order to pay on demand.

New notes and coins are issued to the public by the commercial banks though they originate from the **Bank of England** and the

Royal Mint. Banks also withdraw badly soiled or mutilated notes from circulation.

Cash against documents   For goods imported into a country the terms are nearly always 'cash against documents'. The foreign exporter draws a **Bill of Exchange** against the importing firm; to this document he attaches the **invoice, bill of lading,** and the insurance policy. This Documentary Bill is then sent to the banker in the importing country who will receive payment on behalf of the foreign importer, before the goods are delivered to the importer.

Cash and carry warehouse   These warehouses compete with the traditional wholesaler and are like 'wholesale supermarkets', dealing in bulk; they offer neither credit (though some accept bankers' credit cards) nor transport facilities, this saving on overheads enabling them to charge lower costs to retailers. Their 'cut-price' policy is attractive to the small shopkeeper, for whom they are also open at convenient hours—before and after 'shop hours'.

There is a growing tendency for the 'cash and carry' to open its doors to the public, these 'discount stores' presenting a new type of competition to all retailers.

Cash book   This is really a part of the **ledger** and is not a subsidiary book, although it is a book of original entry. It is kept by the cashier and in it are entered the monies received or paid away by the business.

It provides a suitable record from which entries may be posted to their respective ledger accounts.

Cash discount   A small concession given to customers for prompt payment of a bill.

Cash flow   The money obtained from selling goods or services is used to finance further production. Any major delay in receiving money will probably cause a firm to have cash flow problems and run into financial difficulties.

Businesses should aim to maintain a constant flow of cash into the firm so that working **capital** is always available. Working capital is often more important than profitability.

The price of a product also determines how much income an organisation will obtain from its capital outlay. It greatly influences the cash flow into an organisation, and consequently affects its acquisition of additional resources.

If working capital is insufficient cash will not be available to pay creditors, purchase raw materials, or pay wages; without raw materials production will suffer.

On the other hand, holding too much cash is expensive and inefficient; it should be remembered that money must be employed to generate profit.

Cash limits   Local authorities and government departments do not make profits and are given funds from public sources which they allocate to different (and competing) projects, according to political policy decisions. The Budget sets cash limits on the amounts government organisations can spend, though local government councillors have powers of discretion on expenditure within the cash limits set by central government.

Cash ratio   Early bankers observed that only 8% of their customers' funds were likely to be demanded in cash at any time, which left them free to lend the remaining 92% at interest. In fact the **Bank of England** requires that 10% must be retained by the banks in cash, and a further small percentage—a 'special deposit'—can be called in by the Bank of England to control credit policies. Overall this is the *cash ratio*.

Cash sales/cash transactions   The advantages to a business of the cash trade are—
A smaller **capital** is required;
There are no bad debts;
There is less bookkeeping.

Casting vote   If the **Articles of Association** expressly provide it, the chairman of a meeting has a second or casting vote in addition to his right to vote as a member, and he may use this in the event of an equality of votes.

Caveat emptor   This means 'let the buyer beware', and is an early rule from contract law which still applies today. In placing an order it is up to the buyer to examine carefully what he is about to buy.

Central bank   The central bank, or government's bank of the United Kingdom is the **Bank of England**, which was nationalised in 1946 and which exercises a general control of the monetary and banking systems of the country. Many overseas central banks have accounts with the Bank of England.

Central bank balances   The balances, or deposits, that commercial banks keep with the central bank.

Central government   The three functions of government are the legislative, executive and judicial functions. The legislative function is performed by the Queen in Parliament, the executive function by the Cabinet with the assistance of the *Civil Service*, and the judicial function by the judiciary under the Lord Chancellor.

Central Office of Information   The COI issues many publications, including reports on particular industries and areas; it also runs an intelligence service which answers individual enquiries from commerce and industry.
   The COI offers a very comprehensive publicity service for British exporters, and advice on all aspects of international trade.

Central Selling Organisation (CSO)   This is a London-based marketing organisation whose companies sort, value and sell rough diamonds to the world's major diamond-cutting centres and industries.

Centralisation   The concentration, at one centre, of the government of a country or the administration of an organisation.

Certificate of Deposit (CD)   See **discount houses**

Certificate of Incorporation   Sent by the Registrar of Companies to a newly-registered company as its 'birth certificate', after initial documents (including the **Memorandum of Association** and the **Articles of Association**) have been lodged with him and approved by him. This gives the company a legal personality and allows its shares to be sold to secure the capital it needs.

Certificate of Insurance   This provides proof that the goods have been insured against loss or damage during transit. It is one of the necessary documents which must accompany a Documentary **Bill of Exchange**, others being the **bill of lading** and the **invoice**.

Certificate of Origin   This certifies that goods have been manufactured in the country stated, and is used by customs to indicate the amount of duty payable on a particular item. The duty that an importing country imposes on goods varies according to the country from which they originate.

Certificate of Trading   This must be received by a **public limited company** from the Registrar of Companies before it can begin business. When the **shares** of a limited company have been sold and the minimum **capital** assured, the new company must apply to the Registrar of Companies for a Certificate of Trading which will be granted if all the statutory documentation is in order.

Chain of commerce, chain of distribution, chain of production These are alternative titles for the route by which consumer goods reach the final consumer.

Chain store   The chain store is a multiple which sells a variety of goods; it is one of a large number of branch shops, each of which usually exhibits the same appearance, especially in the shop front and window design.

Challenging   The method of dealing on the London Gold and Silver Bullion Markets. Twice every day (for gold) and once a day (for silver), the **brokers** meet and challenge one another until a firm price is fixed.

Chambers of Commerce   Many towns and cities have Chambers of Commerce. Membership is made up of the representatives of local firms engaged in industry and commerce. Their purpose is to promote trade and help members with problems connected with trade and manufacturing, both at home and abroad. The London Chamber of Commerce also conducts examinations in commercial subjects.

Many Chambers of Commerce throughout the country are concerned with export promotion and will provide information for those wishing to export. In association with trade associations and export clubs they will also undertake specific overseas research, often receiving assistance from the British National Export Council. There is also an International Bureau of Chambers of Commerce.

Chambers of Trade   Many towns and cities have a local Chamber of Trade. Membership is made up of representatives of large shops and smaller shopkeepers. They promote efficient trading and protect the interests of local retailers.

Charter party   In maritime law this is a contract between the owner or master of a ship and a person who hires the ship or part of the ship for the purpose of conveying goods from one port to another. The vessel may be hired for a particular period of time (time charter), or a particular voyage (voyage charter).

Chartering agents   These agents represent merchants or organisations who wish to charter ships. The charter is a 'document of rights' and may be

1   *A Time Charter*, covering a stated period of time.
2   *A Voyage Charter*, covering a particular voyage.

Check trading   This is a type of credit for small purchases. Checks are available in various denominations from agents (tallymen) who make a regular round to collect payments. The checks can be used to buy goods at a large number of shops participating in the scheme. These are often known as 'Provident Checks' because the biggest issuer is the Provident Clothing and Supply Company Limited.

Cheque   A cheque is a written order to a bank to pay on demand a stated sum of money to the bearer of the cheque or to the person named on it. A cheque is a **Bill of Exchange** drawn on a banker and payable on demand (Bills of Exchange Act 1882).

Circulating assets/circulating capital   See **capital** (Types of capital)

Citizens Advice Bureau   A voluntary organisation formed to assist people with their shopping and other domestic problems, and which makes available a considerable network of advice throughout the country. CAB's form an essential part of a nationwide consumer protection service.

Citycall   A telephone service for London giving stock market, foreign exchange and world market reports (British Telecom).

City Working Party on Takeovers and Mergers   This body drew up and supervises the code of conduct to be observed by the various elements in the City of London interested in the securities market. Periodical revisions of the Code will in future be carried out by the Markets Committee of the Council for the Securities Industry.

Civil law   The branches of civil law are contract law, the law of tort, the law of property, the law of succession, and the law of trust. An aggrieved person who seeks justice under any one of these branches must issue a summons against the wrongdoer, so that the action can be heard.

   Civil law is concerned with the rights and duties of individual members of the community towards one another rather than towards the state itself, and is therefore sometimes referred to as private law. It is administered in the civil courts.

Civil Service   The Civil Service attempts to provide impartial advice to ministers and assists and advises any type of government regardless of politics. The knowledge and experience of the Civil Service provides an anonymous and continuous service for the government in power.

Claim   This must be made on the appropriate claim form, and details entered with 'utmost good faith'. If a fair valuation is agreed the insurance company will pay the agreed sum.

If an insurable risk has been 'spread' over several insurers the insurance companies concerned will contribute to the loss proportionately, the exact division depending upon the terms of the original policies. (See **contribution**.)

Clearing banks   The London Bankers' Clearing House consists of six clearing banks, though there are other smaller banks which also avail themselves of the facilities. The six are Barclays, Lloyds, Midland, National Westminster, Williams and Glyns, and Coutts & Co.

These banks together own the Clearing House, contributing to the cost in proportion to the volume of their business.

The prime purpose of the Clearing House is to make a daily settlement of the 'net indebtedness' which exists between the banks. This means that once a day the balance of each bank is altered at the **Bank of England**; all the cheques, standing orders and direct debits transacted between different banks which make up the sum total of this indebtedness are recorded and totalled as they pass through the head offices of the various banks. At the Clearing House these totals are balanced against each other and the debit or credit figures passed to the Bank of England where the final daily adjustment to each bank's balance is effected.

Clearing system of the banks   There is one Bankers' Clearing House in the City of London, where all its members—the clearing banks—also have their head offices.

Closed shop   A workplace practice requiring compulsory unionisation of employees in certain jobs. The Employment Act

1982 extended protection for individuals from compulsion to join a trade union.

Coin   Coins are now used only for petty transactions; larger amounts are paid in bank-notes.

Collateral security   A person borrowing from a bank by means of a loan or overdraft may be asked to offer some sort of security; this is known as collateral—ie, security lying alongside the debt. The deeds of a house, life assurance policy, or stocks and shares may be used as collateral security.

Collective bargaining   The term 'collective bargaining' is applied to those procedures by which the wages and conditions of employment are settled by a bargain in the form of an agreement between employers or associations of employers and workpeople's organisations such as a trade union.

Comecon   The Council for Mutual Economic Assistance whose objectives are to combine and coordinate economic development of the member 'iron curtain' countries,—Bulgaria, Czechoslovakia, the German Democratic Republic, Hungary, Mongolia, Poland, Rumania and the USSR. Yugoslavia is an associate member.

Commerce   Commercial and direct (personal) services together form the third or tertiary branch of production. Commerce covers the distribution and exchange of all the surplus goods produced so that they reach the final consumer in the right place, in the right condition, at the right time, in the right quantity, and at the right price. This involves trade of all kinds—retail and wholesale, home and foreign,—and the ancillary commercial services (the aids to trade): advertising, banking and finance, insurance, transport and warehousing.
  Producers (ie, those who exchange their services for an income) who are engaged in trade or in the ancillary commercial services, are said to be employed in *commercial occupations*.

Commercial banks   See **clearing banks**

Commercial bill   Similar to a Treasury Bill but issued by industrial and commercial companies.

Commercial Court   Queen's Bench Division. This court hears cases on commercial matters, such as banking and insurance.

Commercial invoice   This is very important in international trade; it is one of the three necessary documents sent with the Documentary **Bill of Exchange** to the importer's bank or agent, the others being the **Certificate of Insurance**, and the **bill of lading**.
   The invoice is sent by the seller to the buyer, giving full details as to quantity, prices and descriptions of the goods, method of carriage, name of ship or air freight detail, shipping marks and details of precise terms of sale.
   Many overseas countries require that special prescribed invoice forms be used for all consignments to the countries concerned. If the appropriate form is not used there may be delays or a possible refusal to accept the goods at the port of entry.
   In international trade a **Consular Invoice** is sometimes necessary.

Commercial operations   See **commerce**

Commission   An agreed percentage paid to a company's agents or salesman on sales achieved.

Commission agent   The appointment of a good agent is of crucial importance to an exporter, and it is essential that the agent appointed should be familiar with all aspects of the potential foreign market. There are several organisations—among them the Department of Trade, **Chambers of Commerce** and Trade Associations—who will suggest the names of possible agents.
   The commission agent's renumeration is a commission on sales.

Commission for Racial Equality   The Race Relations Act, 1976, established commissions to investigate discrimination in employment. The Commission for Racial Equality can institute

44

legal proceedings against persistent offenders and must promote equal opportunity and elimination of discrimination.

Committee of Permanent Representatives (Coreper) See **European Economic Community**

Committees   The committee system in a business organisation is the delegation of powers and responsibilites to committees.

A *standing committee* usually covers the activities of a continuous function in an organisation. The members of such committees are drawn from all the departments involved. Standing committees meet regularly, and prepare reports and recommendations for management. The 'reporting back' process is vital, and an effective communication system must operate so that all concerned are supplied with up-to-date information.

Ad hoc committees are called to deal with one particular eventuality which is unlikely to be repeated. They exist only until the matter in hand has been effectively dealt with.

Executive committee   A body with power to govern or administer.

Subcommittee   A committee may appoint one or more of its members to a subcommittee formed to undertake a specific investigation, or to relieve the present committee of some of its routine work.

Joint committee   May be formed to co-ordinate the activites of two committees. It may be a permanent committee, or instigated for one particular purpose.

Commodity markets   The raw material markets or exchanges mostly deal in natural products which are basic to the needs of industry. The **London Commodity Exchange** deals in more than 20 commodities, including coffee, sugar, spice and gums. Other exchanges concentrate on one particular type of product, such as the **London Metal Exchange** (LME) and the **London Wool Terminal Market.** All these markets are highly-organised and only experts may deal on them in very large quantities.

Primary commodities are usually brought in as bulk cargoes, and handled by middlemen whose function it is to finance, transport and warehouse the goods until required.

Common Agricultural Policy (CAP)

Alongside the trade in actual goods are 'futures' or 'terminal' markets, which can only be set up for goods which can be accurately described by grade or quality. In the futures markets the goods being sold are not available but will become available in the future; goods are therefore sold at an agreed price for delivery at a future date. The practice lends itself to speculation since a person may sell for delivery at a future date in the hope that by the time of delivery the price will have fallen, and he can repurchase on the market at a cheaper rate. The risk that concerns the buyer is that the price will rise; by buying on the futures market at an agreed price he can shield against this.

A futures contract is a transaction between two parties; the seller covers himself against a fall in prices, the buyer shields himself from a possible rise.

See also **Baltic Exchange, London Commodity Exchange, Hedging.**

Common Agricultural Policy (CAP)　The variable nature of agricultural production has led the EEC to develop a common agricultural policy to control the price and distribution of goods within the Community. To ensure that farmers are fairly rewarded CAP imposes a minimum price. Since the price cannot fall to an equilibrium position supply exceeds demand, with the result that there are butter mountains, wine lakes, etc.

Common carrier　Common carriers include any person or firm that makes a business of carrying other people's goods from one place to another.

A fixed rate of payments must be charged, and payment can be demanded in advance; delivery must be effected as soon as possible. Common carriers become responsible for the goods, their safety and prompt carriage, as soon as they are accepted.

Common External Tariff (CET)　The members of the EEC permit free circulation of goods manufactured or services provided by its member states. The Common External Tariff operates to exclude foreign goods which could as easily be made by one of the member states; in practice, however, free trade agreements exist between members of the EEC and other countries who have a history of trade with them.

Common law In England this is the body of legal principles evolved by judges from custom and precedents of previous cases. It is complementary to the statute law contained in Acts of Parliament. The term is used to distinguish it from **equity,**—ie, legal principles developed originally by the Lord Chancellor to mitigate hardship caused by the rigid application of common law.

Common law matters are tried by the Queen's Bench, while equity cases are dealt with by the Chancery Division of the High Court.

Common Market See European Economic Community

Common short form bill of lading Introduced by **SITPRO** this form retains all the legal protection of the 'long form' bill of lading, providing a receipt for taking over the goods by the carrier and their surrender by the carrier or his agent against presentation of an original bill of lading, and evidence of the contract of carriage for the goods as described. Like the 'long form' it is a document of title to the goods.

Use of the 'short form' produces savings in direct documentation costs and cuts indirect costs by increased efficiency.

Communist Economic Community See Comecon

Community programme See **Manpower Services Commission**

Community Transit (CT) Goods moving between member nations of the EEC are documented by a system of documents called the Community Transit system, by which goods are enabled to move across frontiers without being inspected by Customs. Goods are sealed into containers on departure and only opened in the country of destination.

Company formation See **floating a company**

Company law This is concerned with the formation, administration and working of limited companies.

The Companies Acts of 1948 and 1967 require plcs to publish annually:

A **profit and loss account**

A **balance sheet**

A directors' report

The main emphasis of the *1967 Act* was to require the disclosure of additional information. Some is required to be shown in the company's accounts, and some to be available for inspection at the registered office of the company concerned.

The Companies Act 1976 codified the appointment and resignation of external auditors, and strengthened the external auditor's position in relation to the disclosure of information by company officials, and access to company records.

By the 1980 Act the promoters of both public and private companies need to find only one other person prepared to join with the promoter as members in signing the **Memorandum of Association.**

Company, limited liability A registered company is distinct from the members composing it; it is an artificial 'person' created (incorporated) by law under one of the Companies Acts. It can sue and be sued in its own name in an action at law, and neither the death or bankruptcy of any of its members, nor any change in the personnel of the membership affects its existence.

There are two kinds of registered companies which are limited by **shares**: these are public limited companies (the companies to which the abbreviation *plc* refers) and private limited companies.

A private limited company is one which, by its **Articles of Association** (statutorily defined in the Companies Act 1929)—restricts its right to transfer its shares, limits its members to 50, prohibits any invitation to the public to subscribe for any shares or **debentures** of the company.

A public limited company (plc) is a company registered under the Companies Acts which invites the public to subscribe to its shares and does not keep the ownership of its share **capital** in the hands of a few persons who have taken up the shares.

Holding companies are companies which have acquired control of another company by the purchase of 51% of its voting shares.

Companies are controlled by the Companies Acts. See **company law.**

Company's risk   Goods carried by common carriers are carried at the carrying company's risk, that is, the carrier is responsible for the safe delivery of the goods.

Compensation fund   A fund maintained by the **Stock Exchange** to recompense investors should a member firm fail to meet its obligations and be 'hammered'.

Competition   Competition in the business world is a desired form of conflict. See **monopoly** and **perfect competition/market**.

Composite offices   These are proprietary offices (ie they have shareholders) usually set up as limited companies, which offer more than one type of insurance.

Compound trading   There is a tendency for retailers nowadays to extend the range of goods handled beyond their expected province. Grocers can sell tights, butchers sell tinned fruit. Pre-packaging of goods by the wholesaler or warehouse has had a considerable influence in this direction.

Computer technology   Computer technology has developed and is developing at great speed. Information systems, assembly-line and clerical operations, warehousing control and electronic traffic control in air, road, and rail transport, are but a few of the areas which have seen amazing applications over the last decade.

In *banking* a combination of modern electronics and a determined marketing policy has been very successful in bringing banking to the masses and profit to the banks.

The Trustee Savings Bank (TSB) Computer Services operate one of the most sophisticated banking computer services in Europe.

In the **commodity markets** the International Commodities Clearing House is an independent organisation which acts as a clearing agent; here all soft commodity futures are checked daily on its own computer.

The **Stock Exchange** has developed its own computerised settlement system known as Talisman.

These are but a few of the many computerised systems which are speeding operations in every sphere of industrial and commercial activity.

Conditional sale agreement　This is a credit sale agreement to sell goods by instalments, the property passing to the new owner at once. It is used for the sale of clothing and similar articles.

Conditions of sale　The general conditions of sale are concerned chiefly with quantity, quality, price, time of delivery and payment.

Conditions of work　The factors of work including pay, hours, holidays etc., that comprise an individual's total employment package. See also **contract of employment.**

Confederation of British Industry (CBI)　This body was formed in 1965 to promote British industry, safeguard its interest, promote its efficiency and maintain close contacts between industry and the government.

Many trade associations are members of the Confederation which is the managers' counterpart of the TUC, and as such is one of the best known pressure groups in business affairs.

Many CBI officials sit on government economic planning bodies.

The CBI is one of the sponsors of the BNEC (British National Export Council) and is deeply involved in export promotion, providing a wide range of information and publications. It also produces, fortnightly, the *Overseas Trade Bulletin.*

Conference lines　See **liner conferences**

Confirmed credit　The best method for financing overseas transactions is a confirmed irrevocable letter of credit. Here the credit arranged by the customer's bank is confirmed by the

London bank, so that it actually makes itself responsible for the payment to the exporter.

Confirming houses   These are specialist firms in the export field which take full responsibility for export orders, the exporter having no worries about payment. A transaction through a confirming house does not deprive the manufacturer of personal contact with the overseas customer, which is preserved because the customer, the confirming house and the exporter act as a team.

Conglomerate   An industrial group made up of companies which often have diverse and unrelated interests.

Consensus ad idem   See **contract, law of**

Consequential loss   See **fire insurance**

Consideration   See **contract, law of**

Consignee   The named receiver of a consignment of goods.

Consignor   The person responsible for transporting a consignment of goods.

Consolidated fund   An account in which are recorded all taxation moneys received and expenditure disbursed.

Consols   Bonds which the owners can never ask to have repaid; an investor in consols simply buys a right to a perpetual annual payment of interest, though investors can, of course, generally recover their money by selling such bonds on the **Stock Exchange**.

Consortium   A syndicate or association common to large-scale enterprise where because of the scale of the business or the amount of capital involved several firms agree to pool their resources.

Constitution 1 The system or body of fundamental principles according to which a nation, state, or body politic is constituted and governed.
2 Also called **standing orders**, these are the rules compiled by an organisation to regulate the manner in which its business is to be conducted.

Constitutional law A system of law which has been established by the sovereign power of the state for its guidance. Its main object is to fix the limits and define the relations of the legislative, judicial and executive powers of the state.

Consular invoice This is a certified invoice which the consul or other representative of the importing country, residing in the country of origin, has certified as showing the correct price. This is necessary when the import duty on goods is to be paid according to the value of the goods, and prevents falsification of the records.

Consultants Individuals or groups of specialists who have gained expert knowledge in a particular field of business and offer professional advice for a fee. The increasing sophistication of business and the accelerating rate of change make it harder for firms to meet the challenge of competition from their own internal staff resources. In recent years the demand for specialist knowledge has led to consultancy becoming one of the major growth areas in the tertiary sector of business.

Consultation Joint consultation provides employees with the opportunity to discuss welfare matters with their employers, and enables employers to assess the impact of policy decisions on employees. Joint consultative committees consist of representatives from all levels of an organisation.
  The changing attitude towards consultation is supported by the European Commission (See **European Economic Community**); in line with this the Employment Act, 1982, requires company reports to contain a statement on the steps the directors are taking to develop employee involvement.

Consumer The consumer is the final link in the chain of
distribution. He buys the goods or services for his own use.

Consumer credit Credit is buying something and being given
time to pay for it, or borrowing money and paying it back later.
In addition to the cost of the goods or services the credit has also
to be paid for; this additional payment is called interest.

There are many different forms of credit: loans may be made
by banks, finance houses, moneylenders, credit unions and
others; a **mortgage, hire-purchase** or credit sale, use of a banker's **credit card**, budget account or monthly account, **mail order**
or the use of trading checks and vouchers are all forms of credit
trading.
The Consumer Credit Act of 1974 applies a comprehensive system
to consumer credit and consumer hire agreements made on or
after 19 May 1985. This Act replaces the Moneylenders Acts and
HP Acts which previously applied, except for parts of the 1964 Act
dealing with the purchase of motor-cars by HP.

There are two new and important provisions in the Act. The first
concerns credit **brokers** who now need a licence from the **Office
of Fair Trading** before they can operate. The second concerns the
rate the credit trader is charging (usually shown as a percentage
rate). Now all traders must calculate their interest and credit
charges in a standard way. The *APR* (Annual Percentage Rate) is
the true cost of credit, and includes in it all the costs which go to
make up the credit charge.

In connection with this act the Office of Fair Trading issues a
great deal of information and advice to consumers. Among their
publications are leaflets on how to cope with doorstep salesmen,
on buying by post, and the right to know what information credit
reference agencies divulge to credit traders about their customers
or would-be customers. The Office of Fair Trading also issues
booklets on the various regulations in force under the Act; to date
they have issued those on Hire Purchase agreements—cancellable
and non-cancellable—and on regulations concerning matters
which may arise during the lifetime of an agreement.

The local Trading Standards Department (sometimes called the
Consumer Protection Department), Citizens Advice Bureaux,

Consumer durables

Consumer Advice Centres, or neighbourhood law centres will all give advice on these matters.

Consumer durables Consumer durables are goods which are purchased and used by the general public, but which do not need frequent replacement. Examples are washing machines, television sets and vacuum cleaners.

Consumer goods In addition to primary (basic) needs people require a range of manufactured goods such as food, clothing, household goods, etc. These are consumer goods; **producer goods** are used by manufacturers to aid them in the production of other articles.

Consumer protection The Citizens' Advice Bureaux, Consumer Advice Centres and Local Trading Standards Department (sometimes called the Consumer Protection Department) will all give advice to consumers on the best action to take if they, as consumers, have a grievance.

The following Acts are the main legislative measures in force for the protection of consumers:

Consumer Credit Act 1974 This applies a comprehensive system to consumer credit and consumer hire agreements made on or after 19 May 1985, and is treated fully under **consumer credit**.

Fair Trading Act 1973 This set up the **Office of Fair Trading** (OFT) to act as 'watchdogs' on traders who break the law. The Director can bring actions in the Restrictive Practices Court against those who do not obey rules of trading.

Food and Drugs Act 1985–8 laid down that ingredients must be displayed on packaging; it became criminal to sell food or drugs unfit for human consumption.

Monopolies and Restrictive Practices Acts 1948–56 outlawed the enforcement of Resale Price Maintenance. Practices considered to be against the public interest could be brought before the Restrictive Practices Court.

Sale of Goods Act, 1893 lays down rules as to when ownership passes from seller to buyer and implies the condition that where goods are bought from a person who deals in those goods, and the buyer relies on the skill and judgement of the seller and makes known to him, expressly or impliedly, the purpose for which he requires the goods, then the goods shall be reasonably fit for that purpose. Goods sold by sample, must correspond with the sample.

Supply of Goods (Implied Terms) Act 1973 protected persons being deprived of their rights by unfair bargaining. (This amended the Sale of Goods Act, 1893.)

Trade Descriptions Act 1968 was designed to prevent misleading descriptions of goods in shops, labelling and advertising.

Trading Stamps Act 1968 stipulated that every trading stamp must have its cash value stated on it, and that holders should be able to choose to exchange them for either cash or goods.

Finally, the Advertising Standards Authority (ASA) provides for complaints by the public about advertisements, to be investigated, and for the authority to make recommendations where appropriate.

Consumer services In some occupations the object is not to provide consumer goods but consumer services. These are part of tertiary production and are known as direct services (direct from the producer to the consumer). They exist in the social, commercial and professional fields. Doctors, teachers, firemen and entertainers provide such services; these producers 'service' the work force and ensure its efficiency.

Consumerism A movement that traces its origins to the campaigns of Ralph Nader in America in the early 1960s for more stringent safety standards in manufactured products. The movement encouraged consumers to be more sensitive to the qualitative factors of products on the market and growing public awareness soon crystallised into a number of major institutions that now protect consumers' interests. As a result, manufacturers and industrialists are more open to public criticism of their products and production methods, and many now take active steps to monitor and evaluate public opinion. We see the results today, for example, in safer motor cars, control of environmental pollution, open dating of perishable foods and generally much stricter regulation of market-place behaviour.

Consumption One of the four main elements of economic activity, the others being production, exchange and distribution. Consumption implies the satisfaction of our demands for goods and services over a period of time. Each individual has a propensity to consume, dependent on income and the utility derived from a particular consumption.

Consumers' Association This is an independent, non-profitmaking body set up in 1957, now strongly established as a watchdog for customers' complaints; it operates mainly by conducting comparative tests on goods and publishing reports on them in 'Which?' magazine.

Annual subscriptions are paid by members of the Consumers' Association, in return for which they receive each month a copy of 'Which?'.

Containerisation Goods packed in containers which look like large boxes can be mechanically transferred from lorries on to purpose-built rail wagons, or on to ships, then back again on to lorries for final delivery.

Containerised goods are safer, protected both from weather and pilfering. Sealed with the authority of the Customs, their use considerably reduces formalities at the port of arrival.

Though containers are best when used with large consignments, small exporters can use the services of a freight forwarding agent, who treats the goods of several consignors as one load.

Although train ferry services have been available for many years, the provision of container services has revolutionised deliveries to the continent of Europe, particularly at the container ports where roll-on roll-off facilities are available. Specially-built vessels now provide the facility for a road vehicle to be packed at the exporter's factory and to make a door-to-door delivery to a customer in Europe.

Contango   The amount to be paid by **bulls** who wish to carry the purchase of shares over to the next **Stock Exchange Account** because the rise they hoped for in prices has not come about.

Contango Day   The last dealing day of a **Stock Exchange Account**, on which Contangos are arranged.

Continuous stock taking   See **perpetual inventory**.

Contract, law of   A contract is a legally enforceable agreement; it is a bargain between two or more persons, either orally or in writing.

The essential element of a contract is that there must be an offer made by one person and an acceptance of that offer by another. Immediately the offer is accepted a contract is concluded, but the parties to a contract must be clear as to what they are agreeing about otherwise there is no agreement. (*Consensus ad idem*— 'agreement to the same idea').

Consideration is another important element of a contract—which is something in return for the promise made by the other party. The most common example is money exchanged for goods or services,—ie, the price in a contract of sale.

The parties must have the intention of creating a legally binding relationship, and must be persons with a legal capacity to contract,—this means that minors cannot enter into a contract with another person.

Basically, the legal rule in contract law is that if an agreement is not carried out, or not performed correctly, the 'injured' party has the legal right to claim some form of redress.

Contract hire fleet   This is where an independent haulier undertakes the entire transport requirements of an organisation. The hiring organisation has complete control over drivers and vehicles, and vehicles are usually painted in the hirer's livery. There are no maintenance costs to the hirer who knows by agreement what the total cost will be.

Contract hire fleets are more expensive for a firm than running its own transport. Ideally the hired fleet should be fully employed, but it is often difficult to organise return loads.

Contract note   Document sent by a **stockbroker** to his client specifying a named amount of **stock, shares, bonds,** etc has been bought at a stated price, together with the amount of **brokerage** charged, and the stamp necessary.

Contract of employment   Under the Contracts of Employment Act 1972 every employer is obliged to give every employee a written statement about his main terms of employment within thirteen weeks of starting work. This must show—
The names of employer and employee
Date of commencement of employment
Title of job
Rate of pay
Whether weekly or monthly paid
Hours of work
Conditions relating to pay when absent through sickness
Pension rights
Length of notice to be given by either side to terminate the contract
Holidays and payment for holidays
The right to belong to a trade union
The right not to belong to a trade union
The procedures for registering a grievance
The steps for the subsequent grievance procedure

Contract of insurance   This is a contract (see **contract, law of**) under which one party undertakes for a consideration to indemnify another against certain forms of loss.

Contract of sale   A properly constituted contract of sale is enforceable by law. To make an agreement legally valid one party must make an offer to perform some function or to pay a particular price, and the other party to the agreement must unconditionally accept that offer. A feature of the sale of goods is that it is the purchaser who makes the offer to buy at a particular price. The price on an article is not an offer, but an **invitation** to offer. The seller can accept or reject the purchaser's offer; usually he accepts.

Contribution   The principle of contribution means that if an insurable risk is 'spread' over several insurers the insurance companies concerned contribute to the loss proportionately, the exact division depending upon the terms of the original policies.

Control accounts   These are memorandum accounts that are maintained as a self-balancing check on small sections of the ledger.

Controlled economy   See **economy, types of**

Co-operation/co-operatives   Co-operation means working together for the production or distribution of goods or services; the capital is subscribed by members, and all profits are shared among members according to an agreed plan. Control of the venture is in the hands of members.

Co-operatives include those in the marketing of farmers' produce, and supply of their requirements and services (agricultural co-operatives), workers' productive societies, fishermen's societies for marketing and supply, and housing societies for financing and building.

Co-operative societies   The Rochdale Pioneers, who opened their store in Toad Lane in 1844, harnessed the co-operative idea to the supply of consumer goods. Basic principles of the Rochdale Pioneers have become those of the whole co-operative movement. The main points were and are:
Open membership
Democratic control—one person, one vote
Payment of limited interest on capital
Distribution of surplus funds in proportion to transactions.

The co-operative societies were pioneers of adult education, and finance a range of educational, political and social activities at the present day.

Co-operative Retail Societies (CRS)   These are the 'traditional' 'co-op shops'—the 'stores'. They are organised by a committee elected by members who have one vote each; the committee directs the society's policy and the trading surplus is shared by members. (Members own shares on which dividend is paid; trading stamps are now given to all customers who purchase goods at the RCS stores).

In recent years the retail societies have lost a large share of the market, and in an effort to make the 'co-op' movement more competitive a large number of retail societies have merged with each other to form regional societies in the hope that a more efficient organisation will result.

Co-operative Wholesale Society (CWS)   This is the national trading and manufacturing organisation of the CRS in England and Wales, and is owned by the CRS whose directors elect the directors of the CWS.

Any trading surplus is returned to the Retail Societies.

The CWS administers the Co-op Bank which offers a full banking service to its customers.

Copyright   The exclusive right of an author or artist to reproduce his works over a fixed period of time.

Corporation (business unit)   A corporation is an association of individuals which by a legal fiction is regarded as a single person. The distinguishing characteristic of a corporation is that a corporation can never die, and consequently the death or change of the persons who administer the corporate property has no effect upon the ownership, which lies in the 'artificial person' or legal entity of the corporation.

Corporation Tax   A tax levied on the profits and **capital** gains of public **limited companies**; companies can deduct allowances from their gross **profits**, and the remaining net profit is then taxed at a standard rate.

Corporation Tax has to be paid before the company can distribute profits to its shareholders.

A high level of Corporation Tax affects growth in the economy because it leaves companies with less finance for capital investment.

Correlation   The reciprocal relationship that exists between sets of figures or variables. Positive correlation is said to occur when an increase in one variable is associated to a greater or lesser extent with an increase in another, (eg, advertising and sales). Negative correlation occurs when an increase in one variable is associated with a decrease in another, (eg, the use of electric light and gas lamp sales).

Cost (economics)   Cost—the use of resources—is measured by the sacrifice of alternatives forgone or opportunities lost. This is because economists are interested in the efficient utilisation of real (as opposed to monetary) resources.

Cost and freight   'Cost and freight' means that the price includes charges incurred for shipping to the port of destination.

Cost centre   An identifiable section of a business—a department, a group of people or machines—in respect of which costs are accumulated and over which cost control can be exercised.

Cost, insurance and freight (c,i&f)   See **delivery costs**

Cost of living   From the time of the First World War, wages have been fixed for very large sections of the community on a cost of living basis, determined since 1947 by the **Retail Price Index Number** issued by the Department of Employment.

Cost-Benefit Analysis   The technique of CBA, where the costs of a project are listed and compared with the benefits, has helped to improve the analysis and understanding of public expenditure. CBA takes into account all the socially hidden costs as well as the actual costs which society will have to pay and balances them against the benefits to society, whether there are actual payment or receipts to be taken into account, or not.

Costing/cost accounting   Describes the procedures for classifying, collecting and analysing costs in respect of a business unit, process, product or service. A good costing system is a necessary prerequisite to management planning and control. See also **marginal costing, standard costing, unit costs, job costing** and **process costing**.

Cost-plus pricing   This is the most common form of pricing; the unit cost is calculated and then a profit margin added.

Costs (of production)   The costs of a firm may be divided into those which are fixed in the short term (ie, those which do not vary as output or sales expand) and those which are variable or *direct* costs.

Fixed costs are those which cover rent, rates, interest on loans, and depreciation which an organisation has to pay, even when production is not taking place.

Marginal cost is the increase in total costs resulting from the production of one more unit of output. An important theory is that any profit-maximising firm will expand output to the point where marginal cost is equal to marginal revenue.

Unit (average) cost   The total costs of production are made up of fixed and variable costs. The unit (average) cost is the total cost divided by the number of units produced.

Variable costs are those which vary with output, such as expenditure on raw materials, fuel, lighting, heating, and the wages of those directly engaged in production. Also known as *direct costs*.

Council of Ministers (EEC) see **European Economic Community**

Country profiles (BOTB)   Country profiles for all markets in Western Europe are available, free of charge, from Exports to Europe Branch of the BOTB.

Coupon   On bearer securities a detachable part of the certificate exchangeable for dividends. Also used generally to denote the rate of interest on a fixed-interest **security**.

Cover   The amount of money a company has available for

distribution as **dividend**, divided by the amount actually paid. If this results in a figure of 1 or more, the dividend is that number of *times covered*. If the result is less than 1, the dividend is uncovered.

Cover note A cover note is issued when insurers agree to insure item(s) detailed on a proposal form. A cover note gives immediate cover on acceptance of risk, pending preparation of a policy.

Credit, bank See **bank credit**

Credit brokers Credit brokers were licensed in July 1978, under the Consumer Credit Act 1974. Credit brokers are those who introduce people to sources of credit or hire, or to other credit brokers. Examples of such brokers are—
A *shopkeeper* who asks a finance company to finance a purchase for a customer.
A *mortgage broker* who helps a house-purchaser to obtain a loan from a building society.
An *electrical dealer* who arranges the hire of a TV set from a rental company.
  All credit brokers must obtain a licence from the Office of Fair Trading.

Credit cards Method of payment through the **clearing banks**. Access cards are issued jointly by Lloyds, Midland and the National Westminster Banks; Visa (Barclaycard) by Barclays Bank.
  These cards enable the holder to buy goods or services at any shop, restaurant, garage, etc, which has joined the scheme, without paying by cash or cheque at the time of making the purchase. Each shop in the scheme is allotted a 'floor limit' beyond which it cannot accept a credit card in payment for goods without first confirming the transaction by telephone with the credit card company. Also each card holder is given an overall limit which cannot be exceeded.
  The card holder is presented with a statement at the end of each month showing all the transactions he has made with the card during the month. This account he settles by one monthly

payment, thereby saving the necessity of carrying cash around; but the card holder may, if he wishes, pay back by instalments each month, at which stage interest will be charged.

The card also enables the holder to obtain cash up to a given limit at any of the branches within the issuing bank's system.

Banks will issue credit cards to customers who do not hold a current account with them.

Credit control   The purpose of credit control is to avoid bad debts. A new customer will be required to establish his 'credit-worthiness' before being granted credit and will be given a credit rating, showing the amount of credit he will be allowed. If he proves to be a reliable customer his rating may be increased.

Every organisation should have a firm policy regarding bad debts and the amount of latitude which customers may be allowed. Customers who do not pay will never help a firm to make a profit.

Credit rating   This is a certificate issued by a bank stating that a firm is financially sound.

Credit sale agreement   This is an agreement to sell goods by instalments, the property passing to the new owner at once. It is usually for the sale of clothing or similar articles where goods are not worth re-selling. (This is also known as the deferred payments system). It is widely used by mail order companies.

Credit scoring   'A Guide to Credit Scoring'—drawn up and published by a number of bodies in the credit industry in consultation with the **Office of Fair Trading**—was the credit industry's response to a consultative document published by the OFT in 1982. At that time the OFT pointed to the risk that some people might feel themselves being unfairly refused credit as traditional methods of credit assessment were replaced by more automated credit scoring systems.

Credit scoring measures the statistical probability that money lent will be repaid. Among the claimed advantages of credit scoring are savings in costs resulting from the increased use of automated techniques and the ability to devolve credit granting authority. By reducing the administrative costs of granting credit, as well as the incidence of bad debts, credit grantors are also better able to contain the cost of credit to their customers.

Credit transactions   These are usual between firms who deal regularly with one another, payment being made at the end of a month. HP (hire purchase) credit transactions may be spread over longer periods.

Creditor   A person to whom a debt is owed.

Credit-worthiness   When buyers wish to purchase on credit the seller has to be satisfied that the customer will be able to pay. It is, therefore, usual for a prospective purchaser to supply references from his banker or other business concerns confirming his ability to pay. See *credit rating, credit scoring*

Criminal law   Crime—an act punishable by law as being forbidden by statute or injurious to the public welfare—affects the whole community. As such, criminal offences are considered to be against the State, and are punished by a system laid down and administered by the State.

Individuals may suffer from the effect of criminal offences and in addition to the punishment laid down by the State, may obtain compensation for personal loss.

Critical Path Analysis (CPA) (Operational Research)   This is a method whereby the policy to be adopted in carrying through a project is represented by a graphical model (network) in which the times necessary for all the different operations are shown. The model is analysed, time required for the total project calculated, and the times available for the different constituent operations worked out.

CPA   is a prediction technique which can shorten the time of projects, especially construction projects such as bridges, roads, buildings and ships. The technique can be refined to indicate the best time to allocate resources.

Cum div,

buildings and ships. The technique can be refined to indicate the best time to allocate resources.

Cum div, *cum dividend*   This means 'together with the dividend'. **Shares** sold 'cum div' are sold along with the dividend due on them.

Cumulative preference shares   See **shares**

Currency and Bank Notes Act 1954   The Government reserves the right to issue notes and coins which reach the public via the **Bank of England**. The size of the note issue is governed by the Currency and Bank Notes Act 1954.
   At the Bank of England the notes pass from the Issuing Department to the Banking Department, then via the **clearing banks** to the public.

Current account (balance of payments)   The current account in this balance covers the difference between imported goods and services and exported goods and services.
   (The balance of payments' *capital account* covers long-term international transactions).

Current account deposits (banking)   Deposits that can be freely transferred by writing a cheque.

Current assets   See **assets**

Current liabilities   See **liabilities, current**

Current ratio   This is a test of **liquidity** and is the ratio between current **assets** and current **liabilities**.
   The current ratio is a quick way of assessing the nature of the working capital. If the ratio is less than 2:1 then the firm could run into liquidity problems and might find it difficult to pay its way.

Customs and Excise   This Department is responsible for
66

collection of the following—
Betting Duty—Gaming and Licensing Duties,
CAP payments relating to the Common Agricultural Policy of the
EEC (for details see **European Economic Community**),
Import Duties—see details under separate entry below,
Revenue Duties—the excise on tobacco and alcohol,
Value Added Tax (VAT)

Customs debentures   The payment of 'process inwards relief'
(this used to be called 'drawback') is made by a Customs document
called a debenture.
   Repayment of duty is claimed when an import pays duty and
is manufactured into a finished product which is subsequently
exported. The exporter can then claim the duty back from the
Customs.

Customs duties   These are indirect taxes raised on goods being
imported into the country, and are used to control imports.
   Customs duties may be **specific duties** which are based on fixed
quantities—ie, the rate is per unit of weight, volume, measure or
number, or it may be an **ad valorem duty** which varies with the
declared value of the goods.
   The amount of duty to be paid can be determined by reference
to the Customs and Excise Tariffs. (A tariff is a list or set of
Customs duties).
   Customs allow goods to be stored in bonded warehouses, and
duty is then paid on any amounts as they are released.

Customs entry   Details of all goods *exported* must be entered and
passed by HM Customs. It is by such entry that the government
is able to build up a comprehensive record of all exports,
subdivided into a range of pre-determined categories.

D

Daily list A list issued officially by the **Stock Exchange** showing quotations for stocks and other securities dealt with on the Exchange.

Daily settlement This is the daily settling up of net-indebtedness between the **clearing banks**.

Data Ideas and facts about people and entities represented in a formal way suitable for communication, interpretation or processing by human or computerised means.

Database A centralised collection of data files logically arranged to serve the needs of users for a variety of applications. Although most usually associated with computer systems a database can comprise manual storage media such as ledger and paper files, as well as magnetic media.

Daybooks Are chronological records of book-keeping transactions. Original documents such as invoices and credit notes are recorded in these books of original entry prior to posting to the ledger.

Debentures 1 See **customs debentures**
2 These are fixed interest loans made to a company; they differ from other loans to a company in that they can be bought and sold on the **Stock Exchange**. They are issued with specific terms regarding interest, capital repayment and security, and are usually redeemable on a set date. They are not part of the share

capital of a company, and the interest on them must be paid
whether there are profits or not.

Fixed debentures are secured against certain fixed **assets**, which
cannot be disposed of in any way by the directors without the
permission of the debenture trustees.

Floating debentures 'float' over the assets of a company,
particularly the current assets.

Mortgage debentures These are 'covered' by a particular part of
the firm's property, which will be sold in order to repay debenture
holders in the event of difficulty.

Simple or *naked debentures* carry no charge on the assets.

　　See also **prior charges**

Debit note A document made out by the seller whenever the
buyer has been undercharged on an *invoice*, or when he needs to
make an additional charge which increases the buyer's
indebtedness.

Debt factoring Factoring is a system of arranging payments
which frees a businessman from the complications that can arise
with debtors, particularly overseas debtors. The factor takes over
the invoices of a firm, paying them up to 80% of the debt
immediately (and sometimes more), after deducting charges.
Factoring is especially effective for overseas debts, as the factors
specialise in specific countries where they have knowledge of the
language, customs, legal system, etc. By using the services of a
debt factor a firm does not have to wait to obtain the cash for goods
sold, which thereby increases the rate of cash flow in the
organisation. The London Finance Houses were among the first
to undertake debt factoring.

Debtor A person who owes money to another.

Decentralisation Centralisation can lead to ineffective
communication and poor control in an organisation. Large
concerns can decentralise in an attempt to overcome these
deficiencies,—authority is delegated by dividing the organisation
into several autonomous units, each unit being responsible for its

69

own performance. Performance is judged in regard to relationships between units and with other organisations.

Central government, because of its size, has problems in internal and external communication, and decentralisation helps to improve the administration of the services and to allow for better communication between the providers of the services and the public.

Decision tables/decision trees A mathematical technique for improving management decision-making when the outcome is uncertain. It is done by quantifying income and costs for all known alternatives to a situation. The purpose is to handle risk in a more certain and objective manner.

Defence Sales Organisation (DSO) This exists to help British firms market and sell their defence products and services overseas. The DSO is part of the Ministry of Defence. It can assist companies with advice on defence market prospects on a worldwide, regional or country basis, by providing military assistance in support of sales, and in other ways.

Deferred payments see **credit sale agreement**

Deferred shares Also called *founders' shares.* See **shares**

Deflation A deliberate contraction in the supply of money available to buy goods and services with the result that demand, production and prices fall, and unemployment tends to rise.

Del credere agent The *del credere* agent believes he has found a buyer who will pay in due course, and agrees to assume the risk of any debts. If the buyer fails to pay, the agent bears the loss; he charges his principal an extra *del credere* commission for this service.

Delegation Describes the management process of releasing to subordinates the authority and responsibility for undertaking particular tasks. Theoretically it should provide each employee with an even workload, allow for individual growth and prevent overloading at senior levels.

Delivery costs   There are several ways in which export prices may be quoted—

Cost and freight (c & f)   This covers the cost of goods and freight, the buyer being committed to making his own insurance arrangements.

Cost, insurance and freight (c, i & f)   The exporter supplies the goods, meets all expenses involved in placing them on board ship or on the aircraft, pays the freight charges and insurance premiums, and renders the bills of lading, invoices and insurance certificates to the overseas buyer whose responsibilities commence when the goods are shipped.

Ex ship   This means that the importer must pay for the unloading of the goods from the ship once they have reached the port of destination, and must make arrangements for their transport therefrom. All charges up to this point are met by the exporter.

Ex works   This covers the cost of goods at the factory, all additional charges being the responsibility of the customer.

'Franco' or 'franco domicile'   This must include in the price *all* prices up to and including delivery *to the premises* of the customer overseas. Such a quotation is made easier if an overseas branch or agent has been organised.

Free alongside ship (fas)   The risks and expenses are the responsibility of the exporter until the goods are delivered to the wharf alongside the ship which will carry them.

Free on board (fob)   The risks and expenses are the responsibility of the exporter until the goods are loaded on the vessel.

free on rail (for)   The risks and expenses are the responsibility of the exporter until the goods are loaded onto the railway vehicle.

Demand   Demand for goods and services is the basis of all business operations, and the changing nature of demand is a permanent feature of business activity. Demand, as used in economics, is the effective demand by prospective buyers who are prepared to pay the market price.

   The ever-changing nature of markets and of needs is the main external risk which an organisation faces.

When the price of a good or service changes and the change in demand is small, demand is said to be inelastic. When demand does respond easily to changes in price then demand is said to be elastic.

Demand and supply, laws of   Under perfect competition price is decided by the interaction of demand and supply; the market price is that price which equates demand and supply—the goods supplied by producers equals the quantity bought by consumers.

Basically, an increased demand or decreased supply leads to a rise in price; in the same way a decreased demand or increased supply leads to a fall in price.

Demographics   The social study of people in their communities. Demography draws on data relating to births, deaths, marriage, health, etc., to draw conclusions about community behaviour.

Demurrage   Charge made by a carrier to cover any delay in loading or unloading.

Department of Trade and Industry   See **Trade and Industry, Department of**

Department store   Large shops in town and city centres, characterised by having 'many shops under one roof', with restaurants and other amenities.

They offer credit facilities to their regular customers, such as budget accounts or account cards—which enable customers to charge purchases to their accounts; the store will send them monthly statements which should be paid, or partially paid, before the end of the following month.

Departments   Within any organisation specialisation is to be seen in the work of different departments.

Deposit account   A form of bank account that entitles the saver to earn interest on money deposited.

Deposit, Certificate of   See **Discount Houses**

Deposit-taking institutions   Under the Banking Act 1979 the term 'bank' is restricted to institutions offering a full banking service, and who have been registered as 'banks' at the **Bank of England**. Lesser institutions are recognized as 'deposit-taking institutions'.

Depreciation   Depreciation of **capital** goods eventually calls for replacement of or repair to premises, plant and fittings, and always leads to a fall in the monetary value of an **asset**.

In accounts, depreciation is a way of measuring the cost of using a fixed asset. A set portion of the asset's cost is treated as an expense each period of its working life. The amount of money used to reduce the cost is deducted from the initial capital outlay in the **balance sheet**, and is also treated as a legitimate expense in the **profit and loss account**.

The purpose of depreciation is to reduce the cost of a fixed asset to a scrap or realisable value and to provide for future purchases.

Desk research   See **Marketing**

Devaluation   Reduction in the value of a currency in relation to the value of another currency or currencies. Devaluation—lowering the rate of exchange—will restrict imports.

Diamond market   See **Central Selling Organisation**

Differential cost analysis   This concerns the physical distribution of goods and is the analysis of the differences of cost involved when various ranges of goods are distributed in different ways.

Diminishing returns, law of   The law of diminishing returns states that as more and more resources are allocated to a fixed asset, then eventually output will diminish.

In all systems there is an optimum mix of resources which will maximise output, and this mix can often be assessed by **Operational Research** (OR) techniques.

Direct controls   Controls on individual banks designed to regulate growth of money and credit. They work through direct instructions rather than through changes in interest rates.

Direct costs   See **costs** (of production)

Direct importation   When a manufacturer needs regular supplies of raw materials, or where a firm has built up a strong link with a supplier overseas, direct importation—importation without the services of a middleman—is customary. Such commodities do not pass through the commodity markets.

Direct mail/direct selling by manufacturers   Selling direct from the manufacturer to the consumer, cutting out both the wholesaler and retailer. Contact with the customer is made by advertisement in newspapers, etc, or by the manufacturer employing door-to-door salesmen.

Direct production   The satisfying of a person's wants without help from any other person. See also **indirect production**.

Direct services   See **consumer services**

Direct taxation   Direct taxation is paid directly by a person or 'legal entity' to the Government. The following are examples: **Income tax, Corporation tax, Schedule D tax** (paid on profits made by businesses operating as sole traders or partnerships), **Capital gains tax.** See also **Indirect Taxation**.

Directors, board of   This is the most important part of any **limited company**, and the chairman of the board is the true head of the firm. The other members of the board are called directors. The managing director actually runs the firm and puts the decisions of the board into effect. Other directors may be heads of departments and are thus executive directors, and full-time employees of the organisation. Part-time directors have experience which will be of service to the company and make a valuable contribution to the organisation.

Everything that happens in a firm takes place through the authority of the board of directors. The main functions of the board are firstly, to determine and clarify company policy, and to formulate plans to put it into effect; and secondly, to ensure that the company complies with the requirements of the Companies' Acts.

Disablement Advisory Service (DAS)   See **Manpower Services Commission**

Discount   Discount is the amount by which a **share** is traded below its original price (see **Premium**).

Discount houses/discount market   There are twelve discount houses—specialist financial institutions who are members of the London Discount Market Association—which operate in the 'money market'. Having obtained very large sums of money from various sources—from individuals or firms, but mostly from the large institutional investors—they specialise in lending it over short periods to the Government, trade and commerce, by means of **bill-broking**.

The discount houses are the only financial institutions who may tender for the Bank of England's **Treasury Bills**. These are 3-month Bills offered by the Treasury as security for a loan. The discount houses tender weekly for these bills at a certain percentage discount, the **Bank of England** accepting the lowest tenders; the discount houses lend the Treasury the amount of the face value of the Bill *less* the discount that has been agreed, and in three months' time receive back the full amount from the Treasury. The 'discount' is thus paid back to the discount houses and is their profit.

75

The discount market also deals in **Certificates of Deposit**. An organisation, such as a bank, which wishes to earn interest on funds lying idle but does not wish to tie up its money in a term deposit, will deposit the money with a discount house and receive a Certificate of Deposit which is negotiable, and can therefore be turned into cash. For the major banks they are a simple way of buying funds in the market, and for the smaller banks they are a liquid asset which can be traded.

Discounted cash flow   A technique for examining the forecasted 'inflow' and 'outflow' of money over the expected life of a project to provide a basis for judging its profitability.

Discrimination in employment   The three Acts of Parliament which relate to this are:
Equal Pay Act, 1970
Race Relations Act, 1976
Sex Discrimination Act, 1975
   Discrimination occurs under these Acts when an employee, or an applicant, is treated less favourably than others because of his or her sex, colour or race.

Diseconomies of scale   Though many advantages arise when large organisations employ effective mass production methods, there are also disadvantages. Among these 'diseconomies of scale' are difficulties in communication (both internal and external), poor co-ordination and control, slow reaction to change, and a failure to keep equipment up-to-date.

Dishonoured cheque   A cheque on which a bank has refused payment. The reasons for this may be that the customer's account has insufficient funds to meet the cheque, or payment has been countermanded. Alternatively a technical error may have invalidated the cheque, or the account may have been closed before all cheques have been cleared.

Disintermediation   The process whereby direct controls or other restrictions on banks lead to a greater amount of lending business being routed through uncontrolled institutions and markets.

Dismissal An employee is dismissed when an employer terminates the contract of employment. This may be done with or without notice, but if the employer fails to establish a fair reason for the dismissal he may be liable in an action for unfair dismissal.

Disposable income The residue of a person's income after taxes and the basic needs for food and shelter have been met.

Distribution, chain (channel) of (also known as the *Chain of Commerce* or *Chain of Production*). The traditional route for consumer goods from the manufacturer to the consumer, involving particularly the commercial services provided by transport and warehousing; usually shown as—
Manufacturer→ Wholesaler→ Retailer→ Consumer

However, with the increased size of many retail shops, often part of a large chain, retail organisations often buy in bulk from the manufacturer and eliminate the wholesaler altogether, providing their own warehousing and warehouse services.

Sometimes these same large organisations manufacture the goods themselves with their own brand names, so that the whole operation needs only a retail outlet to sell to the consumer.

Direct selling is another 'route'. This involves a direct response by consumers to manufacturers' advertisements in the press or on television or radio, which eliminates both the wholesaler and retailer.

Sometimes the wholesaler advertises and sells by means of a catalogue, thus eliminating the retailer.

Perishable goods cannot always be sent by way of the 'traditional' routes. Sometimes they are sold direct by farmers to consumers (particularly the 'pick your own' fruit crops); and there is a strong link between farmers and local markets and shops for many perishable crops. Agricultural cooperatives have their own warehouses from which large retailers obtain supplies, and the large produce markets, both regional and national, receive much of their perishable produce.

The national markets—Covent Garden (now Nine Elms) for fruit and vegetables, Smithfield for meat, and Billingsgate for fish,—receive produce from both home and foreign sources, and both wholesalers and retailers buy from them.

Finally, there may be a law compelling farmers to sell certain produce through a marketing board, which really becomes the wholesaler of that particular product. The Milk Marketing Board is an example of such an organisation. See also **Physical Distribution**.

District auditor   District auditors are government officials who exert financial control by checking the financial records of local authorities and government organisations.

Diversification   The risks encountered by an organisation can be spread by diversification—that is, by an extension of its range of products and/or activities.

Dividend   Payment from a company's profits to its shareholders. It is usually expressed as a percentage of the nominal value of the shares, and the amount is made known at the **Annual General Meeting** of the **limited company**.

NB A dividend is also paid to members of the RCS (Retail Cooperative Societies) who own shares. The 'divi' which used to be paid to members in proportion to the amount of purchases made has been discontinued and replaced by trading stamps, which are given to all customers whether they are 'co-op' members or not.

Dividend mandate   A form, completed by the **shareholder**, requiring the company to pay his dividends direct to a bank, or to some other person.

Dividend warrant   The cheque by which the dividend is paid.

Division of labour   Each industry specialises in one particular type of production, and within each industry there is further specialisation into different organisations, each organisation having its own subdivisions of departments or branches. Even within one department or branch specialisation is apparent. These examples illustrate how work is divided between producers, each producer concentrating on his one particular part of the productive process. The advantages of the division of labour are that one worker, concentrating on one job for which he has an aptitude, can develop his skill to the utmost, and there is a saving of resources as each worker needs only the equipment required for his own adequate performance. A further effect is that an efficient worker will evolve even speedier and more effective patterns of work, all of which leads to increased productivity. The division of labour secures high levels of production and, therefore, a high national income.

There are, however, disadvantages. The main characteristic of the division of labour is that the whole cannot function if one of the parts is ineffective; a breakdown of one section of production can lead to serious hold-ups. The application of new machinery and automation can obviate such occurrences, but usually the introduction of new technology involves redundancy among the workers.

Dock dues   Harbour dues payable when goods pass through a dock either as exports or imports.

Documentation   Details of the following documents used in international trade will be found under their own headings—
Bill of Exchange
Bill of lading or air waybill (also sea waybill)
Certificate of Origin
Commercial invoice
Consular invoice
Certificate of insurance
Letter of credit
Standard shipping note

Documents against Acceptance (D/A)/Documents against Payment (D/P)   See **Documentary Bill of Exchange** under **Bill of Exchange**

Domestic Credit Expansion (DCE)   The chief means by which the **Bank of England** controls domestic credit (the money supply) are—
Open market operations
the issue of **Treasury Bills** requiring special deposits from the banks
the alteration of the reserve ratios of the banks
the use of the **Minimum Lending Rate** (MLR)

Domiciled Bill   A **Bill of Exchange** that requires the holder to present it to a named bank for payment.

Double liability   Wrongful acts can be both criminal and civil, and can be regulated at the same time by criminal and civil actions. This is known as *double liability*.

Double-entry bookkeeping   The feature from which double-entry bookkeeping derives its name is that every transaction is entered twice in the ledger; as a debit to one account and a credit to another. For example a credit sale to a customer will debit his personal account and credit the sales account.

Drawback   See **customs debentures**

Drawee   The bank charged with payment of a cheque.

Drawer   The person who writes and signs a cheque.

Duopoly   A special case of imperfect competition that exists where only two firms compete in the same market.

Duties   See **Customs and Excise**

E

Easements   Easement is a right to use the land of another, such as the use of a right of way.

Economic Development Committees (EDCs)   Like the **National Economic Development Council** the EDCs are tripartite, bringing together leading managers, trade unionists, and civil servants concerned with particular sectors of industry. Their task is to help improve the performance of their sectors by analysing problems, identifying opportunities and making recommendations to help bring about the help needed.
Sectors include
Agriculture and food manufacturing
Construction
Electronics
Project engineering
Mechanical and electrical engineering
Process materials industries
Textiles, clothing and footwear
Service industries (including distributive trades)
Cross sectoral (advanced manufacturing systems group)

Economic rent   This is the surplus earned by a **factor** above the income necessary to keep the factor of production at work.

Economics   Professor Marshall defined economics thus: 'Political economy, or economics, is a study of man's actions in the ordinary business of life; it inquires how he gets his income and how he uses it . . . Thus, it is on the one hand a study of wealth, and on the other and more important side a part of the study of man.'

The study of economics is chiefly concerned with production, distribution, and the exchange of wealth.

Economies of scale There are many advantages attached to large-scale organisation, both within the organisation itself and in its relationships with other organisations which provide it with goods and services external to its own activities. Among these are:
A greater facility to obtain finance for expansion;
More skilled and specialist personnel can be employed, especially as large firms can afford to train their own staff;
Increased output reduces the percentage of fixed costs to total costs, consequently unit costs become lower at each stage of production and profits increase;
Bulk buying improves purchasing power.

Economy, control of Every government tries to control the economy in order to achieve prosperity for the nation.
Financial measures influence the credit policy of the government. An easy credit policy and a low rate of interest encourage investment in new projects; a 'credit squeeze' makes it difficult for businesses to find the capital they require.
Fiscal measures/policy The fiscal policy of the government covers taxation policy in general, and is set out each year in the Budget. On Budget Day the Chancellor of the Exchequer presents to Parliament the Government's plans for raising money in the coming year—the fiscal programme.

In Britain the aim of fiscal and other measures has been to influence the level of activity in the economy. Money can be 'taken out' of the economy by high taxation; conversely money can be 'put back' into the economy by tax cuts and other measures. The Government has to decide the balance between revenue from taxation and public borrowing, as well as between direct and indirect taxation.

Economy, types of The economy of a country is made up of two sectors—the private sector and the public sector. Private enterprises are privately owned and operated; the public enterprise is socially owned and operated, and is run by the public for the benefit of the community.

Controlled economies are those where a high degree of centralised control exists and almost all enterprise is in the public sector. Such economies are found in Communist countries.

Free-enterprise economies are those where most of the wealth is in the hands of private enterprise. The United States has this type of economy, though public sector activity there is increasing.

Mixed economies—such as that of the United Kingdom—have a mixture of public and private enterprise.

Elasticity An economic concept that describes the degree of responsiveness to a change in price. Demand is said to be elastic when a relatively small variation in price causes a marked change in the amount demanded. The same concept applies to supply when a small change in price causes a marked change in the amount supplied. The concept has important implications for government policy, eg, on taxation and tariff setting as well as for the businessman who must monitor closely the effects of price changes on demand for goods and supply of the factors of production.

Electronic funds transfer A system of automatic transfer of money transactions supported by advanced computer and telecommunications systems. Credit transfer between banks is carried out on a large scale using the Society for Worldwide Interbank Financial Telecommunications (SWIFT) network. Messages are sent from bank to bank in 40 countries at high speed, but with complete security and at low cost. At a more personal level, the opportunity of 'cashless' transactions is being offered to more and more shoppers today as retailers increase their use of point of sale terminals for automatic payments.

Electronic office A term used to describe an office setting that is highly computerised and employs the latest techniques and developments in office technology. In such an office the typing,

83

filing, communications and retrieval of information are supported by electronic equipment.

Eligible banks Banks whose bill 'acceptances' the **Bank of England** is prepared to rediscount. In order to ensure an adequate supply of bills through which to conduct its money market operations, the Bank of England has been willing to extend eligibility to a wider range of banks. In judging applications for eligible status the Bank uses the following criteria:

(i) whether the applicant has a broadly based and substantial acceptance business in the United Kingdom,

(ii) whether its acceptances command the finest rates in the market for ineligible bills;

(iii) whether, in the case of foreign-owned banks, British banks enjoy reciprocal opportunities in the foreign owners' domestic market.

On a daily average basis these banks are required to invest 6 per cent of their *eligible liabilities* in secured money with the discount houses and/or secured call money with gilt-edged jobbers and money brokers.

Eligible liabilities Broadly speaking, a bank's **sterling** deposit liabilities, excluding deposits having an original maturity of over two years, and any sterling resources obtained by switching foreign currencies into sterling. See **reserve requirement**

Embargo Embargoes, quotas and **tariffs** are methods of protecting home industries. Embargoes prohibit the import of particular commodities, or goods from certain countries.

Employer's liability insurance See **accident insurance**

Employment, Contract of See **Contract of Employment**

Employment legislation Under the Contracts of Employment Act 1972 every employer must supply a new employee with a **Contract of Employment**. The Employment Protection Act 1975 added further requirements which are now incorporated in the

Contract of Employment; the Employment Act 1982 makes detailed changes to employee/Trade Union relationships within employment.

The three Acts which relate to discrimination in employment are:

Equal Pay Act 1970

Sex Discrimination Act 1975 (which set up the Equal Opportunities Commission)

Race Relations Act 1976 (which set up the Commission for Racial Equality)

Health and safety for employees are covered by:

The *Factories Act 1961*, which consolidated all factory law passed between 1937 and 1959 concerning health, safety, welfare and the employment of women and young persons (the working week for the two categories was limited to 48 and 44 hours respectively, and certain restrictions placed on the night employment of women).

Offices, Shops and Railways Premises Act 1963 covers regulations dealing with the provision of suitable sanitary accommodation, satisfactory standards of cleanliness, ventilation, lighting and heating, the avoidance of overcrowding; fire prevention precautions and the safety of office machinery.

Health and Safety at Work Act 1974 covers everyone at work and also increases the protection of the general public from industrial hazards. The Act sets out certain minimum standards of safety, health and welfare, and employers' and employees' duties in relation to these aspects of the working environment.

INDUSTRIAL TRAINING

The *Industrial Training Act 1964* created the Industrial Training Boards (ITBs) which are now under the direction of the **Manpower Services Commission**. Their aim is to improve the skills and knowledge of employees and to make them more mobile.

Employment and Training Act 1973 established the Manpower Services Commission (MSC).

Employment Rehabilitation Centre (ERC) See **Manpower Services Commission** (Employment Service)

Employment service   See **Manpower Services Commission**

Endorsement   The act of endorsing is the writing of one's name on the back of a **Bill of Exchange**, cheque, note, etc. When endorsed in this way a Bill of Exchange or cheque may be freely transferred from hand to hand and is negotiable.

Endowment assurance   The most popular method of combining life cover with long-term saving is through an endowment contract. This provides a sum of money which is payable by the insurance company either at the end of an agreed period (the maturity date) or at death, whichever occurs first.

The 'with profits' policy entitles the holder to a share in the insurance company's profits; this is called the 'bonus loading', but the premiums are higher than for the 'without profits' policies.

A 'term' policy pays only if death occurs during the agreed period, with no lump sum at the end of the term. This type of insurance is useful for covering the repayment of a house mortgage for dependents. A 'whole life' policy pays out whenever death occurs.

Enterprise Allowance Scheme   See **Manpower Services Commission**

Enterprise Zones   The government has declared certain areas of high unemployment to be Enterprise Zones where employment is encouraged through tax and rate relief.

Entrepreneur   An entrepreneur is one who is responsible for the initiation and organisation of enterprise in capitalist or free-market economies; he is the owner of the business.

The function of the entrepreneur is to control a business, and its success largely depends on his organising ability, foresight and general business capacity. His main function is to maximise profits. This function may be performed by sole traders or partners who own the business, or by professional managers who are employees of an organisation.

Equity

'Entry' form   Goods arriving in the United Kingdom must be entered for Customs clearance on an 'entry' form.
Non-dutiable goods and dutiable goods are required to be entered for statistical purposes; in addition dutiable goods are inspected by Customs and the duties collected.

Equal Opportunities Commission   This was set up under the Sex Discrimination Act 1975 and can institute legal proceedings against employers who do not allow women equal opportunities of employment.

Equal Pay Act 1970   This Act prevents discrimination against women in the terms and conditions of employment.

Equilibrium   An economic term to describe the point at which the amount of a commodity demanded equals the amount offered for sale.

Equity   1   This popularly means natural justice or fair play. Lawyers use the term in a more technical sense as that system of law which has been evolved in the Chancery Court to provide relief for wrongs for which the common law offers no remedy.
   Equity follows the common law but if the common law should suffer a wrong to be without a remedy it will 'see fair play' is administered in the Chancery Court.
2   is the true risk capital of a company. Equity shares have a nominal value which can be anything from 1p upwards. There is no guarantee that an investor in equity shares will get either a dividend or his money back, but he does get the chance of an income and possibly capital growth. Also, being a part owner of the company he has the right to vote proportionately to the number of shares he holds.
   There are more equity shares than any other type. The owner receives a dividend only after other classes of shareholder have been paid the amounts due to them. If a firm is not prospering there is sometimes no dividend, and ordinary shares carry the greatest risk.

Ergonomics The scientific study of the way a human body works, and its physical dimensions. The results are applied to the design of equipment and machines for the workplace with a view to reducing fatigue, discomfort and strain.

Estoppel The fact of being precluded from a certain action as a result of a previous action or statement.

Eurobonds London has established itself firmly in the Eurobond market; outside the United Kingdom gilt-edged market this is one of the largest capital markets in the world. Eurobonds sprang from the Interest Equalisation Tax introduced in the United States in 1963, which made it cheaper for US companies with overseas operations to raise capital outside the US. This gave birth to Eurodollars (the bonds are issued in dollar units). Although most issues are listed in the **London Stock Exchange**, or on a continental bourse, dealing is mostly by international dealers and largely takes place over the telephone.

A recent activity of great importance is the issue of international Eurobonds—sometimes in dollar units (Eurodollars) but also in Swiss francs, Deutschemarks and other units.

Eurocurrency Eurocurrency is paper money on the books of a bank belonging to an overseas customer and can be used to settle debts in other currencies. It originated in Eurodollars which were simply dollar deposits in European centres.

The international banking community in London is active not only in the financing of foreign trade, but in Eurocurrency lending, interbank and Eurobond operations, international **portfolio** management, corporate finance and **consumer credit**, all of which involve Eurocurrency, though this activity is no longer confined to Europe.

Foreign exchange and Eurocurrency are two separate parts of the foreign exchange market. Eurocurrency concerns borrowing and lending—not the buying and selling of one currency against another.

Eurodollars International Eurobonds—once issued only in

dollar units (eurodollars)—are now issued in Swiss francs, Deutschemarks and other units as well as Eurodollars.

Eurolex   The database system for EEC laws.

European Assembly/Parliament   See **European Economic Community**

European Commission   See **European Economic Community**

European Community Law   The branch of law which follows from the United Kingdom's membership of the EEC. The Treaty of Rome, by which the EEC was set up, has the force of law and the Council of Europe can make regulations, directives and decisions which also have the force of law.

European Court of Justice   See **European Economic Community**

European Currency Unit (ECU)   This is a currency 'basket'—it is made up of the currencies of Germany, Great Britain, France, Italy, Holland, Belgium, Luxembourg, Denmark and Ireland—the proportion of each currency being directly linked to the value of international trade carried on by the participating nations. The value of the units is recalculated every day and officially announced, but if the rises and falls within one unit 'balance out' (eg, should the mark rise and the franc fall) the fluctuation in the ECU will be less than that exhibited in a single currency.

This currency unit is used as the unit of measure for all accounts of the member states, and as the medium for presenting financial statements; it may be said to be achieving its objective of a large measure of currency stability between western European countries.

European Economic Community (EEC)   The Common Market. The EEC was founded by the Treaty of Rome in 1957 with six signatories—France, Germany, Italy, the Netherlands, Belgium and Luxembourg—with the intention of setting up a free-trade area and eventually a political and monetary union. Britain joined the EEC in 1973, together with Denmark and Eire.

The aims of the EEC are far-reaching, and go beyond industrial integration; they include a common agricultural policy, free movement of labour and capital, and a unified transport system; in fact, economic integration. Membership of the EEC is changing the patterns of European trade, and increasingly trade is taking place within the Community.

MAJOR INSTITUTIONS OF THE EEC

The EEC studies all aspects of the life of the Community and has five major institutions:

1 *The Council of Ministers*, consisting of one minister from each member state, which takes all basic decisions on Community policy.

2 *European Assembly/Parliament* Members are elected by the electorate of their own states.

The function of the European Assembly is to debate all matters of Community policy, to question both the Commission and the Council of Ministers, and to supervise the Community Budget. It can compel the Commission to resign by a two-thirds majority vote.

3 *European Commission* A major institution of the EEC the Commission consists of two commissioners from each major member and one from smaller powers, chosen by agreement. They act in accordance with powers laid down by the Treaty of Rome, co-ordinating activity in particular fields, considering issues from a Community point of view independent of national interests or aspirations.

The function of the Commission is to formulate proposals for decision by the Council of Ministers and to supply information to, and answers to questions from, the European Parliament. It also provides the day-to-day administration services of the Community.

4 *European Court of Justice* This is composed of learned judges from member nations and has sole authority to interpret the meaning of disputed passages in the Treaty of Rome. All governments, businesses and individuals may appeal to the Court of Justice if they are aggrieved by the application of any

Community regulation.

5 *The Committee of Permanent Representatives* (COREPER), composed of ambassadors to the EEC from all the member states.

Implementation of the Treaty of Rome is through the Common External Tariff (CET), Common Agricultural Policy (CAP), and the Community Transit (CT) System which have the following objectives:

The CET seeks to exclude foreign goods which could as easily be made by one of the EEC member states;

CAP imposes levies on cheap imports to keep up the EEC market price. (If a farmer cannot sell his product on the home market he may sell it to the State Intervention Board at a slightly lower price than the market price; this has created butter mountains, wine lakes, etc.)

Goods moving between member nations are documented by the Community Transit (CT) System which gives entitlement to preferential tariff rates. Tariffs are used to discourage the import of food from non-member states.

EEC FINANCES

The *Regional Development Fund* is used to give direct assistance to investment projects.

The *European Economic Community Agricultural Guidance and Guarantee Fund* supports farm prices and encourages the implementation of agreed agricultural arrangements. (FEOGA is the French abbreviation).

The *European Social Fund* is chiefly used to assist training programmes.

The *European Investment Bank* (EIB) borrows money on the world's capital markets and lends it out on a number of EEC projects, especially in the development of depressed regions, and energy.

European Free Trade Association (EFTA) An economic free trade area created in 1960, but with no common external tariff. The main difference between this and the EEC was that EFTA wished to create a free trade area which would involve minimal erosion of national sovereignties, the object being purely free trade rather than complete economic integration. Since the UK left EFTA and joined the EEC she has enjoyed tariff advantages in the enlarged market, though only at the expense of her privileged position in EFTA and the Commonwealth.

European Monetary System (EMS)   In 1979 the **EEC** (except for the UK, which though not an EMS member has a certain involvement with it) converted to the European Monetary System, by which members' currencies are tied to one another through a grid of currency parities; they are also all tied to the **European Currency Unit** (ECU)—a new international currency. When individual currencies rise or fall the overall value of the ECU changes little, though a country with an obviously weakening currency should take remedial action.

In early 1985 when the pound slipped—not only against the dollar, but also against other European currencies—there was a strong feeling in certain quarters in the UK (among them the CBI in particular), that had Britain been a member of the EMS the situation could have been more easily controlled.

European Parliament   See **European Economic Community**

ex div (ex dividend)   When shares are sold **ex div** the purchaser will not receive the dividend, which will still be paid to the previous owner.

ex ship   See **delivery costs**

ex works   See **delivery costs**

Exchange   1   The term applied to the transfer from one person or institution of goods or services to another person or institution in return for another good or service, or for money.
2   Exchange, in commerce, is used in various senses of the giving or receiving of money or of one currency in return for an

equivalent sum in another currency.

3 Exchange is applied to the assemblage of merchants, bankers and brokers for the transaction of business in commodities, stocks, bonds, bills, etc, and also to the place in which they meet for such purposes, eg, the *Stock Exchange*, Baltic Mercantile and Shipping Exchange, and the Royal Exchange.

Exchange controls These were abandoned in 1979.

Exchange Equalisation Account This contains Britain's gold and foreign currency reserves; it is from this account that the foreign currency ultimately comes when it is needed by an importer to buy goods or by a traveller to spend abroad. It is also used as a defence against currency speculators, and to buy unwanted sterling.

Established in 1932 by the **Treasury**, it was intended for the purpose of buying or selling foreign currencies. The main object of the account is to intervene in the international money market in such a way as to stabilise the value of sterling.

Exchange rates The price of **sterling** (its exchange rate with other currencies) affects the prices of imports and exports. If the exchange rate is low then imports are more expensive and exports become cheaper. If the exchange rate is high, imports are cheaper and exports become more expensive. Movements in the exchange rate affect importers and exporters, and ultimately the whole economy. When the exchange rate gets too much out of line and stability is required the government may step in by raising interest rates; this will attract foreign money to correct the balance. It can also restrict imports by imposing a low rate of exchange by devaluation.

Since 1972 the price of the pound has been determined by the supply and demand for sterling. The **Bank of England** can influence the exchange rate by selling sterling when the government wants the rate to go down and by using foreign currency reserves to buy sterling when the government wants the exchange rate to increase.

The **International Monetary Fund** seeks always to promote harmony in international monetary relations by discouraging erratic movements in exchange rates. See **foreign exchange market.**

Excise duty   This is an indirect tax, imposed on tobacco, petroleum products and alcohol. Excise duties are specific taxes (per unit) imposed at the point of production and which must be paid by the manufacturer before parting with the goods; the tax is later included in the price paid by the final consumer.

Export agents   See **export houses, freight forwarding agents**

Export Buying Offices Association   This is an association of the London buying offices of leading overseas department stores and importers. The majority of consumer goods sold to department stores overseas are channelled through EXBO members who can advise manufacturers on the suitability of their goods for foreign markets.

Export clubs   The idea of the export club is that members (industrialists) should pool their information and knowledge for the benefit of other members. (See also **Inward Missions** and **Outward Missions**).

Export Credit Guarantee Department (ECGD)   This is a separate government department responsible to the Secretary of State for Trade. ECGD provides credit insurance for UK exporters against non-payment risks, guarantees to banks for export finance, and insurance against political risks on new overseas investments. Support is also available against cost-escalation on certain large capital goods contracts, and for performance bonds on large cash or near-cash contracts.

The usual principles of insurance apply to ECGD insurance. The main policies issued are:

Comprehensive policies   The exporting firm insures all its exports to all markets for a specified period. The premiums vary according to the period of time involved, and the market to which the trader is exporting.

Specific guarantees are issued for large, capital projects.

Insurance of investment covers shipping consultant services and other 'invisibles'.

Cover for state-trading company's contracts is given where an exporter has a contract with this type of purchasing organisation, usually in communist countries; compensation is paid if the buyer defaults.

In certain circumstances ECGD will provide a *comprehensive bill* guarantee which will enable an exporter to draw on his bank against outstanding bills drawn against the overseas customer.

ECGD policies are accepted as collateral security by banks financing overseas trade.

Export finance   Can be of three kinds: short- and medium-term, long-term or forward trading.

1   SHORT- AND MEDIUM-TERM TRANSACTIONS

(a) Bank overdrafts and loans can be used by exporters who cannot afford to finance their own sales. Collateral security in the form of an ECGD Policy may be asked for.

(b) Export houses and export merchants can be used by UK-based manufacturers as this is often a trouble-free method of selling. **Confirming houses** and **Export houses** undertake the sale, distribution and delivery to the overseas customer, and assume the financial risk involved in obtaining payment.

(c) **Bills of Exchange** may be used.

(d) **Open Accounts**   If a British exporter has a long-standing arrangement with an overseas buyer, the buyer will make payments directly into the overseas branch of the exporter's commercial bank who will often credit the exporter in advance of receiving payment—especially if the transaction has been backed by an ECGD policy.

2   LONG-TERM PROJECTS

Projects such as the building of dams, oil refineries, etc, may be financed by international organisations such as the **International Bank for Reconstruction and Development** (IBRD), who pays the exporter and assumes responsibility for collecting payments from the countries concerned.

3 FORWARD TRADING

An exporter can suffer serious losses if his export earnings are affected by a falling exchange rate. To prevent this happening the exporter can sell currency 'forward'. 'Forward trading' is buying or selling *currency* forward at an agreed exchange rate for delivery in the future—in 3, 6 or 12 months' time. When the exporter receives payment the exchange rate will be at the 'forward rate', whatever has happened to the £ in the meantime. This is a necessary function to equalise demand and stabilise rates.

Export house/merchant   This type of intermediary functions in one or more capacities as manufacturers' agent, export manager, buying or confirming house, export finance house and so on. Many are members of the British Export Houses Association and they generally specialise in particular markets or goods. Export houses cover the shipping, packing, insurance and finance of export orders. As **confirming houses** they take full responsibility for export orders and remove from the exporter all worries about payment.

These firms may receive their orders in the form of an 'indent' from abroad. An indent requires the export house to find a supplier for the goods required.

Export insurance   See **Export Credit Guarantees Department**

Export Intelligence Service   The Export Intelligence Service receives a non-stop supply of export opportunities from worldwide British diplomatic posts. Each item is given a computer coding and when that matches the type of information which has been requested by a British exporter an immediate printout is posted to him.

The Export Intelligence Service is supported by a range of regional offices throughout Great Britain.

Export invoice   See **commercial invoice** and **consular invoice**

Export licences   The United Kingdom stipulates that a licence must be obtained before certain goods can *leave* this country. This

96

restriction applies mainly to works of art, articles of historical value, and 'strategic' commodities (arms and ammunition), where the restriction may apply only to specified countries.

Export Marketing Research Scheme   This service offers free professional advice on how to set about market research to the best advantage. When a market research project for an overseas market has been decided upon the **British Overseas Trade Board** may make a grant of up to 50% towards the costs.

Export merchant   See **export house**

Export representative service   This is a service which helps exporters to find representatives to handle their trade in an overseas market.

Once requirements are known the BOTB will contact the Commercial Department of the British Embassy (or similar diplomatic post) in the country with which trade is expected to take place. The Department will send back a report listing local businessmen who have been sounded out and will be interested in selling the product or service for the British exporter.

Export restrictions and controls   See **export licences**

Export, risk of   The nature of a consignment determines the type of risk to which it will be subject. Physical journeys by sea or air can present a risk in themselves; rough weather and/or sea water can affect cargoes. Theft at the docks is a very real risk (modified now by containerisation), but the most serious risk is that of non-payment. These risks must be covered by adequate insurance. See **marine insurance** and **ECGD (Export Credit Guarantee Department**.)

Export services provided by the British Overseas Trade Board for UK exporters   The BOTB is an official organisation which directs the Government's export promotion programme.

The following is a list of services provided; details of each will

be found under its own heading.
Country Profiles
Export Buying Offices Association
Export Houses
Export Intelligence Service
Export Marketing Research Scheme
Export Representative Service
Freight Forwarders
Inward Missions
Market Entry Guarantee Scheme
Market Prospects Service
Outward Missions
Overseas Projects Fund
Overseas Seminars
Overseas Status Report Services
Product Data Store
Project and Export Policy Division
Publicity for Exports
SITPRO (Simplification of International Trade Procedures Board)
Statistics and Market Intelligence Library
Store Promotions
Technical Help to Exporters (THE)
Trade Fairs Overseas
Trade Promotions Guide
USA Initiative
World Aid Section
See also **Export Credit Guarantee Department**

Export trade   Britain is an important trading nation, but since becoming a member of the EEC her trading patterns have changed and her overseas markets are now more concentrated on Europe and North America.

The stimulation of exports figures largely in Government economic policies, its aim being to balance exports against imports. Imports are vital to a country which cannot produce all its own food or the goods it requires—nor the raw materials needed by industry.

Goods can be sold on the export market in any of the following ways:

By direct selling from the UK   See **Export services provided by the British Overseas Trade Board**

Selling by overseas agents   These are 'home nationals' who are able to understand the complexities of trade in their own countries.

By setting up an overseas base   This is a typical activity of many international companies who have resources not available to the small exporter.

In the 'invisible' export field overseas manufacturers can be licensed to produce and market British products, 'royalties' being paid to the British firm. The use of licensing enables the British manufacturer to sell goods which otherwise could not be sold overseas by direct exportation. Local import restrictions, prohibitive tariffs, and even a lack of the right currency sometimes make such sales impossible.

Extractive industry (economics)   This is the first stage of production—primary production—and includes the work of all producers engaged in making available raw materials and natural products (food, fishing, agriculture, mining, timber felling).

Most primary production is in the form of raw materials which have to be manufactured into other goods at the secondary stage of production.

Extraordinary General Meeting (EGM)   In addition to the statutory **Annual General Meeting** an EGM may be called at any time to discuss special business which cannot conveniently be held over till the next Annual General Meeting.

F

Facsimile (Transmission)   The transmission of text, pictures, diagrams, etc. An image is scanned by a transmitting device, and reconstructed at a remote receiving machine as a faithful reproduction of the original.

Factor (trade)   An agent who actually has the goods in his possession, sells and delivers them to the buyer, and renders an account, less his commission, to his principal. Factors are particularly useful in the export trade.

Factoring of debts   See **debt factoring**

Factors of production   The factors of production are:
Land, which is of primary importance. The term is used to cover all natural resources available to man, and **land** for factories, warehouses, etc.
Capital is the factor which helps man to produce tools of every sort—both money and goods.
Labour is another essential factor of production,—not only physical labour, but skilful use of human attributes.
The entrepreneur is not regarded by all economists as a factor of production.

Factory Acts   See **employment legislation**

Fair average quality (faq)   This refers to the condition of goods for sale. This type of quotation often refers to goods which are already classified and graded by the trade.

Fair Trading Act 1973   See **Office of Fair Trading**

Family law   The family division of the law covers all matters concerning marriage and divorce, and maintenance claims for wives and children.

Family protection policy   In this type of policy if death occurs during the period stated in the contract the benefit will be paid, not in one lump sum, but by a series of regular payments, terminating with a final sum at the end of a period; it provides useful cover for a widow and young dependents. The period of the contract is usually arranged to cover the time before the children are able to support themselves.

Fee simple   In English law one of the two legal estates in land. 'Fee simple', broadly speaking, covers the term 'freehold'; the other—'the term of years absolute' can be described as 'leasehold'.

FEOGA   These are the initials of the French name of the EEC's **Agricultural Guidance and Guarantee Fund** which supports farm prices and encourages the implementation of agricultural agreement arrangements.

Fidelity bond/guarantee   This is the insurance of interest. For instance, a professional firm may take out cover against the possibility that one of its members may have to answer for giving incorrect professional advice. A fidelity bond is a form of insurance for the benefit of employers, by which they are indemnified against loss through fraud or dishonesty of their employees.

Fiduciary issue   That part of the **Bank of England's** note issue which is not backed by gold but by Government and other securites ('fiduciary' means 'in good faith').

Field research   See **marketing**

FIFO (first in, first out) A method for controlling stock that assumes the goods received first will be the first issued. For stock valuation purposes, the issues are valued at the price paid for the first purchases in the period.

Final dividend The dividend covering the last part of a company's year, recommended by the directors, but authorised by the shareholders at the **Annual General Meeting**.

Finance Finance plays a vital part in both Government organisations and private industry; working within cash limits and providing an adequate cash flow present perennial problems in businesses faced with **inflation** and recession when figures become distorted. Financial information in an organisation is essential to enable managers to formulate a sound business policy for the future; only from the recorded accounts can an analysis be made of the actual cost of goods and services offered, the amount spend on overheads and the exact revenue of the business. Control over expenditure is made possible when figures can be examined and regulated.

PUBLIC SECTOR

Commercial organisations in the public sector face the same problems as those in the private sector—they should pay their way. Often, of course, they do not and run on a perpetual deficit.

Non-commercial organisations in the public sector are given money—and strict cash limits—by the Government, which funds such services from direct and indirect taxes, rates, national insurance contributions and motor vehicle duty.

The Government raises money in other ways: through the 'open market' operations on the **Stock Exchange** (the issue of 'gilt-edged securities' which are central or local government loan stock), through the issue of **Treasury Bills**, and from overseas investment in sterling.

IN THE PRIVATE SECTOR—SHORT-TERM
1 *Bank loans and bank overdrafts* may be obtained.
2 *Hire-purchase* may sometimes enable small businesses to

acquire equipment, but the system is expensive and mostly used when other forms of credit are not available.

3 *Leasing* is becoming increasingly popular—it is a combination of hiring, instalment credit and property leasing. No large sums of money are required to obtain capital equipment, and usually the payment of a fixed cost is made in advance, which facilitates budgeting.

IN THE PRIVATE SECTOR—LONG-TERM

Public and private limited companies obtain their initial capital from the sale of *shares*. Further shares may be issued to raise more capital, but only those of **public limited companies** may be offered to the public for sale.

Debentures may also be issued; though only those of public limited companies are sold on the **Stock Exchange**; they are not shares but *loans* to a company which will ultimately be paid back.

Mortgages enable sole traders and partnerships to purchase premises.

Government assistance is available for industrial innovations, and the construction industry can be given improvement grants and financial aid for inner city projects.

Finance for export   see **export finance**

Finance For Industry (FFI)   This organisation has been replaced by **Investors in Industry**—known as 3i.

Finance Houses Association (FHA)   There are 39 members of the FHA; these include all the larger HP firms. Between them the HP companies provide the money for a continually enlarging market, and without them industrial growth and innovation would stagnate.

Industrial and commercial finance is the main area of activity of the larger finance houses, though all the houses concentrate on particular areas.

Cars and consumer durables are almost always financed for the consumer by a finance house.

The finance houses were pioneers in the field of **leasing** and

debt factoring is another area where they have a substantial stake.

The credit industry itself is financed by deposits from the public, and industrial and commercial companies. They also borrow from the banks. It is because of their high borrowing costs that HP charges are relatively high.

The FHA has its own base rate which is determined by an agreed formula.

Block discounting is another activity of the finance houses. This involves the buying from retailers of blocks of instalment credit agreements, an immediate cash sum being paid to the retailer.

Financial accounting   This covers the recording of all financial activivies as they occur—the record of all transactions (buying and selling), the payment of wages (and payments to other organisations which result from this—to pension funds, inland revenue, national insurance. etc).

The financial accounting department is also responsible for the preparation of the annual accounts of an organisation.

Financial control (of the economy)   See **economy, control of**

Financial control (of businesses)
Public sector   Local authorities and Government departments are accountable to district and internal auditors, and the Public Expenditure Survey Committee (PESC), and should observe 'cash limits' when such restrictions are set.
Private sector   Financial control is exercised by budgeting. Implementation is in the hands of managers and accountants, the accounts being finally passed by external auditors.

***Financial Times (FT)* Index**   The FT Index is the Industrial Shares Index also known as the '30-share Index', and is based on the prices of 30 leading industrial and commercial shares. Government stocks, banks and insurance companies are not included. The FT Index is calculated hourly during trading hours and again as a 'closing index' at 5.00 pm. The movement of the index 'up' or 'down' indicates the mood of the market on that particular day.

Fine rate   This is an agreed minimum rate below which the discount houses will not buy bank bills. (Bank bills are **Bills of Exchange** which have been accepted or endorsed by a reputable bank and are very reliable—hence the competitive minimum rate at which they may be discounted).

Fire insurance   This is a contract of indemnity in respect of loss or damage to material property by fire.

TYPES OF FIRE INSURANCE POLICIES
Straightforward *fire insurance* on domestic and business premises and their contents.
Consequential loss or loss of profits insurance indemnifies an insured party for loss caused by the interruption to business activities resulting from fire. The normal fire policy covers only the value of damaged property, but other losses consequent upon a fire may prove to be even costlier to the business. The type of consequential losses covered by an extension to the fire policy are:
loss of profits   If the annual trading activities of a business are interrupted it cannot continue to earn profits;
additional costs of working   These might include transferring to temporary premises during restoration;
standing charges   These must continue during restoration—eg, rent, rates, bank interest, etc;
insurance of 'special perils', such as flooding;
household policies which cover fire and a very wide range of risks, including burglary.

First entry, books of   Because of the rule in bookkeeping that transactions must be passed through the subsidiary books before being entered in the ledger, the subsidiary books are known collectively as the books of original, or first, entry. The four subsidiary books are the purchases day book, the sales day book, sales returns and purchase returns books. The cash book is one of the books of first entry, but is not a subsidiary book.
stock.

First In, First Out   See **FIFO**

105

Fiscal measures/policy (of Government)   See **Economy, control of**

Fixed assets   See **assets**

Fixed capital   See **capital** (types of)

Fixed costs   See **costs** (of production)

Fixed interest   With *fixed interest stocks* the amount of interest is known in advance and is often included in the title of the security, eg, 7½% Treasury Stock.

Fixings   The name given to the twice-daily meetings of members of the London Gold Market to establish the day's official gold price.

Fixture   A ship chartering deal on the Baltic Exchange which is sealed with a handshake.

Flat yield   This is the income received on *fixed interest stock.*

Flexitime   A workplace practice that allows staff some discretion in the time they start and finish work. It is usual practice for employers to prescribe a core time (say 10.00 a.m. till 4.00 p.m.) when all staff must be present, but outside those hours staff can choose arrival and departure times that best accommodate their personal needs, within a normal working week.

Floating a company   After obtaining clearance from the Registrar of Companies that the proposed name for the company is acceptable the **promoter** joins with one other person in signing—
    The **Memorandum of Association**, governing the relationship of the company with the outside world,
    The **Articles of Association** which control the internal affairs of the company,
    The Prospectus,
    A statement of nominal capital,

A list of Directors with their written consent and promise to take up shares,

A statutory declaration that the Company Acts have been complied with.

These documents are then sent to the **Registrar of Companies** who may grant a Certificate of Incorporation.

When this certificate is received shares can be issued by—

A *private limited company*, the shares being usually bought by the founders.

A *public limited company* (plc). These are bought by the public (directly) or by large institutional investors (indirectly). Often financiers will underwrite public companies to ensure that the minimum capital is subscribed.

When the money is subscribed, documents of confirmation are sent to the Registrar of Companies who, if satisfied, will issue a Certificate of Trading to the new company which enables it to commence business.

Floating capital   See **capital** (Circulating capital)

Floating currencies   Floating currencies are those which do not have a fixed value,—the market forces of supply and demand decide their value, which fluctuates from day to day, and sometimes several times a day.

Floating debentures   See **debentures** (Stock Exchange)

Floating policy   See **cargo insurance**

Flowchart   A diagram that uses special symbols and interconnecting lines to represent the steps in a procedure.

Food and Drug Act 1955   This makes it an offence to sell food which is unfit for human consumption. It also requires the composition of food products to be stated clearly on the packaging.

Forecasting

Forecasting A technique used by governments and business planners to predict future behaviour in the economy or market place. A model is set up, taking account of known variables, and a number of statistical techniques employed to project past relationships into the future. It is a necessary and valuable aid to planning, but as all business and economic activity is dynamic, freezing the system in order to obtain a workable model can lead to unreliable results.

Foreign bill See **bill of exchange**

Foreign exchange market The City of London provides the world's leading market for the exchange of currencies, though it is not based in one building of its own. Foreign exchange dealing is carried on in many separate city locations, but dealers keep in close touch by electronic communication systems. Members of the Foreign Exchange Brokers' Association accept business only from banks actively dealing in the foreign exchange markets.

Exchange dealing is a vital link in the chain of international trade. Exporters buying raw materials from abroad may have to pay in a foreign currency, but may require payment for finished goods in sterling. An exporter's local bank will arrange the necessary transactions through the foreign exchange market.

The Bank of England supervises the exchange rate for the £, and is ready to take action if it moves too far one way or the other; further internal regulation is exercised by the British Bankers' Association. All member countries of the IMF (**International Monetary Fund**) must keep their exchange rates within limits.

Foreign exchange and **Eurocurrency** are two separate parts of the foreign exchange market. The former is the buying and selling of one currency against another; the latter concerns borrowing and lending. Currency speculation must not be confused with forward trading (see **export finance, Exchange Equalisation Account**).

Foreign trade See **export trade** and **import trade**

Forfeiture The procedure by which a company expropriates the **shares** of a member who has defaulted in paying part of the
108

moneys due from him in respect of shares declared forfeit.

Form letters Standardised letters used by businesses for correspondence of a similar or repetitive nature. Examples of their use are to be found in acknowledging employment applications, or in accounts, as reminder letters for overdue payments. Their use helps keep costs down and speed up communications.

Forward dealing   See **Export finance**

Founder's shares   See **shares (deferred shares)**

Franchising   A franchise agreement is made between two parties when an individual or firm sells another individual or firm the right to market something in its possession according to an agreed format. The 'something' can be a process (like the 'secret formula' in so many franchise foodstuffs), a brand good, or a patented device.

   Almost always the agreement will be for a specific area, and other subsidiary agreements (dealing with supplies, equipment, servicing) will be involved with the package. The franchise is not buying just the rights to a name, but the blueprint for an entire, successful operation.

   There is a vast difference between a chain of restaurants and a franchise operation. With the former, a company may start one restaurant, make a profit, and then go on to own other restaurants using the same name. With a franchise operation, the 'parent' company may own one or two of the first restaurants opened—to create a 'name'—but the main part of the operation is to allow others to use its name and product by special agreement.

Franco quotations/franco domicile   See **delivery costs**

Franked income   Dividends received by one company from another company, whose profits have already borne **Corporation Tax**, and which are not subject to further Corporation Tax. *Unfranked Income* has not borne tax, and is subject to Corporation Tax.

Free alongside ship (fas)

Free alongside ship (fas)   See **delivery costs**

Free enterprise economy   See **economy, types of**

Freehold   A business can become the *owner* of land by purchasing the freehold.

Free of Particular Average (FPA)   'Average' in this case means 'the expense or loss to owners arising from damage at sea to the ship or cargo'. An FPA policy covers only against total loss.

Free on board   See **delivery costs**

Free on rail   See **delivery costs**

Free trade   This is trade between nations which is free of all restrictions such as tariffs (customs duties), quotas, and the protection of home industries by subsidisation.

 Though universal free trade could be advantageous, from a national point of view the protection of some home industries is necessary.

 Free trade areas (customs unions) are groups of nations which offer each other reciprocal trading arrangements. The major groups are the EEC, EFTA, the British Commonwealth, and Comecon (the Communist Economic Community).

Freeports   See **ports**

Freight forwarding agents   These agents carry out the handling, through-transport arrangements, and payment collection for the greater part of exports from the United Kingdom.

Freight insurance   *Freight* is the *charge* for carrying cargo. The carriage charges are the income of the carrier, and freight insurance covers the *loss of freight*,—ie, the loss of this income.

Freight market (Baltic Exchange)   This is a highly-organised market where cargoes are arranged for ships and ships for cargoes.

Cargoes are shipped by
Liners operating on regular routes with international calls
Tramps prepared to go anywhere with a cargo for profit
Ships are chartered by
Chartering Agents who represent merchants and others who want to charter ships,
Shipbrokers (owners' brokers) who represent the shipowners
Independent Brokers who arrange both cargoes for ships, and ships for cargoes
Charters
Voyage charters cover a particular cargo for a particular voyage
Time charters give 'rights' over the vessel for a specified period of time.
   See also **charter party** and **air freight market**

Freightliners   The Freightliner system of British Rail is designed to—
run trains in fixed formation between terminals,
run trains to an agreed timetable,
use wagons which convey containers only,
transfer containers from rail to road or to ship, and vice versa, at high speed.
   Freightliners offer customers a fast, reliable, and door-to-door service over medium and long distances. Flexible charging arrangements offer highly competitive prices.

Friction   Friction is any market force which reduces the efficient fixing of prices. Examples are duties imposed on goods and transport costs.

Frictional unemployment   See **unemployment**

Friendly societies   Friendly societies seek to improve the economic position of their members through benefits from subscriptions, which are used for sickness, death, endowment and retirement benefits.

Functional organisation   A form of business organisation where specialists are appointed to undertake and advise on a certain type of work throughout the organisation. These specialists act in an advisory capacity only and do not exercise any authority over line management. The O & M team would be regarded as one such specialist function in most organisations.

Funding   Literally this is the conversion of a floating debt into a permanent one. It may be defined in national terms as persuading citizens and institutions to lend money on a long-term basis (creating a fund) to the Government.

Futures   Futures (or terminal markets) are markets where the goods being bought and sold are not yet available but will be available later. Goods are ordered at a specified price and delivered later at the price agreed, even if market prices have fallen or risen.

A futures contract is essentially a transaction between two parties who require to cover themselves against opposite risks; one fears a rise in price, the other a fall. Speculators are also active in the futures markets and help to stabilise market prices. See also **hedging** and **International Commodity Clearing House (ICCH).**

G

Garnishee order An order on a bank, made by a judgment creditor, for an attachment of funds in respect of a customer's account. The bank stops the account and returns any cheques not yet presented.

Gearing This is the *capital* gearing—the ratio between a company's different sources of finance—ie, between a company's **equity** (ordinary **shares** and dividend capital) and its permanent loan capital (preference shares and **debentures**). When deciding which source of finance to use, the cost of the sources and the company's expected yield will influence the balance between the different sources.

General Agreement on Tariffs and Trade (GATT) Brought into existence at the Geneva Conference 1947, GATT reflected a belief among the members in free international trade for the whole world. It has been very successful in its efforts to simplify and standardise international trade statistics, customs procedures and valuations, and has made valuable contributions to the understanding of international economic relations. A series of very long tariff-bargaining rounds has lowered the overall level of tariffs considerably. Trade agreements now normally follow the pattern of bilateral arrangements between pairs of countries product by product.

Since its creation, GATT has been the only accepted international instrument which lays down rules of conduct for trade on a world-wide basis, and which has been accepted by a high proportion of the leading trading nations.

During the last few years GATT has begun to devote more of its efforts to the task of expanding and stabilising exports of the less developed countries.

General average (g/a) (marine insurance)   'Average' in this case means the expense or loss to owners arising from damage at sea to the ship or cargo. If difficulties occur which make it necessary to jettison cargo or have a ship towed into port by another vessel the cost of such actions is called a *general average*, and must be shared proportionately by all underwriters.

General ledger   The accounts book required for a proper record of the transactions of a business is called the Ledger. In a large firm there may be several ledgers—the sales ledger contains the debtors' accounts, and the purchase (or bought) ledger contains the creditors' accounts. A third ledger—the general or nominal ledger—contains the real and nominal accounts relating to the assets and liabilities and the gains and expenses of the business.

General partners   See **partners**

Geographical location   Some sites are more suitable than others for the location of a business; primarily of course the type of business is the most important factor which influences the choice of site. Following this it is necessary to consider the availability of communications for physical distribution (facilities provided for electronic information technology are available everywhere).

Raw materials and labour should be available for industrial undertakings; commerce seems to function best in a 'commercial centre' where the various services can use common facilities. Direct services will be found wherever there is a need for them.

The government has declared certain areas of high unemployment to be enterprise zones, where employment is encouraged through tax and rate relief. This may provide a strong inducement for a business to choose a particular location.

Giffen goods   A term which refers to those essential and relatively cheap goods for which demand is likely to increase following a rise in price. The Giffen Paradox is named after a 19th century economist who noticed that when the price of bread increased, consumers bought more of it, being unable to afford more luxurious foods such as meat and fruit.

Gilt-edged market   Government expenditure is not met entirely by taxation so there is a constant need for the Government to borrow the money required. This is the primary function of the gilt-edged market, and is achieved by the buying and selling of marketable government and local authority securities. These pay a fixed rate of interest throughout their lives, repayment being guaranteed by the government.

Most new stocks are announced in the financial press and anyone can apply for them, but buyers are mainly institutions—long-term stock is obviously particularly suitable for life assurance companies and pension funds. The banks and **discount houses** trade in short-dated Government and local authority stock.

These 'open market' operations help to implement the Government's monetary policy; by selling such stock the Government siphons money out of the system; to put money back it can buy back stock in the same markets.

Any member of the public can buy gilt-edged stocks on the register at Post Offices, where the commission rates are much cheaper than those of stockbrokers.

Government stocks form the core of the fixed interest investments.

Gold Bullion Market   See **bullion markets**

Gold reserves   Today there is a shortage of gold—British gold reserves represent only part of the face value of the country's issued currency; another part is reflected in the amount of foreign currencies it holds. If the Bank of England intervenes in the foreign exchange market to stabilise the value of sterling against the currencies of other main trading countries, it does this through the Exchange Equalisation Account which includes Britain's gold and foreign currency reserves. The funds can be used by the Bank of England to buy unwanted sterling and stabilise the exchange rate.

115

Goods All the wants of mankind can be classified under the headings of either goods or services. Goods are tangible things such as clothes, motor vehicles, furniture, etc. Services are intangible things such as the services offered by a doctor, solicitor, or entertainer.

Capital goods are produced for other producers to use in a further stage of production; they are also called producer goods.

Consumer goods are those goods required in addition to primary (basic) needs and which have been manufactured, eg, clothing, household goods, etc. They are also called consumption goods.

Goodwill (of businesses) The benefit acquired by an establishment or business beyond the mere value of the capital, stock-in-trade, and funds employed in it, is termed the 'goodwill'; it is the possession of a ready-formed connection of customers, and is considered as a separate element in the saleable value of a business. If demand for the type of business in question is high, then the price paid for the goodwill is high.

Advertising helps to build up an important asset in the form of goodwill.

Government aid for exporters The BOTB is an official organisation with the Secretary of State for Trade and Industry as its president, but its members are mainly businessmen with practical knowledge of exporting. It directs the Government's export promotion programme and offers a large range of market and specialist advice on the rules and regulations which apply to exporting.

A booklet is available from the BOBT called *Help for Exporters* which summarises all the services provided by the British Overseas Trade Board for UK exporters. (See under **export services provided by BOTB**).

In addition, BOTB regional offices offer a complete export advisory service and will put people in touch with organisations which will best help them with export problems.

Government aid for industry The DTI, through its network of

116

regional Development and Investment Grants Offices, offers a comprehensive advisory service on all the types of aid available for industrial development.

Besides covering the broader aspects of government policy in relation to areas of high unemployment, there is a special Small Firms Service, and the department allocates funds for research and development in many different industrial fields.

Government bonds These are documents issued by the Government or public authorities in return for loans to finance expenditure which is not met by taxation.

Government borrowing The main sources of Government borrowing are—
by open-market operations (see **Gilt-edged market**);
by overseas investment in British Government stock;
by the issue of **Treasury Bills**.

Government Broker (Stock Exchange) The Government Broker is an ex-officio member of the Stock Exchange Council, and keeps the Bank of England in close touch with the stock market.

Government departments The aims of government departments are laid down by statute; each organisation in the public sector has legal obligations to provide certain services in such areas as trade, employment, health, education, social services, defence and foreign affairs.

Government expenditure Government expenditure can be classified into two main categories:
(a) *expenditure on goods and services* (defence, education, hospitals, etc); this is, for the most part, composed of salaries and wages, but vast quantities of goods are also required in order for these services to function.
(b) *expenditure in creating 'transfer incomes'* such as social security benefits and unemployment and retirement pensions. This provides personal incomes to the unemployed and retired, who are not supplying any productive services at the time.

117

Government, functions of   The government of a state involves the carrying out of three functions:
the executive function—performed by the cabinet with the assistance of the Civil Service;
the judicial function—performed by the judiciary led by the Lord Chancellor;
the legislative function—performed by the Queen in Parliament.

Government income   (economics) Government income is derived mainly from taxes (direct and indirect), rates, and National Insurance contributions.

Government monetary policy   To a considerable extent the **Bank of England**—acting as the Government's agent—can control the money supply in the following ways:
by open-market operations;
by the issue of Treasury Bills;
by requiring 'special deposits' from the commercial banks;
by using the Minimum Lending Rate (MLR) as a regulator;
by intervention on the foreign exchange market to stabilise the value of sterling against other main foreign currencies. This it does through the Exchange Equalisation Account, which includes Britain's gold and foreign currency reserves.

Government monopolies   In the commercial field some goods and services are by their nature monopolies; examples of natural monopolies are gas, electricity and water. Such enterprises incur tremendous capital costs which make competition impossible.

Grain futures market   A grain futures market operated by GAFTA (Grain and Feed Trade Association) is held in the **Baltic Exchange**. There is now more Government control over the growing and marketing of wheat, to restrict output and preserve prices, and this has done much to reduce the dealing in wheat on the Baltic Exchange. The Grain Market in fact is only concerned with EEC wheat and barley, but non-EEC barley—of particular importance to distillers—is still traded freely.

 Dealing is of the 'ring type'—deals are made across a wooden circular rail on the 'floor' of the Baltic Exchange—and by 'open outcry'. This means that bids and offers are shouted out so that all can hear the prices clearly when bargains are struck.

Green Paper Before a Government Bill is introduced into Parliament a pamphlet—called a Green Paper—may be issued to explain the proposals being put forward. This is done to promote public discussion.

Gross (Investment) Before deduction of tax. *Grossing up* is calculating the amount that would be required, in the case of an investment subject to tax, to equal the income from an investment not subject to tax.

Gross Domestic Product (GDP) Total value of output produced within the country's physical borders.

Gross National Product (GNP) Equals GDP plus net property income from abroad accruing to residents of the United Kingdom.

Gross profit The difference between cost price and selling price.
   To calculate the gross profit made by a business, the cost of the goods sold during a particular period is deducted from the total value of sales made during the same period.

Gross profit percentage (accounts) Gross profit is the difference between the cost price and the selling price of the goods sold.

$$\text{Gross profit percentage} = \frac{\text{Gross profit}}{\text{Turnover}} \times \frac{100}{1}$$

Group life insurance Small employers may take out insurance to cover an agreed sum on each member of staff. An employee leaving such employment can usually arrange to commute his benefits to a personal insurance on terms suitable to his own requirements.

Growth (economics)   New capital resources in an organisation provide the capacity for expansion. One of the main reasons for the growth in the economy during the nineteenth and twentieth centuries has been the development of organisations.

Guarantee   An agreement undertaken by product manufacturers to indemnify customers against faulty goods over a limited period of time.

Guarantee, companies limited by   These companies may or may not have a share capital. The guarantee consists of an undertaking by members to contribute up to a stated amount in the event of winding up, such a guarantee being incorporated in the **Memorandum of Association.**

Guarantor   A person who undertakes to be responsible for the liabilities of another.

Guillotine closure   A form of closure of a meeting or debate (rarely used outside the House of Commons) in which a time limit is fixed for debate on each section or stage of a bill. When the time limit expires discussion ceases, whether the business is concluded or not.

H

Hammering   Announcement of the failure of a **Stock Exchange** firm. A compensation fund is maintained by the Stock Exchange to recompense investors should a member firm fail to meet its obligations.

Hansard   The official, printed reports of the proceedings and debates of the Houses of Parliament.

Hardware   The physical components of a computer system. These include input and output devices, the central processing unit itself, and any auxiliary storage devices.

Hatton Garden   Site of the London diamond market where many independent traders have their offices. It is close to the offices of the Central Selling Organisation (CSO) whose companies sort, value and sell rough diamonds to the world's major diamond-cutting centres and industries.

Hawkers   Itinerant dealers who carry their goods for sale from place to place, using a cart or van to bring goods to the customer's door.

Health and Safety at Work Act 1975   See **employment legislation**

Health and Social Security, Department of (DHSS) Government department responsible for the administration of the National Health Service (NHS) in England, and for the Welfare Services run by local authorities for the elderly, infirm, handicapped and other persons in need.

The Department is also responsible for the social services in Scotland, England and Wales; these services comprise schemes for war pensions, national insurance, family allowances and supplementary benefits.

Hedging   An attempt by an investor or speculator on the futures or terminal markets to safeguard the real value of his investments is known as hedging. The *buyer* of physical goods—sugar, cocoa, or any other commodity for which there is a terminal market (ie, he has bought them for payment and delivery at some *future* date) will protect himself by *selling* a balancing amount on the futures market.

The net effect is that whether the commodity value rises or falls, the buyer or seller is assured of a minimum price. A loss on the physical side is offset by a gain on the futures markets—or the other way round.

Highly-organised market   Market where the whole range of buying and selling takes place through institutional or other arrangements. The organisation of such markets depends on the rules under which the market operates; examples are those which deal in commodities such as coffee, cocoa or silver, or the **Stock Exchange** with its numerous special markets in foreign stock, mining, gilts and ordinary shares.

In these markets buyers and sellers are numerous and communication between them is rapid; only experts are permitted to deal and the minimum contracts allowed are set at a very high figure.

High Street banks   Also known as clearing banks, joint-stock banks, or commercial banks. They handle the accounts of millions of depositors through a countrywide network of High Street branches.

Hire-purchase   A hire-purchase agreement is an agreement to hire goods for a specified period, with an option for the hirer to

122

purchase the goods at the end. The property does not pass to the hirer until the last payment has been made, therefore he cannot sell while it is still under an HP agreement. The hirer may terminate the agreement, but must allow the seller to take possession, bring the total payments up to 50% of the purchase price, and pay for any damage. The seller may retake goods if instalments are overdue; notice of default requires payment within seven days.

After one-third of the purchase price has been paid the seller cannot recover the goods except by Court order.

The agreement must contain:

a heading—'Hire-Purchase Agreement regulated by the Consumer Credit Act 1974'—shown prominently on the first page, the name and postal address of both trader and customer, a declaration of the cash price, the amount of any advance payment, the amount of credit to be provided, the total charge for credit and the total amount payable by the customer, the timing and amounts of repayments of credit and credit charges, the **Annual Percentage Rate** denoted as the APR of the total charge for credit, statements about the main rights of customers provided by the **Consumer Credit Act 1974.**

An agreement must be recorded in a document which embodies all its terms, is signed by both trader and customer, and is readily legible when given or sent to the customer for signature.

No right of cancellation exists on a contract made on trade premises.

A right of cancellation exists on all contracts signed elsewhere—ie, doorstep sales, etc. Such a sale will be cancelled if the hirer gives notice within five days of receiving the second statutory copy (or fourteen days if bought from a mail order company). This is the cooling-off period.

All agreements are to be signed by both customer and trader or their representatives and the date of signature entered. The customer's signature must be inside a box. The signature of the trader must be outside the customer's signature box; similarly the signature of any witness and its date must also be outside the customer's signature box.

Copies of agreements must be given to a customer—when and

how depends on the circumstances in which the customer signs the agreement.

ADVANTAGES OF HIRE-PURCHASE

The consumer is enabled to enjoy possession of goods before he has paid for them,

the retailer increases his turnover and profit,

the manufacturer also benefits from increased sales which enable more fully specialised production techniques to be introduced with a consequent reduction in unit costs,

the community prospers because HP keeps demand for mass production at a high level.

Retailers do not usually finance HP sales themselves, but use the services of a finance house—often a member of the **Finance Houses Association**. To the financier this is, in spite of its highly speculative nature, a most rewarding field of investment, yielding higher than average results. This is due to the nominal rate of interest being in fact doubled up by repayment systems—a fact that the *Consumer Credit Act 1974* has tried to make clear to the public by making it compulsory to reveal the true APR on all HP sales.

Hire-Purchase controls are one of the means used by the Government to control the economy. They do this by varying the HP deposit, and by varying the period of repayment. See also *consumer credit*

Hire-retailing   This is a relatively new development; the retailer hires out equipment for use in the hirer's own home or garden. Equipment used for 'do-it-yourself' activities is particularly popular, such equipment being expensive to buy and not frequently used by the amateur. Hiring such items for short periods is a very satisfactory arrangement.

Another area where hire-retailing is developing rapidly is in the holiday trade; bicycles, camping and skiing equipment are among items which can be hired.

Holding companies   A holding company is an essentially financial company, the purpose of which is to maintain or gain control of other trading companies by acquiring a majority sharehold in them, and bringing the subsidiary company within the direct influence of the parent company. It is one way of building up a large-scale business, as subsidiaries may supply the parent manufacturing company with particular components; it may also present the possibilities of diversification where there is a fear of decline in any particular market. The term multinational is commonly used to describe a holding company with foreign subsidiaries.

The shareholders of subsidiary companies are in the minority; the Companies Acts protect the rights of such minority shareholders by allowing them to appeal to the Department of Trade and Industry against unfair treatment.

Where a company is a holding company there must, with every **balance sheet** and profit and loss account laid before a general meeting, be presented also—
a consolidated balance sheet dealing with the state of affairs as at the end of the financial year of the company and its subsidiaries;
a consolidated profit and loss account dealing with the profit or loss for the financial year of the company and those subsidiaries.

The financial years of the holding company and its subsidiaries, shall, if possible, coincide.

Home Office (HO)   This government department is responsible for law and order and for all home affairs except those specifically assigned to other departments. Most of the Home Office's responsibilities are limited to England and Wales, but in some matters they extend to Scotland and Northern Ireland. Among the more important duties of the Home Office are the administration of justice; police administration; provision of prison services; control of aliens and naturalisation.

The Home Secretary acts as a channel of communication between the Queen and her subjects; other functions include the conduct of elections, community relations, and supervision of the BBC and IBA.

Home trade   The buying and selling of goods and services by persons living in the same country. This can involve extractive and manufacturing industry together with commercial services connected with the chain of distribution, through the wholesale and retail markets.

'Home produce' usually refers to such perishable items as milk, butter, cheese, and other fresh foods and vegetables which are bought either direct from the farmer or through farmers' co-operatives. A large amount of produce is sold through the produce markets in London and other large cities.

Home trade may be protected from foreign competition by the application of embargoes, quotas and tariffs to imported goods.

Horizontal integration (of business units) This is where firms which are engaged in similar activities join forces to gain greater market penetration.

Hot money Funds transferred suddenly from one country to another because conditions on the international money markets make transfer financially advantageous.

Household protection insurance Many insurance companies offer a household policy which generally covers the complete contents of a home against various types of risk. See also **fire insurance**.

House of Commons The United Kingdom Parliament legislates (makes law) by means of Acts of Parliament, and has two chambers. The lower chamber is the House of Commons, the upper chamber is the House of Lords. Members of the House of Commons are elected at a general election by voters over the age of eighteen, normally for a parliamentary term of five years. By-elections occur when a member dies or resigns during such a parliamentary term.

After a general election the Queen asks the leader of the party which has gained most seats to form a government. The leader—the Prime Minister—then selects ministers who are approved by the Queen; other ministers are also appointed by the Prime Minister who fill positions below cabinet rank.

Ministers share responsibility for Government actions, and also have individual responsibility for the work of their own departments. See also *Cabinet*.

House of Lords The upper chamber of the Parliament of the United Kingdom, composed of the Lords spiritual (two archbishops and twenty-four bishops of the Church of England), and the Lords temporal. The Lords temporal are those peers holding peerages in Great Britain; some are hereditary peers, but the Crown is enabled also to confer life peerages on both men and women.

Hovercraft Hovercraft are particularly effective over water and a cross-channel ferry operates carrying vehicles and passengers between England and France.

Hull insurance The hull of a vessel, which includes the machinery, can be covered against damage or total loss by storm, stranding, fire, collision or other perils of the sea.
Time policies usually last 12 months.
Voyage policies cover the hull from the port of departure to the port of arrival with no specific time limit.

Human relations Describes the activities of management in attempting to achieve the best possible fit between workers and their jobs. Problems involving morale, teamwork, creativity, introduction of change, etc., are the concern of human relations practitioners, who draw upon a wide range of social sciences to achieve a better understanding of inter-personal relationships and foster improved job satisfaction.

Human resources (economics) The labour market is a market where employers can buy human resources and where workers can sell their labour.
Labour is one of the factors of production, the others being land and capital.

127

Hypermarkets

Hypermarkets (trade) Very large retail establishments, hypermarkets with ample parking are usually situated outside large towns, and offer a tremendous range of consumer goods. Like **supermarkets** their prices are highly competitive.

I

Imperfect competition   See **monopoly**

Import broker/commission agent   Deals with goods for foreign exporters on a consignment basis. A consignment in mercantile law means a particular lot of goods sent or consigned to an agent, usually in another country, for disposal on behalf of his principal. The agent makes arrangements for the landing of the goods and sees to the Customs formalities; if necessary he arranges warehousing before selling the goods. When the goods are sold he renders an **Account Sales** to his principal, which details expenses incurred in the transaction, including brokerage or commission (possibly also an additional *del credere* commission). These expenses are deducted from the gross proceeds of the sale and the agent then remits the amount due to his principal.

Import documents   The main documents of the import trade are the **bill of lading** (or air waybill), **invoice**, **certificate of origin**, and the **insurance certificate**. In addition, goods arriving in the United Kingdom must be entered for Customs clearance on a form known as an 'entry' form.
   Possession of the consignment cannot be obtained from the shipping company until the necessary documents are presented to them.

Import duties   See **customs duties**

Import licences   If goods are not listed on the schedules of goods which may enter the country without restriction a licence must be obtained. Such licences are often called 'quota' licences, as they restrict imports to a given quota which has been approved.

Import merchant An import merchant usually has connections with a particular country or area, buys goods from manufacturers or growers there, and sells them for his own profit. He may deal on the commodity markets or direct with wholesalers and retailers in this country.

Import trade Trade between nations takes place because, for climatic reasons, a country may not be able to produce all its natural products; on the other hand it may be able to produce a surplus which it can export. A further reason for trading lies in the international specialisation of labour.

A nation which wishes to import must be prepared to export, but exports must be of the right quality and price to achieve a favourable balance of trade. Many of the raw materials which are imported into Great Britain are manufactured into goods which are then exported.

British imports of *primary products* are mainly bought as *bulk cargoes*,—eg in oil tankers or refrigerated meat carriers. They are— handled by the **Commodity Markets**, financed, transported and warehoused until required by middlemen, *or*
directly imported by a manufacturing firm which has built up a special link with an overseas supplier.
Secondary products (manufactured goods) are imported directly by importing organisations or by agents appointed to handle goods in this country. (See **import broker commission agent** and **import merchant**).

Imports are controlled by Customs Duties and Import Licences

Customs can give the 'most favoured nation' treatment to a particular country or countries.

Repayment of duty can be claimed when an import pays duty and is manufactured into a finished product which is subsequently exported. The exporter can then claim the duty back from the Customs. This payment of 'process inwards relief' (which used to be called *'drawback'*) is made by a Customs document called a **debenture**.

130

Goods for trans-shipment—that is, for immediate re-export—which are transferred to another vehicle for onward delivery to an overseas port, are entered on a specal 'entry' form and are not liable for duty.

Duty is normally payable in advance before 'entry' is allowed. A system of **bonded warehouses** permits landing of cargo on which duty has NOT been paid. See also **balance of payments, balance of trade,** and **invisible trade.**

Imprest   Is a sum of money advanced to a person for a particular business purpose. Today the term is mostly associated with petty cash. The cashier starts off the petty cash fund with an amount of money deemed sufficient to cover expenditure for a limited period (usually a week). Records are kept of each item of expenditure, and at the end of each period are checked by the cashier who then restores the imprest. This means that the petty cash fund is reimbursed with the amount of money spent, which makes up the money left in the cash box to the original imprest again.

Incentive schemes   Incentive schemes enable employees to become more effective and so ultimately reduce wage costs. Usually the incentive involves financial reward of some kind, but flexible working hours and a less rigid demarcation between jobs also have an effect on an employee's contribution to the general effectiveness of an organisation.

Income and expenditure account   An income and expenditure account is more than a mere statement of cash transactions; it is credited with all income pertaining to the period whether received in cash or not, and is debited with all expenses. All transactions of a capital nature are excluded. The income and expenditure account is normally used only by clubs and other non-trading societies.

Under the Companies Act 1948 it is compulsory for a company registered under the Act as not trading for profit to lay an income and expenditure account before the company in general meeting.

Income tax   Income tax is a *direct tax* on personal income, graduated according to the amount of such income. It is a statutory deduction made by employers from salaries and wages (PAYE), and in general is a tax levied on earnings to help meet the expenses of the government.

Income velocity of circulation of money   The ratio of money income to money. If money income rises but the stock of money remains constant then the velocity of circulation has risen.

Incomes policy   The aim of an incomes policy is to curb inflation and avoid unemployment. Incomes policies range from statutory policies (laid down by Act of Parliament), voluntary policies (social contracts between governments and representatives of the trade unions), to 'market policies' where controls are released and the free play of market forces is supposed to take charge.

Incorporation, certificate of   This is sent by the Registrar of Companies to a newly-registered company and is its 'birth certificate', after initial documents (including the **Memorandum of Association** and the **Articles of Association**) have been lodged with him and approved by him. This gives the company a legal personality and allows its shares to be sold to secure the capital it needs.

Indemnity   The object of all insurance (except for life insurance and personal accident insurance) is to restore the insured to the position he was in before the event which was insured against took place,—ie, to indemnify him.

Indent   Export houses or merchants may receive their orders in the form of an 'indent' from overseas. An indent requires the exporter to find a supplier for the goods required.

Index-linked stock   A type of government stock where the value of the principal and the interest are adjusted in line with the increase in price level.

Index of Retail Prices   See **Retail Price Index (RPI)**

Index numbers   A single figure which summarises a comparison between two sets of figures. To construct an index number we need:
(a) A starting point or 'base' year,
(b) A set of figures for the base year and year of comparison.

   If the index number is to compare a 'basket' of commodities (as in the Index of Retail Prices) we would also need to compute an average basket and 'weight' the contents. For many purposes 100 is used as a base, since comparison then becomes much clearer.

Indicator system (Bank of England)   A system whereby the central bank adjusts short-term interest rates according to a predetermined formula relating to the growth of the money stock. If the money stock is growing faster than the official target then interest rates will automatically be increased.

Indirect costs   For most costing purposes, the term may be treated as synonymous with 'overheads', meaning those expenses which cannot be directly traceable to a cost unit. There are three categories of indirect costs—materials, labour and expenses. Indirect materials consist of 'consumables' such as machine oil or rubber gloves used by the production department, but only in the course of manufacture. Indirect labour refers to functional sections of the business such as R & D, administration, sales, etc. The balance of indirect costs is in the expenses incurred by the production department and these inlcude heating, lighting, rent, rates, insurance and depreciation.

Indirect production   Indirect production (mass production) is production by specialisation—each worker contributing a part of the whole product. Mass production is a system which seeks to make the greatest number of goods with the least number of workers (cf **direct production**).

Indirect taxation   These are taxes on expenditure such as VAT and duties collected by the **Customs and Excise Department**.

Induction courses Induction courses for new members of staff are often provided in large organisations to help new employers to get used to the new environment and to see their own work in relationship to the work of all other employees in the establishment.

By visits to other departments, lectures and films the new employee can be introduced to the organisation's structure, its products or services, the availability of welfare facilities, health and safety measures, and the operating 'rules of the house'.

Industrial disputes See **Advisory, Conciliation and Arbitration Service (ACAS)** and **Industrial Tribunals**

Industrial life offices (Also known as home service offices). These offer most types of insurance cover, including life assurance. The premiums are collected by agents who visit the homes of the insured.

Industrial property The description 'industrial property' refers to such intangible assets of a business as patented inventions, goodwill, trademarks, and copyrights. These non-physical properties can be owned and sold.

Industrial relations The academic study of the rules and procedures which govern employment and the organisations that regulate them.

Industrial Society, The The Industrial Society began its work in 1918 and was granted a Royal Charter on 20 February 1985. It is a self-financing and non-profitmaking organisation, is independent and non-party political, and it enjoys the support of employers and trade unions.

Industrial Training Act 1964 See **employment legislation**

Industrial Tribunals These are concerned with disputes arising out of a person's employment, such as claims for redundancy payments, equal pay and complaints of unfair dismissal. If the

matter is not settled by the Industrial Tribunal it may be taken to
the Employment Appeals Tribunal: this consists of judges and
members from both the employer's and employee's side of
industry.

Industry, Department of   See **Trade and Industry, Department
of**

Inelasticity of demand   When the price of a good or service
changes and the change in demand is small, demand is said to be
inelastic.

Inflation   Inflation is an undue increase in the quantity of money
in proportion to buying power, so that if the value of money in
circulation is not matched by earnings, that country is suffering
from inflation. The Government can curb excess demand by
increasing taxation and/or reducing public expenditure.

Monetarists argue that inflation only occurs because the money
is available to permit price increases, but so far there has been no
successful formula for permanently reducing inflation.

Inflation is the most serious threat of all to investors, since it
causes the value of money to fall. The nominal value remains the
same, but the real value is diminished.

Inflation accounting   During an inflationary period it becomes
increasingly difficult to assess the assets of a firm in real terms.
Constantly increasing prices mean that all figures need constant
adjustment to keep pace with inflation. The cost of depreciation
of fixed assets, for example, should keep pace with inflationary
prices; stock may increase in value but the increase is not profit.
In times of rapid inflation cash resources lose their value, but
borrowed money (because the interest rate does not reflect
inflationary rates) remains 'cheap'.

It is difficult to measure the value of money at such times,
because the valuation of assets and the calculation of profit
become increasingly difficult.

The Accounting Standards Committee has put forward
suggestions to assist accountants to present a true and fair picture
of a company's accounts which take into account the fact of
inflation.

Informal organisation A type of organisation in which relationships and communications are not rigid and restrictive, but emphasise team-work and co-operation. The organisation becomes a dynamic and flexible system which uses people's expertise more effectively. Conventional principles and lines of command tend to fall into the background while staff are expected to display more self-discipline and responsibility in their highly flexible roles.

Information Technology The Department of Trade and Industry defines Information Technology as 'The acquisition, processing, storage, dissemination and use of vocal, pictorial, textual and numerical information by a microelectronics-based combination of computing and telecommunications.'

The Information Technology Division of the Department of Trade and Industry co-ordinates all Government activities in the IT area (telecommunications, computing and microelectronics). The minister responsible is advised by an inter-departmental committee of senior officials and by an IT advisory panel of senior industrialists.

Until the British Telecommunications Act was passed by Parliament in July 1981, IT was committed to providing a national telecommunications network capable of stimulating, and meeting, demands for a new service. The new Act, by liberalising the Post Office's telecommunications monopoly, laid the foundations for the modern telecommunications network Information Technology needs.

The cornerstones of the Government's policy for IT are:

The development of a statutory and regulatory framework favouring the growth of IT products and services;

action to make individuals and firms more aware of what IT offers, and so enable them to take advantage of the new services and equipment;

the development of new products and techniques through direct support and enlightened public purchasing.

136

Specal initiatives to date include:

Support for R & D in the IT field which helps firms research and develop new and improved IT products and processes.

Microelectronics Application Project (MAP) which promotes the use of microelectronics in product and process control in manufacturing industry.

Microelectronics Industry Support Programme (MISP) which provides support for companies engaged in the development and manufacture of integrated circuits.

Fibre Optics Scheme   A programme of assistance to build up a fibre-optics and opto-electronics supply industry, and to stimulate the development of new applications by support for R & D and the imaginative use of public- and private-sector purchasing power.

CADCAM awareness and training campaign (computer-aided design/computer-aided manufacture) seeks to accelerate CADCAM's uptake by the engineering industry of systems which are far cheaper, more versatile and easier to operate.

Electronics CADMAT Programme (computer-aided design, manufacture and test) seeks specifically to extend and accelerate the use of CADMAT by small and medium-sized firms. In the electronics industry computer-aided engineering has developed a different range of techniques from those in the mechanical- and electrical-engineering industries.

Micros in Schools Schemes; Microelectronics in Education Programme   This is designed to put a microcomputer into every primary, secondary, and special school in the country. The Education Department's Microelectronics in Education Programme helps teachers acquire the skills and educational material needed to enable the computer to be used as an aid to teaching and learning.

Information Technology Centres are a joint DTI/MSC initiative. A national network is being set up to give young unemployed people the type of training and work experience in Microelectronics and in computing which will create permanent jobs.

Microsystem Centres   The DTI is supporting the establishment of a country-wide network of Microsystems Centres to provide the businessman (particularly the small businessman) with

137

independent advice, training and information on microcomputers and microcomputer systems.

Demonstration projects The DTI is supporting a number of projects aimed at exploring, developing and demonstrating salient sectors of IT technology. In one, twenty different 'makes' of automated office are being set up in twenty different public sector organisations to demonstrate their scope in actual working environments. In another—a combined exercise with the Science and Engineering Research Council, British Telecom and various industrial and academic organisations—six local-area networks in different parts of the country have been linked together by satellite on a terminal-to-terminal basis.

In addition, as part of their current 'awareness' programme, the Department of Industry's Ashdown House Library has produced a comprehensive IT Bibliography, which is available free of charge from IT Awareness Programme, Department of Industry, Gorringe Building, 29 Bressenden Place, London SW1.

Initial deposit Sum which a broker requires a client to deposit with him before he starts trading on his behalf in the futures markets.

Inland bills See **Bill of Exchange**

Inland Revenue The three sources of Inland Revenue are death duties, stamp duties, and taxes.

Insolvency (of businesses) Denotes inability to pay one's debts. The term is for most practical purposes replaced by the term **bankruptcy**.

Institutional investor (Stock Exchange) An institutional investor collects the savings of many people and invests them for the good of the saving public.

Banks, building societies, finance companies, insurance companies, investment trusts, local authorities, the national savings scheme, pension funds, trade unions, and unit trusts are all institutional investors.

Each institution holds a 'balanced portfolio'—a mixture of **shares** and other securities in both the public and private sector of industry. These 'safe' investments yield a reasonable return.

Insurable interest   An insurance policy is not a legal contract unless the person insured has a direct interest in the matter insured. The insured person cannot improve his position through a loss covered by insurance which can only indemnify him—ie, bring him back to the state he was in before the loss occurred. If the insured himself does not suffer from the loss he cannot be indemnified.

Insurable/non-insurable risks   Insurance rates are based on the probability of the risk which has been insured against actually occurring. If there are statistical records available, the 'probability' of the event can be estimated by an insurance underwriter and the correct amount of the premium worked out. Some eventualities, because there are no records to work on, are non-insurable. For instance, a business cannot insure against failure to make a profit because there are so many reasons and causes for this that the insurance company could not work out the probability.

Insurance   Insurance provides one of the main commercial services, being an important aid to trade. It relieves traders of the risks involved in developing trade and encourages them in enterprise.

The purpose of the contract of insurance is either to indemnify against a loss which may occur if a certain event takes place, or to pay upon some event occurring a sum of money to the insured person.

Insurance is a 'pooling' of risks. The success of such an insurance pool depends on adequate contributions to cover losses (the pool must never be allowed to 'shrink' but must grow bigger annually), and it is essential that claims are paid promptly and in full.

The three main principles of insurance are insurable interest, utmost good faith (*uberrima fides*), and indemnity:
Insurable interest   The insured must be in danger of suffering loss

should the thing concerned be destroyed or damaged in any way.

Utmost good faith (*uberrima fides*)   On the basis of truthful facts a fair premium is decided.

Indemnity means the restoring of someone to the position they were in before the event concerned took place.

Note: Insurance against death or injury can never be indemnified—it simply provides money called 'benefit' to the injured or to relatives and dependents after the death of the insured.

The principle of contribution lays down that if a person insures twice or three times for the same risk, the companies concerned must each contribute to the loss a half each or a third each, so that the insured is *indemnified.*

Subrogation   It is wrong for an insured person to accept an agreed sum in compensation and then continue to have other rights as well. A car that is a 'write-off' may have good tyres, but they belong to the insurance company after the insured person has been indemnified.

Doctrine of proximate cause   When insurance is taken out it covers certain eventualities which must be the *primary cause* of a loss if a claim is to be made against the insurer.

There are four main types of insurance: marine, fire, life, and accident.

ARRANGING AN INSURANCE POLICY

A *proposal form* must be completed. All questions on Proposal Forms must be answered honestly—with *utmost good faith.* Not all risks are insurable—insurance depends on the calculation of probabilities made by statisticians called underwriters (actuaries deal with life assurance). Provided there is evidence of similar events over a fairly lengthy period of time these can be worked out, but if there are no records there is no possibility of insurance.

The *premium* to be paid is assessed on the basis of answers given to the questions on the Proposal Form.

When the premium is decided the insurance company makes an *offer* to insure the proposer for a certain sum.

The person desiring insurance accepts by paying the first premium whereupon a *cover note* is issued and insurance commences.

An *insurance policy* is drawn up giving full details of what has been agreed. Any inaccuracy voids the contract; the declaration on the Proposal Form is the basis of the contract of insurance.

The insurance company takes care of the pool (the sum total of all premiums collected) by acting as an institutional investor; it invests wisely in a balanced portfolio.

Insurance brokers Brokers are agents who undertake to get the best rate from underwriters and carry through the insurance on behalf of their customers. A Lloyds underwriter will deal only with brokers and cannot be approached by a member of the public.

Insurance certificate See **Certificate of Insurance**

Insurance claim When an insured person has suffered a loss against which he has insured he should complete a Claim Form, which should be filled in with utmost good faith—ie, only the truth must appear. The insurer will wish to confirm that the insured peril was the proximate cause of the loss, and that liability exists. It must also be ascertained that there were no breaches of the conditions of the policy. Depreciation must be taken into account when the amount of **indemnity** is calculated. When a 'fair' valuation is agreed the insurance company should pay promptly.

Very large disasters which have been covered by several syndicates at Lloyds, may involve the selling of an insurance company's investments to meet the claim.

Insurance Market The British Insurance Market is the largest insurance market in the world. Besides **Lloyds Corporation** there are many large insurance companies—the Prudential, Equity and Law, Commercial Union, etc.—who offer a very wide range of insurance cover.

Insurance of exports Marine insurance, which includes cargo insurance, is largely the concern of the insurance market of **Lloyds**

of London, where marine insurance originated in Britain.

The **Export Credit Guarantee Department** of the Board of Trade (qv for further details) provides *credit* insurance for UK exporters.

Insurance of interest   See **fidelity bond/guarantee**

Insurance of liability   See **accident insurance**

Insurance Ombudsman   If a policy holder is in dispute with his insurance company the Insurance Ombudsman can try to settle matters, but only if the insurance company concerned is a member of the Insurance Ombudsman Scheme, (the Citizens Advice Bureau will know).

The Ombudsman may only be approached if the policyholder and insurance company have finally failed to reach an agreement, and this must be done within six months of the company's final decision having been given. The Ombudsman's decision may be accepted or rejected, but if the policyholder rejects it his rights to take legal action remain unchanged.

Insurance, parties to   In any contract of insurance the first party is the insured person, the second party is the insurer, the third party is any person affected by the contract. (In motor vehicle insurance the third party may be passenger, pedestrian, or cyclist).

Insurance policy   The document which sets out the terms and conditions of the contract between the person taking out the cover (the first party) and the insurance company or underwriter (the second party). It also shows the value covered, the premium(s) payable, and the date(s) on which payment is due.

Insurance premium   The sum of money payable by a policyholder to the insurer for the protection being given. The amount of the premium is calculated from information given on the Proposal Form, and on past statistical records relative to the proposal. If there are no records no calculations can be made so there is no possibility of insurance.

Insurance, principles of   See **insurance**

Integration   Integration—businesses joining together to increase size—may be either horizontal or vertical.
Horizontal integration occurs where firms which are engaged in similar activities join forces to gain greater geographical control.
Vertical integration occurs where a holding company controls all the stages of a particular product by taking over the companies which supply components.

Interbank market   The market on which banks borrow and lend large sums of money among themselves.

Interest (Finance)   The price paid for the hire of money by the hirer, and received by the lender of money. (The same rates do not apply to borrowing and lending).
   Interest is a reward paid to lenders for the use of capital.
   See also **insurable interest.**

Interest rates   Domestic interest rates printed daily in the press are:
The Bank Base Rate
The Finance Houses Base Rate
The Discount Market Loans Rate (fixed weekly)
3 month interbank rate

Interest-Bearing Eligible Liabilities (IBELS)   The interest-bearing element of **eligible liabilities**.

Interim dividend (Stock Exchange)   A dividend declared part of the way through a company's financial year which is authorised solely by the directors.

Internal audit (Accounts)   See **audit**

International Bank for Reconstruction and Development (IBRD)   Commonly called the World Bank. Its function is to assist in the reconstruction and development of member countries by facilitating the investment of capital.

The IBRD raises funds by the sale of stock to member countries and from the issue of bonds in the world's financial centres.

International Commodities Clearing House   An attraction of the commodity markets is that the speculator never has to lay on line the full amount of his stake, but if the price of his commodity fluctuates unduly he will receive a 'margin call'—a demand for more cash to keep his deposit percentage in line.

Deposits or margins on soft commodity futures contracts are lodged with the ICCH, an independent organisation which acts not only as a clearing agent, but as guarantor for deals on the London, Paris and Australian markets.

International company/corporation   A multinational firm which operates outside its own country of origin as well as in it.

International Labour Organisation (ILO)   This is an inter-governmental agency but employers and workers as well as governments take part in its work. Its three major areas of interest are—

human resources and economic development,

the development of labour relations and social institutions in the labour field,

living and working conditions, with special reference to labour legislation, social security and occupational safety and health.

International Monetary Fund (IMF)   Established in Washington in 1945 this may be regarded as a co-operative deposit bank

The objectives of the IMF are—

to assist nations with temporary balance of payment problems,

to provide guidelines for economic policy to nations with a permanent disequilibrium on their foreign trading,

to monitor foreign exchange rates.

International trade   See **export trade** and **import trade**

Intervention Board   The variable nature of agricultural

144

production has led the EEC to develop a common agricultural policy to control the price and distribution of goods within the community. To ensure that farmers are fairly rewarded the **Common Agricultural Policy** (CAP) imposes a minimum price. A farmer who cannot sell his produce in the market can sell it to his state Intervention Board; the intervention price is usually about 90% of the target or guide price.

Products bought by Intervention Boards are then kept off the ordinary channels of trade for a while to avoid upsetting market prices.

Intra vires   A legal expression meaning within the power of the person or body concerned.

Investment trusts   Limited companies who issue shares to the public in the ordinary way, and invest the funds obtained in other securities.

Investors in Industry (3i)   Investors in Industry is an independent private sector group whose business is the creative use of money. They provide long-term and permanent capital to businesses of all sizes, through innovative investment schemes tailored to meet their individual requirements. For companies seeking advice rather than capital, they have management consultancy, corporate advisory and portfolio management services. Most business is done in the UK but 3i is now established in Europe and the USA, both important UK export markets and sources of technology.

Investors in Industry is owned by nine London and Scottish banks (85%) and by the **Bank of England** (15%). They raise their funds on the finest commercial terms through a highly sophisticated treasury function in the domestic and international money markets.

The group has a unique knowledge of the small company sector, but invests in businesses of all sizes, from small-scale family firms to major multinational companies.

Invisible trade   This involves invisible earnings—the export and import of services as opposed to goods. Invisible earnings make a substantial contribution to the UK's balance of payments; these consist primarily of shipping and banking services, interest on loans and overseas commitments undertaken by insurance in the British insurance market, and tourism.

Invisible imports into Great Britain consist mainly of British Government spending overseas, expenditure by British tourists abroad, and additional imports of services.

Invoice In *home trade* this is the bill for payment for goods or services rendered and is sent from the seller to the buyer; it gives details of the goods or services to be paid for, names the terms and any discounts and shows the method of delivery.

In *international trade* it is the export invoice/commercial invoice: there are certain requirements of an export invoice which do not have to be considered for home market transactions. All the following information should be included:

Name and address of the supplier and the buyer,

Date and reference number of the buyer's order,

Details of method of carriage (name of ship, air freight details, etc),

Shipping marks in full,

Details of packages and individual contents, with package numbers,

Net gross weights and measurements of packages,

Total value of invoice (but not including cash discount),

Details of terms of sale (fob, cif, etc) and port of destination.

See also **consular invoice.**

Inward Missions The BOTB can often provide support when a big retail outlet overseas puts on a 'theme' promotion. The BOTB 'Help for Exporters' booklets include one on 'Store Promotions'.

IOU These documents have no legal properties. The debtor in accepting an IOU is simply taking a written acknowledgement of a debt.

Irrevocable credits (Letters of credit) Once established, and confirmed by a bank in the exporter's country, an irrevocable credit may not be revoked by the overseas buyer, and therefore

146

offers complete security for the exporter.

Issue Department   See **Bank of England**

Issuing Houses Association   Some merchant banks are Issuing Houses and organise the sale of shares for public limited companies. The company will sell its new securities to an Issuing House, which then offers the shares by an 'offer for sale' to the public. The Issuing House may ensure that all the shares are sold by asking institutional investors to underwrite the issue; this means that any shares not taken up by the public will be bought by institutional investors. (See also **offer for sale** and **placings**).

J

Job analysis This involves the breaking down of a particular job into the different skills and knowledge required for its performance. The purpose of job analysis is to produce a job description or specification for a particular position in an organisation.

Job costing A method of costing that is particularly appropriate for firms such as builders or contractors, where each job or contract is regarded as a separate and distinct unit. The unit may be anything from a 'one-off' job to build an extension to a house, to a large contract for a power station.

Job description/specification This is sometimes given to applicants for a position in a firm or organisation. It lists the tasks involved in the job, and identifies the position of the particular post in the overall organisation.

Job evaluation A phase in establishing job requirements which determines the value of a particular job relative to others. Several methods are in use, from the simple ranking of jobs to the points rating system. This latter method identifies the characteristics of jobs which are held to deserve payment, such as skill, experience, responsibility, supervision exercised, etc.; weights these according to their relative importance in the eyes of those making the judgment and awards points to each job accordingly. The total points rating for each job can then be compared to a scale to establish the appropriate *grade* for a job and its relative claim to a salary.

Jobber Professional dealer on the **Stock Exchange** whose business it is to buy and sell a particular line of securities. Members of the public cannot approach jobbers direct on the floor of the Stock Exchange—stockbrokers are the intermediaries. Stockbrokers approaching jobbers are given two prices—one at which the jobber is prepared to buy and another, higher, at which he is prepared to sell. Having agreed a transaction broker and jobber note the 'bargain' in the books. The difference in the prices quoted is the jobber's turn, and therefore his profit.

Jobcentres   See **Manpower Services Commission**

Joint European Torus (JET)   The JET development involves the construction near Oxford of one of the most powerful experimental stations in the world. It was launched by the EEC to research the production of energy by nuclear fusion rather than by nuclear fission.

Joint-stock banks   See **clearing banks**

Journal   An accounting book of original entry. The types of entries that would be passed through the journal are correction of errors, sales of worn out or obsolete assets, the issue of **shares** or **debentures**, goodwill valuations, and some adjustments to final accounts.

Judicial function   The judiciary is one of the three divisions of government, the others being the Cabinet (the executive) and the legislature. The judicial function is to interpret the laws passed by Parliament, and the law courts provide the framework for the enforcement of the law.

K

Kangaroo closure   A method for controlling debate used in the **House of Commons**, where the chairman of a committee is empowered to 'jump' from one amendment to another, omitting those he considers to be repetitive or of minor importance. This saves time by cutting down unnecessary discussion.

Kerb dealing   Dealing which takes place after the official market has ended. Originally it took place in the street on the kerb outside the market. In modern times it also refers to trading on the telephone or by other dealing outside the ring or market.

Kondratieff curve   The term applied to long-term swings in economic activity named after its 19th century discoverer. Kondratieff claimed that over a period of 50 or 60 years one could find evidence of a long general upswing in the economy followed by a similar decline.

L

Labour   The factor of production known as labour covers the productive services rendered by human beings: the man hours worked in production of all kinds, using man's ingenuity and skill in producing what is wanted by the community. Labour as a factor of production ranges from the work of the unskilled through the various ranks of specialists to the highest professional experts. All are producers doing all kinds of work which has to be paid for.

Labour turnover   A measure for assessing the stability of a workforce. It is calculated by comparing staff replacements with the average number of full-time staff over a set period. Although labour turnover will vary from industry to industry and with the prevailing economic climate, a high relative labour turnover is considered damaging to a firm. It means increased costs in recruiting and training new staff, loss of efficiency whilst they are learning new duties, and often means low morale amongst other workers when staff keep leaving.

Lading, bill of   See **bill of lading**

Land   **1**   Land is one of the three factors of production (the others being labour and capital); the reward received by the factor *land* is commercial rent.
2   In economics, land is also understood to include not just the land itself but all its geographical features and its products, such as minerals and forests, the seas and the products of the seas, rivers and lakes, water supplies and the gases of the atmosphere; in fact all the natural resources of the earth. In common with all

resources they demand the best price which can be obtained on the market.

Large-scale production   Large-scale production is sometimes thought to be undesirable as it tends towards monopoly; it also faces central management with ever-widening and less accessible areas to control. Nowadays, with computerisation, it is much easier to run a large-scale enterprise and inevitably successful firms will get larger.

The 'economies of scale' which attend such large enterprises still exist and may be summarised as follows:
the ability to effect bulk transactions;
the use of expensive work-study and O & M techniques, possible only in large organisations, which produces a more efficient use of human resources and machinery and better production planning;
the diversification of output, markets, sources of supply and processes of manufacture which help to maintain satisfactory output when breakdowns occur in any area, including the spreading of resources to reduce vulnerability.

Law, classification of   The principal sources of English Law are legislation and the principles worked out in decided cases in the Courts (judicial precedent or case law).

There are two categories of English Law—public and private.
Public Law involves — Administrative Law
                                        Constitutional Law
                                        Criminal Law
Private Law
(*Civil Law*) involves — Company Law
                                        Family Law
                                        Law of Contract
                                        Law of Succession
                                        Law of Torts
                                        Law of Trusts
In 1972 the UK joined the EEC and thereby added a new source of law to those already existing. European Law covers very few subjects, but if it is different from English Law it prevails over it.

152

Law of demand and supply   See **demand and supply, law of**

Law of diminishing returns   See **diminishing returns, law of**

Leasehold land   A tenure of land by lease. As the name implies the tenure has a definite date of ending. (cf the indefinite end of a *freehold* estate).

Leasing   If a business is expanding, or if it finds it necessary to replace outdated capital equipment, it could cost a great deal of money. Leasing is the answer to this problem. It is simple, tax-efficient and inflation-proof. It is becoming increasingly popular as a flexible form of medium-term finance. The equipment is selected by the firm that requires it, and this firm negotiates the purchase terms with the seller. The financier—usually a merchant or commercial bank—will then place the order, and the firm requiring the equipment will lease the goods from the bank for an agreed period. The bank will claim the capital allowances and any regional development grants from the government, and this is passed on to the leasing firm in the form of reduced rentals. Usually the rental is fixed at the outset, so the firm's budget is not pressurised by increases in interest rates, tax changes, or inflation, since the rental payments will be coming out of future earnings. Leasing can be the most economical way of financing new capital equipment without laying out capital.

Most large leasing organisations are members of the Equipment Leasing Association Limited (ELA).

Ledger   The principal book of accounts required for a proper record of all the transactions of a business. In theory the ledger is one book, but in practice it is convenient to divide the book into several volumes. A special volume is usually set aside for the reception of the personal accounts of customers and is known as the sales or sold ledger. Another book is devoted to the personal accounts of creditors and is known as the purchase or bought ledger. A third ledger, called the general ledger—sometimes the nominal ledger—contains the real and nominal accounts relating to the assets and liabilities and the gains and expenses of the business.

In sole trading and partnership concerns a fourth ledger, known as the private ledger, may be used to contain the capital account, drawings account, trading and profit and loss accounts, and the balance sheets for each period. It is also kept for the final accounts of limited companies.

Legal aid A system under which those whose means are insufficient to enable them to pay for legal representation may have their legal costs paid wholly or in part from public funds (Legal Aid and Advice Act 1949).

Legal rights Legal rights stem from the **common law**; a legal estate is a right to hold land that the common law will recognise.

Legal tender Under the law of legal tender a creditor cannot refuse payment of a debt in notes and coins of the realm.

Any debt may be settled by payment in notes, which are legal tender up to any amount. The £1 coin is also legal tender to any amount. Other limits to legal tender are as follows:
Up to £20 may be paid in 50p coins
Up to £10 may be paid in 20p coins or crowns (25p)
Up to £5 may be paid in 5p and 10p coins
Up to 20p may be paid in 1p and 2p coins

Legislative function The legislative function is performed by the Queen in Parliament; the UK Parliament legislates (makes laws) through its two chambers—the House of Commons and the House of Lords.

Sometimes delegated powers of legislation are conferred on local authorities and statutory undertakings to make rules such as bye-laws, which come under the general heading of delegated legislation.

Legislative process Legislation is by Bill introduced in either House of Parliament, passed by both Houses, and formally assented to by the Crown.

Legislature One of the three functions of government, the others being the executive and judicial functions. The legislature consists of the Queen in Parliament, the **House of Lords** and the **House of Commons**. It is a 'bicameral' parliament—ie, having two chambers.

Lender of last resort It sometimes happens that those who have deposited money at the **discount houses** demand immediate payment; this may leave the discount houses 'short' because they will probably have lent their borrowed money for three months or even longer. They endeavour to obtain money from every source available, but if they fail are forced to turn to the Bank of England—the lender of last resort—and pay at the bank's MLR, which will probably involve them in a loss.

Letter of credit Document in the form of a letter given by a bank to a client. It serves to introduce the client to that bank's branches or agents, to whom the letter is addressed, and authorises them to make payments in favour of the client up to the amount stated in the letter of credit. On the back of the letter columns are ruled for details of the payments made, and after payment of the last amount the letter of credit is returned to the issuing bank.

An importer may arrange to pay the exporter by means of a letter of credit. The importer sends a letter of credit with his order, and the exporter can then collect payment by presenting the signed bill of lading to his bank. This is a common method of settlement, but denies the period of credit possible where payment is made by means of a Bill of Exchange.

There are three principal categories of letters of credit—

The *unconfirmed irrevocable letter of credit* is opened through an overseas bank and *not* confirmed by a bank in the country of the exporter. Such a credit can only be cancelled or revoked with the consent of the exporter and does provide the exporter with a certain measure of protection.

The *irrevocable and confirmed credit* is also opened through an overseas bank but *is* confirmed by a bank in the exporter's country, thus ensuring that the exporter is paid promptly on presentation of the specified documents.

155

The *revocable credit*, which can be revoked at any time by the overseas buyer, is rarely used.

Letter of indemnity   Request to a company's registrar to issue a replacement stock or share certificate when the original has been lost, destroyed or stolen. In it the holder undertakes to indemnify the company for any loss incurred as a result of issuing a duplicate document; most companies require this undertaking to be countersigned by a bank or insurance company.

Letter of renunciation (Stocks and shares)   Form attached to an allotment letter which is filled in should the original holder wish to pass his entitlement to someone else. See **renounceable documents**.

Liabilities, current   The current liabilities of an organisation can include trade creditors (for goods supplied), expense creditors (for services supplied), and bank overdraft.

Liability   When a dispute occurs the courts decide which person or organisation represented in the case is liable for any wrongful act.

Liability can be strict when the person who commits the offence can be held liable, or vicarious when—as could happen in the case of an organisation—the employer is liable for the actions of one of his employees.

Liability, insurance of   See **accident insurance**

Licensed dealer   A dealer in securities licensed by the Department of Trade and Industry under the Prevention of Fraud (Investments) Act 1958, but not a member of the **Stock Exchange**.

Licensed deposit-taking institutions   Institutions licensed by the **Bank of England** to take deposits from the public. Licensed institutions and recognised banks (together with a few other institutions) make up the monetary sector.

Life assurance   The term assurance is often applied especially to *life* as distinct from fire and other classes of insurance, but in fact the words assurance and insurance are used indiscriminately. Death or physical injury cannot be indemnified—life assurance policies provide benefits rather than compensation. The aims of the various policies vary; they may cover the death or retirement of the insured, or provide for dependents.

In certain cases building societies may insist that a mortgage be backed by life assurance, so that in the event of the mortgagor's death dependents own the property without further repayments.

Limited company   Limited companies may be either private or public, but the abbreviation plc refers only to public limited companies. One of the important functions of the **Articles of Association** is to fix the distinction between the two. Features of both types of company are—
Private Limited Companies
must have one director and at least two shareholders but not more than 50,
shares can only be sold with the permission of the other shareholders,
shares cannot be issued for public subscription,
the capital is usually small,
the accounts have to be published.
Public Limited Companies (plc)
must have two directors and at least seven shareholders,
shares may be sold to anyone and may be quoted on the Stock Exchange,
public subscription for shares can be invited,
the accounts have to be published.

Limited liability (of companies and partnerships)   Both public and private limited companies have limited liability, which means that the personal liability of the owners is restricted to the amount of each investor's stake in the company.

Company *limited by share* means that the extent of the member's risk is limited to the amount of his shareholding (all companies quoted on the Stock Exchange are in this category).

157

Limited partner

Company *limited by guarantee* may or may not have share capital. The guarantee consists of an undertaking by members to contribute up to a stated amount in the event of winding up, such a guarantee being incorporated in the Memorandum of Association.

Limited Partners are accorded the privilege of limited liability.

Unlimited liability means that in the event of loss all the members would be liable for all the debts which have been incurred, and would have to sell their private possessions to repay the debts.

Limited partner   See **partners**

Line and staff organisation   A combination of the functional and line organisation types which in theory is designed to take advantage of the best features of each.

Line management (Organisation)   The formal relationships between departments can be illustrated by an hierarchical organisation chart, indicating the lines of communication. Where instructions are passed along lines in the hierarchy the system is referred to as line management.

Authority and responsibility are passed downwards; accountability is passed upwards.

Liner, cargo   Nearly all cargo liners take cargo to and from major ports and have a few cabins for passengers; most passenger liners are now cruise liners used for holidays at sea.

Liner Conferences   The International Chamber of Commerce, which represents Liners' customers, approves the system of Liner Conferences which charge a steady rate for carrying cargo, unlike 'tramps' whose freight rates fluctuate with supply and demand. As long as customers are 'regular' customers rebates are allowed, and the service provides security and reliability.

Liquidation   A company may cease to exist by winding up or liquidation. The appointed liquidator proceeds to realise the assets and pay off the creditors, after which the company is dissolved and ceases to exist.

Liquid capital   See **capital (types of)**

Liquid capital ratio   See **acid test ratio**

Liquidity   The ease with which a firm can convert its assets (such as debtors and stock held) into cash is known as liquidity.

The following is a list of liquid assets (in descending order of liquidity)—
cash,
current account deposits at banks,
other bank deposits and deposits at non-bank financial intermediaries (NBFI's),
short-term securities (bills and bonds) which can be sold for money on organised markets. (NB the price of securities tends to fluctuate),
long-term securities,
physical assets such as property and machines which may be sold, though the prices they fetch may be very uncertain.

Liquidity ratio   Early bankers observed that only 8% of their customers' funds were likely to be demanded in cash at any time, which left them free to lend the remaining 92% at interest. In fact the **Bank of England** requires that 10% must be retained by the banks in cash, and a further small percentage—a 'special deposit'—can be called in by the Bank of England to control credit policies. Overall this is the **cash ratio**.

In order to meet any sudden demands for cash, bankers keep a further 20% of their deposits in 'near-cash' investments which can be turned back into cash immediately. These investments plus the cash ratio form the bank's liquidity ratio, which is about one-third of the bank's total deposits.

Listed company   Also **quoted company**. A company whose shares are listed on the **Stock Exchange**.

Listing agreement   A company whose shares are listed on the **Stock Exchange** must abide by the Stock Exchange's Listing Agreement. This insists on the prompt release of any information which could affect the market price of the shares. A serious breach of the Listing Agreement can result in suspension of dealing in the company's shares.

Litigation   To carry out an action in law. The process of carrying on a judicial contest.

Lloyds brokers   All business is brought to Lloyds of London by Lloyds brokers who represent the public and who obtain for their clients the best insurance terms available.

Lloyds Corporation (Lloyds of London)   The London insurance market. The Society of Lloyds was first incorporated by Act of Parliament in 1871, and is controlled by an elected committee of twelve members. The actual insurance is done by **underwriters**. It is the modern practice for them to work in syndicates, sharing the risks they insure; they may not be approached by members of the public—a Lloyd's broker is a middleman who acts as an agent between the public and the underwriters.

Traditionally Lloyds is noted for marine insurance (which now includes aviation), but in fact it carries on business in all classes of insurance, though the bulk of insurance in Britain is transacted through the large composite companies.

Lloyds List is published daily; in it is recorded all the shipping information available on a world-wide scale. It is Lloyd's own and London's oldest daily newspaper. In addition to general shipping news it gives arrivals and sailings of merchant vessels throughout the world besides coverage of marine and aircraft casualties.

Lloyds Register of Shipping (Lloyds Shipping Index)   This gives full descriptions of 20,000 ocean-going vessels, current voyages and latest reported positions; also the classification of ships according to their strength and efficiency for carrying cargo.

Lloyds syndicates   A syndicate is a combination of firms for some common purpose or interest. The Lloyds syndicate system developed from an old-time practice whereby an **underwriter** would 'write a line' on behalf of others. Members of a syndicate take no part in the mechanics of underwriting, which is left to the syndicate's professional manager, who corrects an imbalance on his book by **reinsurance**. There is nothing to stop an independent member from insuring personally against unacceptable loss, and a Lloyds member is not confined to one syndicate, and often works in both the marine and non-marine sectors.

Lloyds underwriters   Lloyds underwriters are the members of Lloyds Corporation who alone may accept insurance risks in Lloyds insurance market. They must be elected and prove their financial ability to the satisfaction of the committee of Lloyds. They are formed into **Lloyds syndicates**—groups of a few to several hundred individuals—which are represented at Lloyds by underwriting agents who accept insurance risks on behalf of members of their syndicates. All business is brought to Lloyds by brokers who obtain for their clients the best terms available in the competitive market.

Loan   Bank loans may be made for a specific reason and for an agreed length of time. Interest is paid on the loan, repayment of which may be by instalments or a lump sum. Collateral security may be asked for by the bank for the duration of the loan. To be granted a bank loan the client need not necessarily be already a customer of that bank.
   Loans to a company which can be bought and sold on the Stock Exchange are called **debentures**. These are fixed interest loans made to a company and are issued with specific terms regarding interest, capital repayment and security, and are usually redeemable on a set date.

Loan capital   This is money a company has borrowed, either on mortgage or by the issue of **debentures**.

Loan stock   See **gilt-edged market**

Local authorities/local government   Local authorities or councils are given the power by a number of Statutes to administer many services in their own areas. The work of these authorities is called local government. Local government consists of County Councils and District Councils.

The Department of the Environment supervises the work of local authorities.

Loco price   This is the price of the goods as they lie in the seller's warehouse, or some other specified place, at the time of sale. In cases where packing is necessary, the buyer has to bear the extra cost of this, and he has likewise to pay the cost of transport to his own warehouse.

Lomé Convention   This is an agreement between the **EEC** and African, Caribbean and Pacific States. Besides providing financial assistance the Common Market is almost entirely open to exports from the sixty developing countries which are parties to the convention. Specific advantages are granted under other agreements.

London Bankers' Clearing House   The Committee of the London Clearing Bankers on which each bank is represented by its chairman, is responsible for the management of the Clearing House.

See **Clearing system of the banks.**

London Commodity Exchange Group   Terminal or *'futures'* markets in 'soft' commodities—cocoa, coffee, sugar, rubber, vegetable oil, soya bean meal and wool—are operated on this exchange, which also provides a centralised market for all kinds of cereals produced in Britain.

London Discount Market Association (LDMA)   See **discount houses/discount market**

London foreign bond market   Although most issues of foreign bonds are listed on the **Stock Exchange** or on a continental bourse, dealing is mostly by international dealers and largely takes place over the telephone.

London Metal Exchange   The primary function of the LME is to provide a protective mechanism against price fluctuations for producers, merchants and users of metal. This mechanism is the terminal market where sales and purchases can be covered by **hedging**. This attracts speculators.

In the past 'ring trading'—members stood around a chalk circle drawn on the floor and conducted their business by 'open outcry'—was confined to copper and tin; these days grading has been extended to a range of metals which makes it possible for ring trading to take place, but the ring now consists of a circle of curved benches.

In the LME the buyer and seller are directly responsible to each other for carrying out the deal as agreed.

London Option Clearing House (LOCH)   With a traded option the buyer and seller each has an option with the LOCH, a special corporation controlled by the Council of the **Stock Exchange**. A traded option has a market price which can be traded from day to day, and has a life of up to nine months; it can be bought and sold throughout its period of currency. See **options dealing**

London Stock Exchange   Though there are other stock exchange 'floors' in Birmingham, Dublin, Glasgow, Liverpool and Manchester the main trading floor is in Throgmorton Street in the City of London. See **Stock Exchange**

Longs/long gilts   These are gilt-edged securities without a redemption date within fifteen years.

Loss leader   An item sold at a loss by a retailer to attract other custom.

Lutine Bell   The bell which was salvaged from *HMS Lutine* which

163

sank in 1799 with a cargo of gold bullion which has never been recovered, and which is now in Lloyd's of London.

The bell is now rung mainly for ceremonial occasions but used to signal news about overdue vessels. One stroke may still be sounded for bad news and two strokes for good news.

M

M0, M1, M2, M3   See **money stock**

Macroeconomics   The study of the aggregate flows of expenditure between household and firms, and through the financial markets; the overall working of, and interconnections between, the markets in goods, in factors, and in finance. (See **microeconomics**.)

Mail order   There are three main types of mail order business.

The most familiar is the very large mail-order firm which sells through expensively produced catalogues, operating through agents (usually housewives) who receive a commission. One of the attractions of such buying (mostly of clothes and other non-durable goods) is that customers are allowed to buy on credit—usually over 20 weeks—the basis of the transaction being a Credit-sale Agreement.

These large firms combine the roles of wholesaler and retailer, thereby gaining the profits of both functions. A further financial advantage is that they operate from premises which need not be easily accessible and need not, therefore, be situated in 'prime' or expensive sites. In addition, by dealing in very large quantities they enjoy the economies of bulk buying. On the other hand, these large mail order companies have enormous postage bills and pay all their agents a commission. They are also particularly vulnerable to bad debts.

The second method of selling by mail order is by advertising in the daily press and magazines; this is done by manufacturers, wholesalers and retailers. The advertisement requires a direct response from the buyer, who is thereafter kept on the advertiser's mailing list.

A third method is by the use of a mailing list. A firm may send advertising literature through the post to selected addresses—their names being usually obtained from a mailing list which a supplier has bought.

Making-up day   The second day of the **Stock Exchange** account on which speculators can make arrangements to carry bargains over to the next accounting period.

Management   (of organisations) An organisation's policy decisions must be put into effect by those in management, and those in management must not only be good organisers but also possess the qualities of leadership. All managers are experts in a particular departmental function, be it marketing, finance, personnel, production or office administration; managers must implement policy decisions by planning, co-ordinating and organising their departments to obtain an optimum result, working at all times within budgetary controls. 'Reporting back'—for example, in the case of a limited company to the managing director—is a managerial function which is extremely important. It is from departmental reports that top management is able to assess whether policy decisions are being implemented and how successful they are.

Management by objectives   An approach to management that begins with a broad statement of what a company seeks to achieve over a planned period. This is narrowed down to individual objectives, with subordinate managers being asked to suggest possible objectives for their departments for producing certain results that will contribute to overall objectives. It requires free discussion and free exchange of ideas, and relies on each manager knowing what he has to do and why and agreeing that what is required is achieveable.

The approach is considered successful for providing an achievement motive, leaving people to develop better ways of doing things if they find that new methods will produce better

166

results. It also makes overall goals the concern of every manager and helps to break down the narrow restricting departmental view of business activities.

Managing director (MD)   The **Articles of Association** usually give authority to the board of directors to appoint a managing director. After the chairman he is the most important director. As the chief administrative officer he has the responsibility of running the organisation according to the decisions made by the board.

Manpower Services Commission (MSC)   The aims of the Commission are:
to contribute to efforts to raise employment and reduce unemployment;
to help assist manpower resources to be developed, and contribute fully to economic well being;
to help secure for each worker the opportunities and services he or she needs in order to lead a more satisfying working life;
to improve the quality of decisions affecting manpower.

EMPLOYMENT SERVICE
The aims of the Employment Service are:
to help people choose, train for and get the right job,
to help employers recruit the right people as quickly as possible.
    Through its nationwide network of *Jobcentres*, the Employment Service provides a wide range of MSC services. Jobcentre staff assist disabled people who need to find jobs. The *Disablement Advisory Service* (DAS) provides employers with advice and guidance on how to make full use of the skills and abilities of disabled workers and on the practical and financial assistance available from MSC.
Employment Rehabilitation Centres (ERCs) run courses to help people who have been ill, injured or unemployed regain their working ability.
Professional and Executive Recruitment (PER) is organised and managed separately from the other Employment Service programmes. Employers using PER's selection and Executive Post advertising services are charged a fee.

Manpower Services Commission (MSC)

The *Careers and Occupational Information Centre* (COIC) publishes a wide range of literature, games, video tapes and computer software to support the New Training Initiative.

THE ENTERPRISE ALLOWANCE SCHEME

This helps unemployed people set up in business by paying an allowance for 52 weeks. The scheme also helps by providing advice and guidance from experienced business counsellors of the Department of Industry's Small Firms Service.

COMMUNITY PROGRAMME

This is a scheme to help people who have been out of work for some time and to help local communities.

Typical projects include: turning a disused building into a community centre, making parks from derelict sites, helping disabled people, building a children's adventure playground, gardening and decorating for old people, and building a day centre in a church hall.

THE VOLUNTARY PROJECTS PROGRAMME

This provides a range of constructive voluntary opportunities designed to help unemployed people develop their existing skills, learn new work skills or provide part-time work preparation and rehabilitation without affecting their entitlement to statutory benefits.

Typical projects include: volunteers helping disabled people to live as independently as possible, adult education classes for ex-offenders, volunteers providing a gardening and household repair service for elderly or disabled people, basic skills training in woodwork, dressmaking, catering and computer programming, conservation and landscape improvement schemes.

YOUTH TRAINING SCHEME

This is successfully established as a carefully planned high quality training scheme, equipping today's young people to meet the requirements of tomorrow. It offers a permanent bridge between school and work to all sixteen-year-old school leavers, both

168

employed and unemployed, and also to some seventeen-year-olds and disabled youngsters.

Employers can expect: a better trained and better motivated workforce, more confident and competent staff with the basic skills they need at work, and in everyday life, grants from the MSC towards the financing of approved schemes, help from MSC Training Division, Area Offices and Accredited Centres in setting up quality schemes.

TRAINING FOR ADULTS

As well as providing a strategic framework for all those involved in adult training, MSC itself adds to the total training effort by providing training directly, and by facilitating and assisting action by others, in particular employers.

The MSC works in partnership with both statutory and non-statutory industry training organisations on the provision of training for all sectors of industry. Grants for training in priority economic and occupational areas are made available to employers through these organisations.

Other MSC provision in this area includes: grant schemes for employers; direct training services, including the Skillcentre Training Agency's service for employers provided on a cost recovery basis.

OPEN TECH PROGRAMME

This is intended to make training more accessible to adults by expanding open learning provisions, initially at technician and supervisory levels.

The Commission is now taking ahead action on its Adult Training Strategy, which the Government broadly endorsed in January 1984.

TECHNICAL AND VOCATIONAL EDUCATION INITIATIVE

TVEI is a five-year pilot scheme to stimulate the provision of technical and vocational education for 14–18 year-olds in the education system.

The projects differ but all: offer a four-year course starting at 14 of full-time, general, technical and vocational education, with

169

appropriate work experience; are for young people across the ability range; lead to nationally recognised qualifications; are being run in existing schools and colleges; are optional for pupils.

SKILLCENTRE TRAINING AGENCY (STA)
The MSC's skillcentres now operate on a commercial basis, covering their costs from fees charged.

The MSC will remain a large customer of the STA but an increasing proportion of STA's business will be directly with employers.

Manufacturing industry This forms the second tier of production and involves the use of the raw materials of primary production, using them to produce 'manufactured goods',—it changes the form of raw materials. It also covers all building and constructive work.

Manufacturing industry requires materials, power and labour; choice of location is often dictated by their ready availability.

Margin Money put up as security that a contract will be fulfilled. A margin is usually deposited with the clearing house of a commodity exchange.

Margin call If the market moves against an investor after he has entered into a *futures* contract, the *broker* will ask him to provide more money to top up the deposit payment to cover his loss and maintain the deposit at the original percentage level. A margin call is normally made when one quarter to one half of the original deposit has been lost.

Marginal costing A technique for ascertaining the marginal cost of a product, ie, the amount by which aggregate costs are changed if the output is increased or decreased by one unit. In marginal costing, *fixed* expenses do not form part of the marginal cost, as they are incurred irrespective of the volume of output.

Marginal revenue The increase in total revenue to be achieved by selling one further unit of output.

Marginal utility The term 'utility' is used to mean the satisfaction which, at a given time, is derived from a good or service. The utility derived from the *last unit purchased* by a consumer is known as marginal utility. The law of diminishing marginal utility is based on the principle that the more a person possesses of a particular commodity the less satisfaction he will derive from a further increase. The law states that as a general rule the marginal utility of a commodity will diminish with every increase in the supply of the product. Money is considered to be an important exception.

Marine insurance A large share of marine insurance is transacted by Lloyds **underwriters** (see **Lloyds Corporation**) and is of particular importance to shipowners.

Apart from hull, cargo and freight insurance, which are treated separately under their own headings, the shipowner is faced with many risks against which he can insure. These include events which may result from his own or his employees' negligence; examples are collision with other vessels or shore installations, injuries to those on board, and water pollution.

Mark A price given in the **Official List** under the heading 'Business Done'. Though under **Stock Exchange** Rules marking is not compulsory, (except in a few specified instances) the use of computers to compile this information has meant that it is now the rule rather than the exception.

Market 1 The market system assumes that prospective buyers and sellers satisfy their needs by the **price mechanism**, particularly if there is a choice of identical products.
2 A place where buyers and sellers are in contact with each other.

Market Entry Guarantee Scheme The **BOTB** promotes a scheme to assist the financing of new ventures based abroad. The scheme will help businesses through the early stages of the venture by assisting in the cost of on-the-spot office accommodation, staff training, sales promotion, etc. Funding is repayable with interest, but if the venture is unsuccessful any shortfall at the end of the agreed period will be cancelled.

Market forces   See **price mechanism**

Market price   **1**   The short-term equilibrium price on the market which equates demand and supply.
2 (Stock Exchange)   The price at which shares actually change hands. Because shares can vary in price through the day an average is therefore taken, and the 'average market price' is often used for valuation purposes.

Market prospects service   This supplies reports drawn up by the commercial staff of the British Embassy in the country selected by the prospective exporter. These are intended to enable a clearer picture to be formed of the prospective market, and provide the names of contacts in the market-place who might wish to trade.

Market research   Concerned with supplying information to manufacturers and wholesalers about consumer market trends.

Marketing   Marketing, basically, is discovering what the customer wants, and selling it to him.
Market research and analysis is concerned with present and future needs of users, monitors present and potential competition in the field, and consumer trends and preferences. This is market intelligence.
Desk research consists of analysing in-house information over a previous period, so that trends and tendencies can be identified; it also involves the analysis of statistics published by official bodies and trade associations.
   Desk research should reveal the potential market and size of the market for a projected product or service.
Field research involves actual entry in the field in which the research is interested, sampling the opinions of customers and clients first-hand. Many organisations undertake such market research on behalf of other businesses. See also **sampling**.

172

Planning Goods must be available in the right form and of the right quality; this is the function of secondary production (manufacturing). They must also be available at the right price, time and place; this is the function of tertiary production employing commercial services. Co-operation and co-ordination between research and development, basic engineering, production control, financial control, sales and promotional functions are essential to the successful marketing of a product, and the changing nature of demand makes it necessary for these co-ordinated functions to be constant factors during the life of a product.

Specialised marketing activities include branding and packaging, merchandising, pricing, physical distribution, selling, advertising (large organisations make use of the services of advertising agencies), public relations and provision for after-sales services.

Marketing boards These were established in the 1930s by the Agricultural Marketing Acts which empowered ministers to set up marketing boards for agricultural produce, but they were only to be established on the initiative of independent farmers themselves. Marketing boards may be empowered to buy all produce from farmers, and have been associated with guaranteed prices and production grants.

Markets Committee of the Council for the Securities Industry (Body responsible for the City Code on Take-overs and Mergers) The 'Markets Committee' (full name above) has succeeded the *ad hoc* 'City Working Party' as the body responsible for carrying out periodical revisions of the Code.

Mark-up Mark-up is usually a percentage of the cost price, added to the cost price, to produce the selling price of an article.

Mass production The manufacture of goods on a huge scale by automation. Standardisation, simplification and specialisation are essential to its success.

Mechanism of price See **price mechanism**

173

Mediums/medium gilts   These are gilt-edged securities with a redemption date between five and fifteen years ahead.

Medium-Term Financial Strategy (MTFS)   The collective term for the Conservative government's plans for monetary, public spending and tax policies. The MTFS was introduced in 1980 and has involved the setting of targets and projections for monetary growth, public spending, etc, for a number of years ahead.

Meetings (of limited companies)   Company 'general meetings' (of members) are of three types:

The Statutory Meeting   This must be held not earlier than one month and not later than three months, after the company is entitled to commence business. Its purpose is to inform members of the state of the company's affairs, and to give shareholders an opportunity to discuss any matter concerning the formation.

The Annual General Meeting (AGM) of a limited company must be held at least once a year in addition to any other meetings in that year, and not more than fifteen months must elapse between one AGM and the next. If a company fails to hold an AGM the DTI may call or direct the calling of a meeting. Matters generally dealt with at the AGM are:

declaration of a dividend;

presentation of the accounts and an auditor's report;

submission of the directors' report (under the 1982 Employment Act this must include a statement showing how employee participation has been developed in the organisation);

election of directors;

appointment of auditors and fixing of their remuneration.

Extraordinary General Meeting (EGM)   In addition to the AGM and any other general meetings of members a company may hold an EGM at which the special business set out in the notice convening the meeting may be transacted.

Other company's meetings may be held—eg, meetings of a class of member, meetings of debenture holders, meetings of directors, and meetings relevant to winding up.

Memorandum of Association (Limited companies)   After

obtaining clearance from the Registrar of Companies that the proposed name for the company is acceptable, the promoters join in signing, among other documents, the *Memorandum of Association*. This sets out:

the proposed name for the company which must have the word 'limited' for the last word;

the address of the company's registered office;

the objects of the company;

a statement that members' liability is limited;

the amount of nominal share capital and its division into shares of fixed amounts;

in the case of a company limited by guarantee a statement that each member undertakes to contribute to the assets of the company in the event of winding up (but not exceeding a specified amount).

Merchandising A marketing term that describes the promotional activities (excluding media advertising) that are designed to stimulate purchasing at the point of sale. In its broadest sense, merchandising means any special short-term promotional scheme, device or activity. There are numerous forms of merchandising employed in the market-place today, ranging from gift coupons, free samples, premium offers and competitions to the special in-store displays using show cards, mobiles and dummy packs.

Merchant Middleman who trades on his own account.

Merchant banks The term merchant bank is properly applied only to the members of the Accepting Houses Committee— finance houses whose primary business is the finance of overseas trade, but which also raise capital for industrial expansion, and generally take care of mergers and take-overs, and the needs of commercial and industrial companies.

Some merchants are also 'Issuing Houses' which organise the sale of shares for public limited companies. The **Gold Bullion Market** is operated by five merchant bankers, the **Silver Bullion Market** by three.

Merchant bankers are also very active on the **Foreign Exchange Market**, especially in the issue of **Eurobonds**

Both the Accepting Houses Committee and the Issuing Houses Association are represented on the Panel of Take-overs and Mergers which prepares the City Code for the Council for the Securities Industry.

Mergers (of businesses)   Firms agree to amalgamate to achieve rapid expansion. *Horizontal integration* involves the merging of firms which have an identical market. *Lateral integration* is the combination of firms with fairly similar markets. Combinations of different firms to achieve diversification usually involve all the firms in the group with a common 'holding company'; holding companies may also achieve *vertical integration* by taking over the subsidiaries which supply a parent manufacturing company with particular components.

Merit rating   A regular periodic assessment of a worker's job performance. It is undertaken to assess a person's abilities for promotion purposes and/or to reward a pay increase for extra achievement.

Metal exchange   See *London Metal Exchange*

Method study   The critical examination and recoding of work techniques with a view to developing and applying easier and more cost effective methods.

Methods of dealing   There are four methods of dealing on the *commodity markets*; these are by auction, by challenging, by private treaty, and by ring trading, which are all explained under their own headings. See also **'open outcry'**.

Methods of payment   Prompt payment in cash or Cash with Order are recognised methods of payment. **Promissory Notes** and **Bills of Exchange** are promises to pay by a certain date and are legally binding; they are therefore regarded as fairly secure methods of payment.

The clearing banks offer current account customers the following payment facilities: banker's draft, bank giro credit, cheques, credit transfers, direct debits and standing orders. A banker's credit card is another method of payment, but not restricted to current account customers.

Girobank also offers banker's drafts, Girobank cheques, Girobank payment services, direct debits, standing orders, and transfers, to its current account customers. (Transcash is a method of paying money *into* a Girobank current account to clear a debt if the payer does not have such an account himself).

The *Post Office* offers postal orders for the payment of small debts, and also an international payment service.

The *Royal Mail* offers a Cash on Delivery (COD) service.

See also **Bill of Exchange, letter of credit** and **open accounts** and **electronic funds transfer**.

Microeconomics The study of the 'small' elements of economics—individual buyers, sellers and firms (cf **macroeconomics**).

Microelectronics The Department of Trade and Industry launched its Microelectronics Application Project (MAP) in 1979 with the aim of encouraging UK manufacturing industry to use microelectronics in its products and processes.

Now a Minister of Information Technology has been appointed within the Department to co-ordinate all government activities in the IT area.

See **information technology**.

Microprocessors A term which is normally used to mean the single chip containing the central processing unit, but it can also be used to mean the complete microcircuit or computer system. In word processing the microprocessor is a small electronic package that controls the hardware of the word processor, under the guidance of software.

Microsystems centres The rapid growth of microcomputer technology presents a bewildering array of equipment, software and services for business computing. In order to assist businesses

177

to make effective use of this, a Federation of Microsystems Centres has been established across the UK to provide a range of services for users or intending users of microcomputers.

Supported by the Department of Trade and Industry and co-ordinated by the National Computing Centre, Microsystems Centres provide open access workshops, and training and advisory sessions.

A common code of practice ensures the impartiality of Centres, and, by working together, each has access to a wide range of information about computing systems and applications.

Middle price   The price half-way between the two prices shown in The **Stock Exchange** Daily Official List under 'Quotations', or the average of both buying and selling prices offered by a *jobber*. The prices found in newspapers are normally their estimate of the middle price.

Middleman   A middleman is a commercial intermediary or wholesaler who acts between producers of primary products (such as perishable foodstuffs) and the retailer, or between manufacturers and the retailer.

Minimum capital   See **capital (types of)**

Minimum Lending Rate (MLR)   The minimum rate of interest at which the **Bank of England** would normally lend to the discount houses. In 1981 the Bank suspended its practice of setting the MLR formally every Thursday, but does on occasion—when necessary—designate the rate.

Minimum reserve ratio   Since 1981 the **Bank of England** has kept the ratio of a bank's assets which must be kept in cash or near-cash to 10%.

Minority shareholders (of companies)   The right to make decisions concerning a company's affairs rests with those holding the majority holding power. If the majority support the directors there is nothing the minority can do about it, but provision is made for the protection of minorities where the majority rule operates against them unfairly; this can happen in the case of shareholders in a company which has merged or been taken over by another.

Minutes   The written record of business transacted at a meeting. As minutes may be required as evidence in a court of law they must give a precise account of the proceedings. The chairman usually signs the minutes at the subsequent meeting after their accuracy has been verified.

Misrepresentation Act 1967   The Misrepresentation Act established that innocent, negligent or fraudulent misrepresentation invalidates a contract.

Mixed economy   Mixed economies—such as that of the United Kingdom—have a mixture of public and private enterprise.

Mobile shop   Mobile shops selling bread, fruit and vegetables, meat, etc. are of particular benefit to those living in outlying areas.

Model(ling)   In its broadest sense a model is a representation of a real world situation. It may be three-dimensional, or simply a verbal or mathematical expression describing a set of relationships in a precise manner. A model can be useful in explaining or describing the behaviour of a system or it can be used to predict actions and events. The chief advantage of using models is that they permit alternative courses of action to be evaluated before implementation and at less risk. Also they provide a formal and structured description of a complex problem. However, the model-building process is often difficult and expensive, and many models assume a constant relationship between variables that is not consistent with the real world.

Monetarism (Economics)   A school of thought which emphasises the importance of controlling the growth of the money stock. Monetarists believe that the rate of growth of the money stock should be reduced over time in order to eliminate inflation.

Monetary authorities   The collective term for those responsible for monetary policy—usually this means the government department responsible for financial policy and the central bank. In Britain the monetary authorities are the **Treasury** and the **Bank of England**.

Monetary base   The banks' deposits, or balances, with the central bank. The monetary base can also be defined to include cash held by either, or both, the banks and the public.

Monetary base control   A method of monetary control in which the central bank seeks to control the growth of the money stock by regulating the growth of the monetary base.

Monetary demand   The level of overall demand for goods and services in the economy measured in terms of money. Monetary demand means the same as expenditure or money income.

Monetary policy   Regulation of the monetary system designed to contribute toward the objectives of economic policy. The basis for monetary policy is the belief that such things as the stock of money in circulation, or the level of interest rates, have important effects on the development of the economy.

Monetary sector   The monetary sector in Britain is made up of recognised banks, licensed deposit-taking institutions, the **National Girobank**, the **trustee savings banks** and the Banking Department of the **Bank of England**. Broadly speaking the money stock in Britain includes cash held by the public plus the deposits of the public with the monetary sector.

Monetary systems   As soon as a market develops with frequent exchanges of standard commodities a measure of value becomes necessary. Many commodities—shells, tobacco, all the common metals—have been used for this purpose; these have given way to a standard abstract unit of exchange—money—which means that goods can be priced to a monetary scale and exchange of goods effected between parties where a coincidence of needs and produce does not exist.

Bank money   In modern economies the main means of payment are cash (notes and coin) held by the public, and bank deposits. The depositor can withdraw cash up to the value of his deposits, or transfer them to someone else by writing a cheque. Because bank deposits can be exchanged for goods and services in this way they qualify as a means of payment.

It is important to note that not all bank deposits are a means of payment. This is true only of those deposits which can be transferred directly in exchange for goods and services, that is, current account deposits. Other, non-current account deposits are not a means of payment and should not be counted as 'money'. However, in some cases such deposits can either be withdrawn in cash or transferred to the customer's current account with little delay, so they are almost as convenient as current account deposits as a store of purchasing power.

It is not just banks that accept deposits that can be withdrawn with little delay. In Britain most of the deposits with the building societies can be withdrawn at any time. These, with the current account deposits with banks are important examples of 'liquid assets' or liquidity. Broadly speaking it can be said that an asset is more liquid the more swiftly it can be converted into the means of payment and the more certain (or less variable) its monetary value.

Monetary targets   Targets for the growth of the money stock.

Money   The main functions of money are: a specialised means of payment; a store of value; a unit of account; and a standard of deferred payments.

The properties of money are: stability of value, durability, divisibility, transferability, and recognisability.

Money incomes   These are the actual amounts of money earned; *real incomes* refer to the actual goods and services which can be purchased with those incomes. In times of inflation a static income means that over a period of time fewer goods and services can be purchased.

Money market   Market where large sums of money (or wholesale funds) are borrowed and lent for relatively short periods. Amongst the most important of the money markets in London are the markets for bills, for certificates of deposit and for interbank deposits.

Money market intervention   The **Bank of England** intervenes in the money markets in order to set very short-term interest rates. It does this mainly through intervention in the bill market (by buying and selling **Treasury Bills**).

Money stock/money supply   Money stock can be defined in various ways. Central banks have to decide which monetary aggregates are important for policy purposes, and in terms of which aggregates they should express their targets.

M0 equals notes and coin in circulation with the public *plus* banks' till money and banks' balances with the Bank of England. (M0 is a measure of the 'monetary base'.)

M1 equals notes and coin in circulation with the public *plus* private sector holdings of sterling 'sight' bank deposits (ie deposits withdrawable without notice).

M2 equals the non-interest bearing component of M1 *plus* private sector holdings of interest-bearing sterling bank deposits of a 'retail' nature (ie deposits that can readily be used for transactions purposes), 'retail' building society deposits and National Savings Bank ordinary accounts.

£M3 equals M1 *plus* private sector holdings of sterling 'time' bank deposits (ie deposits which require notice before withdrawal) and sterling bank certificates of deposit.

M3 equals £M3 *plus* private sector holdings of foreign currency bank deposits.

PSL1 equals £M3 *less* bank time deposits with an original maturity of more than two years *plus* private sector holdings of money market instruments and certificates of tax deposit.

PSL2 equals PSL1 *less* building society holdings of money

market instruments and bank deposits etc *plus* private sector holdings of building society deposits (excluding term shares and SAYE) and national savings instruments (excluding certificates, SAYE and other longer-term deposits).

Monopolies and Mergers Act 1965   This set up the Monopolies Commission which investigated those mergers likely to operate against the consumer's interest—ie, if, by the merger, 25% of the market would be controlled by one supplier.

Under the *Fair Trading Act of 1973* the Commission was renaméd the Monopolies and Mergers Commission, and now includes services as well as goods.

The Commission conducts enquiries and investigations into the organisation's pricing policies, profit record and general practice of any firm or industry referred to it. Its recommendations will then be a matter for the Minister to take action upon and secure improvements to ensure fair trading.

Monopoly   A firm which has more than 25% of the production of a particular product or service under its control. When such a producer dominates a market then market forces play a smaller part in price decisions, and 'imperfect competition' exists. See also *natural monopolies*.

NB: *Monopoly rights* are granted by the Crown to an inventor who patents his idea. Patent rights can be sold, or another party granted a licence which allows use of the invention.

Monopsonist   A single buyer. Organised employers are monopsonists—single buyers of labour. (*NB:* A monopolist is a single seller).

Monorail   Monorail transport systems have been built to carry passengers on elevated tracks through cities,—eg, the line between Tokyo and its airport.

Monthly statement   All businesses make a practice of balancing their debtors' accounts at regular intervals, usually monthly. At the end of each month a statement of account is made up and sent

183

to each debtor, setting out his/her dealings with the firm during the month just passed. 'Account customers' do not pay cash for each transaction, but are able to avail themselves of short-term credit.

Mortgage   A building society or a bank can offer loans of money to prospective home buyers by means of a mortgage.

The borrower of the money is the *mortgagor*; the lender of the money is the *mortgagee*.

Mortgage debenture   This is covered by a particular part of the firm's property, which will be sold in order to repay the debenture holder in the event of difficulty.

Mortgage security policy   In certain cases building societies may insist that a mortgage be backed by life assurance, so that in the event of the mortgagor's death dependents own the property without further repayments.

Motion   A proposition put forward for discussion and decision at a meeting.

Motor vehicle insurance   A motor vehicle owner's comprehensive policy may cover damage to the car as a result of an accident, theft, fire, injury to the insured, and third party risks. (The first party is the insured, the second party is the insurer, the third party may be other persons affected by the contract—passengers, pedestrians, cyclists, etc). Car insurance is compulsory before using a vehicle on the road.

Multilateral clearing   See **clearing banks**

Multinational company/corporation   This is a company with productive facilities in more than one country, but under ownership based in one country only. It may be a holding company with foreign subsidiaries.

Multiple store   A group of similar shops operated by one large-scale retailer, with numerous branches. Such organisations can be operated by manufacturers to sell their own goods, or they may produce some of the commodities they sell, but also offer a wide range of other consumer goods.

Multiplier (the)   An economic concept that describes the effect of changes in investment on consumption and income. It demonstrates that a small change in investment can exert a magnified effect on income and hence on employment and consumption. The size of the multiplier effect depends on the marginal propensity to consume. Where this is high the multiplier will be high since the additional spending released into the economy will generate a knock-on effect amongst subsequent consumers.

Municipal undertakings   Commercial enterprises can be operated by borough and district councils. Examples of these are swimming baths, bus services, leisure centres and theatres.

Mutual insurance offices   These offer insurance to members who have mutual interests, such as belonging to a particular trade or profession.

N

Naked debentures   These **debentures** carry no charge on the assets of a company.

Name of limited company   This must not be the same as that of any other company. It must be followed by the word 'limited'. The usual procedure is to gain clearance from the Registrar of Companies before flotation so that the proposed name is known to be acceptable.

National bank   The central bank of a country, in the UK the **Bank of England**.

National Debt   In developed countries the government often borrows money from the people in order to finance its expenditure, particularly in times of war. It pays interest on the money and may give a date of repayment. Nowadays the borrowing is for permanent public works ('productive' loans) and various schemes have been mooted over the years to bring about a reduction of the debt.

The National Debt is administered by the National Debt Commissioners who, among other things, invest deposits from the ordinary account of the **National Savings Bank** (under the NSB Act 1971) in government securities. Marketable government stock comprises more than 70% of the National Debt.

National Economic Development Council (NEDC)   Part of the 'Neddy' organisation. The Council, set up in 1962, meets monthly under the chairmanship of the Chancellor of the Exchequer or, occasionally, the Prime Minister. Leading government economic and industrial ministers, top level representatives of the CBI and TUC, and representatives of certain other important interests, discuss topics of national importance. The Director General of NEDO is a member of the Council, and is the link between it and the other parts of the Neddy organisation.

National Economic Development Office (NEDO) Part of the 'Neddy' organisation. NEDO provides the support staff for the Council and EDCs (Economic Development Committees), but also has an important independent role.

National Enterprise Board (NEB) This has now combined with the **National Research Development Corporation** to form the **British Technology Group (BTG).**

National expenditure Very broadly, the total national expenditure can be used for calculating the national income—ie, the total expenditure of citizens and firms, government departments and local authorities.

National Freight Consortium The enthusiastic participation of employees as majority shareholders in the NFC public limited company has created a unique industrial partnership. In February 1982 the NFC was bought from the Government by employees, pensioners, and their families. They oversubscribed by nearly a million pounds for the 6,187,500 £1 shares on offer, the purchase price being completed by a loan from a syndicate of major UK banks.

Employee ownership and professional management make a powerfully motivated combination, committed to a successful response to customers' requirements. About 13,000 managers, staff, pensioners and their families hold 82½% of the NFC's issued share capital between them, the rest being held by the banks.

The NFC is Britain's biggest and most diverse freight transport, storage, removals and travel business. It is a market leader in important sectors of transport and distribution, operates some 13,000 vehicles and has over 700 locations throughout the UK and several overseas, including Australia and the USA. Its physical resources include over six million square feet of warehousing and more than thirty million cubic feet of cold storage, and it commands considerable in-house computer power. Annual revenue exceeds £500 million.

Its principal areas of activity are as follows:

British Road Services Group (Contract Hire and Fleet Management; BRS Distribution Consultancy; Truck and Trailer Rental; Engineering Services; AA-BRS Rescue; BRS TRANSCARD—a free charge card which enables drivers to buy a full range of supplies and services without the need to carry large sums in cash).

National Services Group (National Carriers Contract Services; Fashionflow Ltd—specifically serving Marks and Spencer's stores; Freight Computer Services Ltd—which includes a commercial printing works; Tankfreight Ltd; Felixstowe Tank Developments Ltd).

Parcels Group (Roadline UK Ltd; National Carriers Parcels; International Carriers combines freight forwarding skills with the parcels distribution to provide co-ordinated export and import freight facilities).

Property Group—one of the Group's main tasks is to provide the operating companies with the properties they need to run their business cost-effectively.

Special Traffics Group (Cartransport Ltd; Containerway and Roadferry Ltd; Cotrali-Pickfords Ltd—wine shippers; Fleetcare; Sonitrol Pickfords Ltd—protection for industrial, commercial and domestic premises; Waste Management Ltd).

The Regional Group provides a range of services in Scotland and Northern Ireland (Scottish Freight Company Ltd; Scottish Road Services and Scottish Parcels; Northern Ireland Carriers Ltd).

Pickfords Removals; Pickfords Travel Service Ltd; Tempco Union Ltd (temperature-controlled food distribution and cold storage).

NFC International (Downard Pickfords Pty—Australia; Merchants Home Delivery Service Inc—Oxnard, California, Texas, and Los Angeles; Pickfords International).

National Girobank   The national banking system operated from the post offices, offering a competitive service to that of the

clearing banks. It enjoys no special privileges and has to compete in the market place with other banks.

Girobank offers its customers current, deposit and budget account facilities. Further facilities are fixed interest personal loans, travellers' cheques and foreign currency through Thomas Cook.

National income   The national income relates to the total income of the members of a community, not to that part which passes in rates and taxes to public authorities; it is a measure of the economic well-being of the community. Increases in the national income may be due to inflation and may simply reflect a fall in the value of the units of money; or it may be due to a growth in population.

National Insurance (NI) (DHSS)   This is a form of direct tax, payment of which is shared between employers and employees. The money is raised specifically to fund the National Health Service, the National Insurance Fund and the Redundancy Fund.

NI is a statutory deduction from salaries and wages and the money is used by the government to provide many cash benefits. These include payments to the unemployed, the sick and those permanently unable to work. Retirement and widows' pensions, together with maternity and child allowances, are funded in this way. The amount of contributions paid is related to the amount of money earned, and the money, when deducted by the employer, is entered on the Deductions Working Sheet and is subsequently sent with the **Income Tax** that has been deducted, to the Income Tax Office.

All school-leavers are issued with their personal National Insurance number which remains the same throughout life. It is essential that the number is retained for reference.

National Loans Fund   This records the government's lending and borrowing. Money invested in savings certificates, **Premium Bonds**, and SAYE contracts (the latter being now replaced by the Yearly Plan Scheme) are authorised under the general borrowing powers conferred on the Treasury by the National Loans Act 1968;

189

money invested in these is paid into the National Loans Fund, from which all payments (including prizes) are met.

National output The national output is the total production of goods and services, plus the total of producer goods created by all the industrial firms of the nation. Figures are collected on a 'value-added' basis to avoid counting them twice. The total figure is the Gross National Product (GNP).

National Research Development Corporation (NRDC) This has now combined with the **National Enterprise Board** to form the **British Technology Group**.

National savings

NATIONAL SAVINGS BANK

There are two kinds of National Savings Bank Account:

A *Savings Bank Ordinary Account* may be opened with £1 or more at any Savings Bank Post Office, which will issue a bank book in which transactions are recorded. The bank book may then be used to make deposits and withdrawals at any post office transacting Savings Bank business. Repayment of deposits with interest is guaranteed by the State.

An *Investment Account* may be opened with £1 or more at any Savings Bank Post Office. All withdrawals are subject to one month's notice of withdrawal in writing. Payments on demand are not allowed.

NATIONAL SAVINGS CERTIFICATES

These are issued for different amounts and on different terms from year to year. They can be cashed at a few days' notice, but have to be kept to maturity to gain the full amount of interest.

PREMIUM BONDS

Premium Bonds are a government security for which winning bond numbers are selected each month by ERNIE (Electronic Random Number Indicating Equipment). The only essential difference between them and other forms of small savings is that instead of earning interest the bonds carry, after a qualifying period, a chance of winning a tax-free prize.

Premium Bonds are £1 each, but can only be bought in multiples of £5.

YEARLY PLAN

This is a new scheme (1984) from National Savings for regular savers. Monthly payments (in multiples of £5, with a minimum of £20 and a maximum of £200) can be made for as little as one year, and they can continue for further years if required. It is an easy way of building up a lump sum for a major purchase or retirement, and offers guaranteed returns on the investment with tax-free interest.

Under Yearly Plan the contributor makes monthly payments for one year, all payments being made by Standing Order. At the end of that year he or she will receive a Yearly Plan Certificate showing the value of the monthly payments, including the interest earned in that year. This certificate will then earn interest every month for the next four years, and can be left in the scheme to earn further interest.

National Standard Shipping Note   An **aligned document** which can be used by exporters and forwarding agents when delivering cargo to any British port, container base or other freight terminal.

Nationalisation   The nationalisation technique is essential to the institution of state ownership and to public control of the means of production, distribution and exchange in an industry.

Nationalised industries/public corporations   A nationalised industry or public corporation is set up by Act of Parliament to carry out the duties entrusted to it by Parliament. A minister is appointed to achieve general control and direction when the national interest demands it. A board is appointed by the minister which is responsible for the management of the industry; it recruits its own staff and is not run by the Civil Service.

An annual report and the annual accounts must be presented to Parliament, which gives the House an opportunity to discuss the industry's work if it seems necessary. The accounts are investigated by the Public Accounts Committee.

Any surplus in trading belongs to the state, but is mainly 'ploughed back'. In the event of a loss the state bears the liability.

Each nationalised industry has a consumer council which represents the users of the product or service, and which deals with complaints.

Natural monopolies In the industrial and commercial fields certain goods and services are by their nature monopolies. Examples are gas, electricity and water supply.

Natural resources Primary products from the earth's fields, rivers, lakes, seas, forests and mines, and gases such as 'natural gas'.

'Neddy organisation' 'Neddy' is the only forum in the country where senior representatives of employers, trade unions and government meet regularly to discuss ways of improving our economic and industrial performance. See **National Economic Development Council; Economic Development Committees; National Economic Development Office.**

Negotiable instruments Any document which is negotiable can be passed into the possession of another person. Such documents are called 'negotiable instruments.' Most cheques are negotiable; when they pass into the possession of another they should be endorsed (signed on the back). **Bills of Exchange** are also negotiable. Bus and train tickets must be used by the person for whose use they were bought and are not negotiable.

Net capital formation This is the total amount of capital assets which a country has created over a given period, less depreciation of capital assets for the same period.

Net National Product The Gross National Product (GNP) after the figures for depreciation have been subtracted from it.

Net profit   All the expenses associated with running a business (the overheads) must be deducted from gross profit to give the net profit figure.

Net turnover   The word 'turnover' refers to the total value of the sales of a business. If goods are returned to a trader they are 'sales returns'. 'Net turnover' is therefore turnover minus the figure for returns. This is often referred to briefly as 'sales less returns'.

Net worth   **Capital** is the accumulated wealth contributed to the firm by its proprietor; it is the net worth of the business to the owner.

Network analysis   See **Critical Path Analysis**

New issues market   *New issues* may represent the first issue of **shares** by a new company or the issue of additional stock by an established company.
Issuing Houses undertake the administration of new issues; they will buy the new issue from a company, re-selling to the investing public at a profit.
   Large issues are usually underwritten. Issuing Houses arrange with large institutional investors to accept responsibility for a part of a new issue. They will only be called upon to take up their undertaking if the issue is not fully subscribed by the public.

New Shares   Term used to indicate that new shares can be transferred on **renounceable documents.**

New time (Stock Exchange)   'New time' dealings may be done by special arrangements in the last two days of an account, and settled as if they had been done during the following account.

Nil paid   A new issue of shares, usually as a result of a **rights issue**, on which no payment to the company has yet been made.

Nine Elms   The site of the London Produce Market dealing in fruits, flowers and vegetables which has transferred from Covent Garden.

No par value (NPV)   See **par**

Nominal accounts   The **ledger** contains all the accounts—whether personal, real or nominal. Nominal accounts represent the expenses of a business; credit balances are profits, debit balances are losses.

Nominal capital   See **capital**

Nominal ledger   Also called the general ledger. The accounts book required for a proper record of the transactions of a business is called the **ledger**. In a large firm there may be several ledgers—the sales ledger contains the debtors' accounts, and the purchases (or bought) ledger contains the creditors' accounts. A third ledger—the general or nominal ledger—contains the real and nominal accounts relating to the assets and liabilities and the gains and expenses of the business.

Nominal price/value   The par value of a share given to it on its issuing day. This nominal value is retained throughout its life but its actual value varies with supply and demand, and the extent to which profits have been ploughed back since the share was issued. By law a company must have set a **par** value to its ordinary **shares**. In some countries shares have **no par value** (NPV).

Nominee name   Name in which a security is registered that does not indicate who the **beneficial owner** is.

Non-bank financial intermediaries   Financial institutions none of whose liabilities are means of payment.

Non-insurable risks   See **insurable/non-insurable risks**

Non-profitmaking organisations   With non-profitmaking units the ownership rests with the members—for instance, of a club or co-operative society. Profits are not made; any money 'made' is a surplus.

Non-shop retail outlets   Shops form an overwhelmingly large proportion of retail outlets, but some retailing is effected away from 'shop' premises. Examples are automatic vending machines, door-to-door salesmen (these sometimes represent manufacturers and eliminate both the wholesaler and the 'shop'), mail order, mobile shops and street markets.

Non-trading concerns   Under the Companies Act 1948 it is compulsory for a company registered under the Act as not trading for profit to lay an income and expenditure account before the company in general meeting.

   Some clubs, benevolent and similar institutions come into this category.

Normal profit   The concept of normal profit in economics describes a hypothetical figure considered to be the minimum level of return necessary to induce an entrepreneur to remain in an industry.

North Atlantic Treaty Organisation (NATO)   The treaty was signed in 1949 in Washington by the USA, Great Britain, Canada, France, Belgium, the Netherlands, Luxembourg, Norway, Denmark, Iceland, Italy and Portugal. By it the USA associated herself with the Western European countries in security arrangements for their common or mutual defence against possible aggression.

'Not negotiable'   A special crossing added to a cheque as an additional safeguard to protect the legal title of its true owner.

Note issue   The Issue Department of the **Bank of England** issues bank notes as required by the public, within the limits set by the gold reserves + a fiduciary issue which has no gold backing but is backed by government-held securities.

O

Objects clause The objects clause in the **Memorandum of Association** establishes what the purposes of the company are and what it may do to achieve its objectives.

Occupational Pensions Board Provided a company pensions scheme at least matches the benefits, an employer can opt out of the earnings-related part of the State scheme, but he cannot withdraw his employees from the basic part. Many thousands of firms with schemes approved by the Occupational Pensions Board have contracted out. Others use the company scheme to supplement the State provisions.

Occupier's Liability Act 1957 This states that occupiers of property have a duty to ensure that visitors will be safe when visiting the premises for a permitted purpose. Adequate warnings can free the occupier from liability, but visitors themselves have a duty to take care.

The law does not expect the occupier to safeguard a trespasser's interests.

Offer for sale Some **merchant banks** are 'Issuing Houses' and organise the sale of **shares** for public limited companies. The company will sell its new securities to an Issuing House, which then offers the shares by an 'offer for sale' to the public. As the public applies for the shares the Issuing House renounces its rights so that the purchasers become allottees of the company.

Copies of the 'offer for sale' must be lodged with the Registrar of Companies.

Office of Fair Trading   The Office of Fair Trading, set up by the Fair Trading Act 1973, is a government agency whose job is to keep watch on trading matters in the UK and protect both consumers and businessmen against unfair practices.

The Director of Fair Trading looks after consumers' and traders' interests in various ways. To do so he works very closely with local trading standards departments and advice agencies.

He publishes information to help people to get to know their rights and obligations. He encourages members of trade organisations to draw up and abide by codes of practice. These help to raise standards of service and set out special ways of dealing with complaints. The products and services which are covered so far include: buying by post, cars, double glazing, electrical goods, furniture, launderers and dry cleaners, funerals, package holidays, photography, shoes, the **Post Office**, and buying from doorstep sales-people and at parties.

He keeps a look out for traders who persistently commit offences or break their obligations to consumers; he can ask offenders to give assurances that they will mend their ways; and those who refuse to give an assurance, or break one that they have given, can be taken to court.

He checks on the fitness of traders who provide credit or hire goods to individuals, and issues licences. He publishes guidance for traders and is concerned with enforcing the safeguards which consumers have under the Consumer Credit Act. These include resolving disputes which people may have over the accuracy of information held on them by credit reference agencies.

He collects information about trading practices and if he thinks they are unfair he can suggest changes in the law or other remedies. Complaints reported locally are the main source of information.

Encouraging competition   Lack of competition in business may be against the public interest. The Director General has a duty to keep a watch on monopolies, mergers and other trade practices which may be restrictive or anti-competitive. He provides guidance for traders.

Monopolies, mergers, and *anti-competitive practices* can be referred to the Monopolies and Mergers Commission.

Office of Telecommunications (OFTEL)

Restrictive trade practices may be referred to the Restrictive Practices Court.

The Office of Fair Trading cannot take up people's complaints, but a local consumer adviser at a Citizens Advice Bureau, Trading Standards/Consumer Protection Department or Consumer Advice Centre is best able to help with these problems.

Firms or individuals can help the OFT in its work involving monopolies, restrictive trade practices, and anti-competitive practices by sending any details of such practices direct to the OFT.

Office of Telecommunications (OFTEL) Set up by the government after British Telecom had 'gone public', to regulate telecommunications. (It was consulted for the first time in November 1984 to sort out a dispute between British Telecom and Mercury, its rival business network.)

Offices, Shops and Railway Premises Act 1963 See **employment legislation**

Official List Short for the *Stock Exchange Daily Official List*

Official Receiver The collection and distribution of a bankrupt's property is now carried out by a DTI official called the 'Official Receiver in Bankruptcy'.

Oil and oilseeds market This market deals on the **Baltic Exchange** in primary commodities which yield vegetable oil, and also in the 'cake' which is left over after the extraction of oil which is used to feed cattle and poultry. Further commodities dealt in are linseed, castor seed, soya beans, groundnuts and cotton seed.

Oil tankers Cargo ships specially built to carry oil and oil products. These large bulk carriers with weights between 50,000 and 500,000 tons are too large for many ports to handle; 'outports' with refining facilities—such as that at Milford Haven—have been specially designed to accommodate such carriers.

The largest are very large crude carriers (vlccs) which operate

198

from the oil-producing countries to Europe, North America and Japan.

Freight rates per ton for return journeys are based on the 'Worldscale' system which is operated in US dollars.

Oligopoly   A situation in which there are few sellers, and a small number of competitive firms control the market; it approaches monopoly, and is a major incentive to form 'cartels'—firms forming a 'ring' to preserve their own positions by mutually agreed output, price and marketing arrangements.

In the UK the Monopolies Commission seeks to control such situations.

Ombudsman   In 1967 the **House of Commons** appointed a 'Parliamentary Commissioner for Administration'—the Ombudsman—who investigates complaints of maladministration by government departments, brought to his notice by MPs on behalf of their constituents. (Maladministration means delay, neglect, incompetence or prejudice.)

Complaints concerning the running of nationalised industries do not come within the ambit of the Commissioner's work, nor do complaints against individual policemen, though the Ombudsman may deal with complaints against a police authority.

The method of complaint is to fill in a *Form of Complaint* obtainable from Consumer Advice Centres. This is then presented to the authority concerned.

In addition to the Parliamentary Commissioner the Local Government Act 1974 established a Commission for Local Administration in England and another for Wales, to investigate complaints about injustices suffered as a result of maladministration in local government.

See also **banks' Ombudsman** and **Insurance Ombudsman.**

Open accounts   See **export finance** (short- and medium-term)

Open cheque   An uncrossed cheque which can be cashed over the counter of the bank on which it is drawn.

Open cover agreement   See **cargo insurance**

Open market operations   One of the **Bank of England's** measures for controlling the money supply is by its operations on the open market.

Treasury Bills are sold to the **discount houses** to remove a surplus of money on the market and bought back (thus repaying the loan and redeeming the Bill) to relieve a shortage, and prevent the discount houses having to seek help from the **Bank of England** ('the **lender of last resort**').

The Bank of England also borrows money by the issue of gilt-edged securities on the **Stock Exchange**. These operations help to implement the government's monetary policy; by selling such stock the government siphons money out of the system; to put money back it can buy back stock in the same market.

Open outcry   In some of the London **Commodity Markets** where 'ring trading' takes place, the bids and offers are shouted across the ring (open outcry) so that all are aware of the prices prevailing.

Open tech programme   See *Manpower Services Commission*

Opening price (Stock Exchange)   The price at 9.30 a.m. for commercial securities or 10.00 a.m. for Gilts.

Operating statement   An accounting report produced for the purpose of control or communication. No hard and fast rules regulate their preparation since each operating statement should be designed to serve the needs of the recipient. Where necessary each type of expense—wages, salaries, materials, rates, etc.—can be shown and the difference between budgeted and actual cost can be identified to stimulate remedial action.

Operating targets   In order to achieve its intermediate targets a central bank usually needs to influence key conditions in financial markets, such as money market interest rates or the banks' central bank balances. These conditions are known as operating targets.

Operational Research (OR)   Describes a series of techniques—of which CPA (**Critical Path Analysis**) is one—which assist managers in planning and decision-making.

Opportunity cost   The term 'opportunity cost' or 'alternative cost' expresses the cost of a commodity, not in money, but in the terms of the alternative forgone.

In making business decisions it is necessary to weigh up the opportunity costs of the alternative uses of resources.

Optimum firm   A firm operating at a scale which gives it the lowest unit cost possible.

Optimum population   The optimum population of a country will combine exactly with the available natural resources and the average stock of capital to give the highest possible output of goods and services per head of population.

Options dealing   An option is an agreement to buy or sell a security at a specified price on a specified date.

A *call option* is an option to buy **shares** at a future date at an agreed price, whatever happens to the market.

A *put option* gives the right to sell at a stated price at an agreed time.

A *double option* gives the right to buy or sell.

With a *traded option* the buyer and seller each has a contract with the LOCH (**London Option Clearing House**) instead of with each other, and one can trade his rights in the market without the consent of the other.

Order cheque   A cheque which can be negotiated by endorsement to a third party.

Ordinary shares   See *Shares*

Organisation and Method (O & M)   The application of time and motion assessment to office procedures by systematic analysis of office methods. Simplification and improvement can be achieved in most clerical practices by the use of O & M.

Organisation chart

Organisation chart This is an attempt to portray the responsibilities (areas of activity) and relationships in an organisation or part of an organisation, such as an office. Large charts can give very little detail; more information can be obtained if a smaller area is analysed.

Organisation for European Co-operation and Development (OECD) This now serves to bring Europeans, Americans and Canadians together. The headquarters is in Paris. Its aims are:
to achieve the highest sustainable economic growth and employment and a rising standard of living in member countries, while maintaining financial stability, and thus to contribute to the development of the world economy
to contribute to sound economic expansion in member as well as non-member countries;
to contribute to the expansion of world trade on a multi-national, non-discriminatory basis in accordance with international obligations.
   The Council produces statistical and economic publications and co-operates with other international bodies.

Organisation of Petroleum Exporting Countries (OPEC) Members of this organisation co-operate to fix oil prices in a cartel, which seriously hampers a free market in the commodity concerned.

Original entry, books of Also called books of first entry. Because of the rule in bookkeeping that transactions must be passed through the subsidiary books before being entered in the ledger, the subsidiary books are known collectively as the books of original, or first, entry. The four subsidiary books are the purchases daybook, the sales daybook, sales returns and purchases returns book. The cash book is one of the books of first entry, but is not a subsidiary book.

Output and costs Assuming that everything else remains constant as production increases, then unit costs will fall, but the

202

law of diminishing returns states that as more and more resources are allocated to a fixed asset, then eventually output will diminish.

Outward missions   Members of a **British Overseas Trade Board** supported outward mission qualify for travel grants. These missions enable the prospects for the sale of goods and services to be explored at first hand.

Most missions are run by **Chambers of Commerce** or **trade associations.**

Over capitalisation   When a firm has bought too many fixed assets and left itself short of working capital, this is over-capitalisation.

Overdrafts   See **bank credit**

Overfunding   Sales of public sector debt to non-banks limit the effect of public sector borrowing on the growth of the money stock. And when sales of debt exceed the public sector borrowing requirement they offset part of increase in the money stock generated by other factors. This is known as overfunding.

Overhead expenses (overheads)   The general expenses of running a business, including rent and rates, heating, lighting, etc.

Overseas agents   One method of selling on overseas markets is by the employment of overseas agents who are 'home nationals' and able to understand the complexities of trade in their own countries. The Overseas Status Report Service of the **BOTB** will help to assess the suitability of suggested agents.

Overseas Projects Fund   The Projects and Export Policy (PEP) Division of the BOTB brings together all the various government support measures for large international projects. The PEP is divided into sectors according to the type of industry.

Overseas sales base   Goods can be sold abroad by setting up an overseas base. This is a typical activity of many international companies who have resources not available to the small exporter. The **BOTB** offers help and advice.

Overseas Seminars   Overseas Seminars are supported by generous help with costs and organisation. The BOTB is interested in events which will enable British companies to bring their products or services to the attention of a specific audience.

Overseas Status Report Service   Appointing an agent or distributor abroad can be profitable—or perilous. The **BOTB** will provide impartial reports on the trading capability and commercial standing of possible agents. These will be drawn up by the Commercial Department of the relevant British Embassy or Diplomatic Post and will complement a financial report from the enquirer's bank or commercial enquiry agency.

Overseas trade   See **import trade** and **export trade, balance of trade, balance of payments**

Over-The-Counter (OTC) Market   (in securities) The development of a British OTC Market has had significant advantages for companies and investors alike; companies have access to new sources of capital without losing independence, and investors are able to trade in smaller companies' securities where faster than average rates of growth might be obtained.

The OTC Market in Britain has been pioneered on the lines of that in the United States, but adapted for local market conditions; since 1972 it has grown substantially. The securities of a wide range of companies are now traded and held by a large number of financial institutions and several thousand individuals. Price information on all OTC-traded securities, together with their dividend yields and price/earnings multiples, is published daily in the *Financial Times* and is available on Prestel.

Overtrading   If a firm leaves itself short of working capital it is said to be overtrading.

Own account transport Owners of a business can effect deliveries by road by the use of their own fleet of vehicles (own account transport). This gives complete control over drivers and operations, vans can be used for advertising, and vehicles can be available for other uses.

Disadvantages lie in the fact that return loads are difficult to organise and garaging and maintenance can prove to be expensive.

Alternative methods are by the use of leasing (a contract hire fleet) or making use of the services of a public haulier.

Ownership of organisations The type of business unit which will describe a particular organisation can be determined by identifying who provided the **capital** (the owner) and who receives the profits.

The *sole trader* owns his own business.

Partnerships are owned jointly by the partners.

Both *private and public limited companies and holding companies* are owned by the shareholders.

Co-operative societies, friendly societies and clubs are owned by all the members.

All organisations in the public sector are publicly or 'socially' owned.

Owner's Risk (OR) Goods may be sent 'Owner's Risk' (OR) in which case the carrier is only responsible for damage caused by the deliberate neglect of his employees or their dishonesty. Rates are lower than those for 'Company's Risk' (CR).

P

Packaging It is inevitable that costs must be incurred in the packaging of goods,—it is therefore worthwhile considering how a novel or enterprising form of packaging may be able to contribute to the total marketing operation.

The pre-packaging of goods has been accompanied by the branding of goods, so that they are readily identifiable.

The fact that so many commodities are pre-packed has meant an increase in **compound trading**.

Pallets A platform or tray for lifting and stacking goods, used with a fork-lift truck, and having a double base into which the fork can be thrust.

Pallet loads can be deposited in a container and provide very economical lifting operations.

Par The *nominal value* of a security (always taken as £100 in fixed interest stocks). By British and Irish Company Law, a company must set a par value on its ordinary **shares**. In some countries shares can have no par value (NPV).

pari passu (Latin) Equal in every respect: used to describe new issues of **shares** in relation to shares already in issue.

Parliament The legislative function of the constitution is performed by the Queen in Parliament.

Parliament, which makes laws, consists of three components: the Queen, the Lords and the Commons. Acts of Parliaments have to be approved by all three. The Government translates its policy

206

into Bills which having been approved by Parliament (the Government usually has a majority) become Acts of Parliaments or Statutes.

Private members are also allowed time to introduce their own Public Bills.

Participating preference shares   See **shares**

Partners   *General partners* who actually run the business cannot be limited partners, and are liable for the partnership's debts to the full extent of their share in the partnership, and their private fortunes.

Limited partners   By the Limited Partnership Act 1907 the liability of a partner for the debts of the firm may be limited to the amount of his fixed stake in the business, but in exchange for this limited liability he is required to remain a dormant partner and to take no part in the management of the business.

Partnership   Partnerships are suitable for commercial and professional services such as doctors, solicitors, decorators, etc. It is not lawful to have more than twenty partners in a partnership or ten in the case of a banking business.

The Partnership Agreement, often called the Articles of Partnership is a formal agreement, mainly regulated by the Partnership Act of 1890. All the terms of partnership, other than those contained in the Act, must be stated in the agreement.

All matters are settled by a simple majority; each partner is allowed 'drawings' which are really profits taken in advance.

The Articles of Partnership must be maintained; if the nature of the business is to change all partners must agree to it. Once a firm is liable under the contracts entered into by a partner, all the partners are jointly liable.

Books of account must be kept at the principal place of business and each partner has access and the right to copy them.

The advantages of partnerships are that they are simple to establish, make more capital and better management available, and personal contact with clients or customers makes for a keener interest in the business.

Among the disadvantages are the risks of dissolution, and liability in the event of a failure in the business. There is a certain limitation of size, and the actions of one partner being binding on all partners can cause problems.

Part-paid stock   In recent years there have been a number of important innovations designed to improve the borrowing options open to the government. For example, since 1977 a number of stocks have been issued in part-paid form. With these stocks the investor pays only part of the subscription money on application, the remainder being payable in a series of instalments designed to coincide with the expected needs of the government for finance.

Passenger liners   Nearly all cargo liners take cargo to and from major ports and have a few cabins for passengers; most passenger liners are now cruise liners used for holidays at sea.

Patents   More correctly letters patent—documents in which the Crown vests a subject with special rights and confers on him the sole right to make, use and vend an invention for a limited period of time.

Such a grant creates a monopoly in favour of the patentee.

Patent rights can be sold, or another party can be granted a licence allowing him to use the invention.

Applications for patents are processed by the Patent Office in London (DTI).

Pay As You Earn (PAYE)   This is the system used in Britain to collect **income tax** from the employee as he earns his money. The amount due is collected from employees' earnings each pay-day and sent by employers to the Tax Office.

Pay-back method   The pay-back period is the time taken for an investment to 'pay for itself'. The investment programme should be the one which repays the initial cost in the shortest time.

Payments   See **methods of payment**

Pedlar   A pedlar travels and trades on foot. A certificate must be obtained before a person can trade as a pedlar; this is normally issued by the Chief of Police of the area for which it is required.

Pension funds   The large amounts of money collected for occupational pension schemes are invested in stocks and **shares** to produce the regular payments promised upon retirement. As institutional investors the pension funds are a very powerful force in the stock markets.

   These pension funds are in no way connected with the State pension, which is financed out of employers' and employees' National Insurance contributions.

Perfect competition/perfect market   In a perfect market there are many buyers and sellers, none of whom is such a large dealer that he can influence the price. The price which is charged in a perfect market is determined by the interaction between consumers and the most efficient suppliers. The market mechanism sets the price and determines how much is supplied. For perfect competition to exist products should be homogenous (ie identical) and there must be no barriers or restrictions on entry into the market by any firm as a result of governmental or any other type of intervention.

Perpetual inventory   A stock control procedure that involves checking small sections of stock at regular intervals throughout the year. The book figures are checked against actual stock count and any discrepancies reported for immediate investigation. Although it may take more time overall than a one-off stock take, it avoids the upheaval associated with the latter, and it is also claimed to discourage pilfering and fraudulent stock entries since staff may not know in advance which stock items are being checked. It is also more effective in highlighting slow moving stock items and problems over damage or deterioration.

   See **Stocktaking.**

Personal accident policies   See **accident insurance**

Personal accounts   Personal accounts are the accounts of a firm's dealings with other persons or firms. A debit balance on a personal account is an asset and represents the right to receive corresponding value (usually cash) in the future. A credit balance is a liability and represents the obligation to refund corresponding value in the future.

Personal credit agreements   Consumer credit arrangements confer great advantages on the retailer, the financier and the manufacturer, and should do so also on the consumer, but the fact that consumers need protection in this field led to the **Consumer Credit Act 1974.**

Personal credit agreement can be either a **credit-sale agreement**, conditional-sale agreement, or **hire-purchase** agreement.

Personal loans   These bank loans are normally made to bank customers to enable them to purchase a particular item, such as a car. Repayments are normally made monthly.

Personal services   Part of tertiary production, these are services rendered by producers who are not concerned directly or indirectly with material production, but whose services are necessary in so far as they 'service' the work force and ensure its efficiency. Examples of such services are those provided by doctors, teachers, the police, army and navy, and those who provide entertainment. The services offered by **commerce** also form part of tertiary production.

Personnel Department   The Chief Personnel Officer is responsible for recruiting staff and interviewing applicants. He is responsible also for the work records of all members of the work force and for holiday arrangements.

In a large firm a Training Officer will be a responsible member of the Personnel Department. He will provide induction courses for new members of staff, and technical and supervisory training in all departments and at all levels.

All employees should be regularly assessed and promotions and transfers between departments arranged where necessary.

The Personnel Officer will advise on all aspects of salary structures within the firm, and will also act as a Labour Relations Officer in negotiations with union officials.

The welfare of the workforce is also the responsibility of the Personnel Officer, as is the implementation of all government Acts regarding the health and safety of staff.

Persuasive advertising This uses persuasive advertising techniques which may be harmful if, as a result of them, consumers buy anything dangerous or anti-social.

Physical distribution   When studying production and the vast quantities of manufactured goods produced by it, the chain of distribution is seen to be of vital importance; sometimes called the **chain of commerce** or the chain of production it is the route taken by goods from their place of manufacture to the place where they are finally purchased by the consumer. Without it there would be little consumption and no point in producing anything that could not be 'consumed' at the point of manufacture. The distribution of the raw materials and components from which manufactured goods are made is not covered by the term 'physical distribution'; this is concerned solely with goods between their manufacture and the point at which they are sold to the consumer. The whole activity is part of tertiary production and is a commercial service. Commerce is that part of production which ensures that goods and services reach the final consumer at the right place, in the right condition, at the right time, in the right quantity and at the right price. Below is shown the fundamental contribution which physical distribution makes in achieving this.

At the right place—Wherever the goods are to be sold they have to be taken to the place of sale. This involves transport, finance, insurance and sometimes warehousing—all commercial services.

In the right condition—Consider the use of specially constructed vehicles: refrigerated vans; vans for carrying large panes of plate glass; road and rail tankers of many types.

At the right time—'Movement through time' belongs particularly to the distributive trades. Consider the uses of warehousing in retaining ice-cream in cold storage which enables the trade to cope with a high demand during a heat-wave; the warehousing of seasonal goods which are manufactured throughout the year but which the average retailer has no room to stock far in advance of requirements; the daily and unfailing delivery of food stocks which, though primary products, have been processed in some way.

In the right quantity—The cost of distribution is increasingly heavy and the distributive trades endeavour constantly to provide services at the most reasonable rates. Containerisation has made a substantial contribution in this area, particularly in overseas trade, and in 'door-to-door' journeys generally, where more than one type of transport is involved.

The costs of distribution always add to the *price* of an article; the greater the efficiency of the means of transport, the greater the advantage to the customer.

The manufacturer or wholesaler who offers his own delivery service has a choice which—from the point of view of both actual and cost efficiency—can be difficult. He may own and maintain his fleet (see **own account operations**); he may contract out the whole operation to an independent organisation (see **contract hire fleet**); he may lease the vehicles (see **leasing**) or, again, may use the services of a common carrier, the latter having the disadvantage that the vehicles can have no distinctive and easily recognisable livery—important from the point of view of advertising.

Pipelines Modern oil and natural gas trunk pipelines have three basic functions:
to transport crude oil from oilfields to ocean terminals, and from ocean terminals to refineries, or where no sea voyage is necessary from oilfields direct to the refinery;
to carry refined products from refinery to tanker terminals or to large consumers or to local distribution depots;
to transport natural gas from the fields to local distribution centres or direct to large consumers.

Placings A system of issing **shares** by asking institutional investors to buy up the extra issue. It is cheaper than the usual way of issuing shares and is often helpful to the institutional investors who are glad to purchase shares in reliable businesses. See also **Issuing Houses Association**

Planning   All business activities must be planned to avoid wasting resources, and this is true of every type of organisation. The greater the complexity of an organisation the more it will benefit from expert planning in every department—planning based initially on forecasts of how customers and clients will act.

Planning permission   Under the Town and Country Planning Act 1971, planning permission must be sought for all proposed developments, including changes of use of land or premises, and the construction or alteration of buildings, roads, etc. There is a right of appeal to the Secretary of State against local planning decisions, and in important cases public enquiries are held.

Plantation House   The Federation of Commodity Associations has its Headquarters at Plantation House in Mincing Lane in the City of London. It also has an EEC office in Brussels.

'Ploughing back'   Using the profits to buy new equipment, premises, or any services which will enable the firm to expand.

Point of order   An interruption of a meeting by a member drawing the chairman's attention to some irregularity in the proceedings.

Policy (Insurance)   See **insurance policy**

Policy   The policy decisions of any organisation affect all aspects of that organisation. They provide a guide to the further decision-making which will implement the policies.

Policyholder's Protection Act, 1975   In the event of an insurance company going into liquidation, customers are protected by the Policyholder's Protection Act, 1975, which provides that up to 90% of the company's liabilities will be met out of a levy on other companies, and 100% if the insurance is compulsory.

Policyholders' interests are also under the constant surveillance of the Investment Protection Committee of the British Insurance Association.

Pollution   Many waste products are harmful and it costs money to make them safe. Industrial development often produces pollution and much of the waste is disposed of without any attempt being made to render it harmless. Pollution is at its most dangerous when it is hardest to detect, and often cannot be detected without scientific apparatus.

The United Nations Environment Programme (UNEP) has been set up to monitor the environment globally, and the EEC is conducting massive investigations into the presence of heavy metals and chemicals in water and root crops, and into sewage pollution of beaches and estuaries.

In the UK the Deposits of Poisonous Wastes Act makes the dumping of poisonous materials illegal. The United Nations Food and Agriculture Organisation monitors the impact of pesticides on food products.

Pooling of risks   An insurance pool is the money contributed (in the form of premiums) by all the policyholders; it is kept in a central fund from which those contributors who suffer loss can be indemnified. In the case of injury to life or limb, of course, indemnity cannot be effected, and the sufferer—or his dependants—receive cash benefits instead.

An insurance pool must fulfil three obligations:
the money collected from premiums must be adequate enough to indemnify those who suffer loss,
the pool should never be allowed to shrink, but should, by careful investment, increase in size,
claims should be met promptly and in full.

Population   Population changes may involve an increasing population or a decreasing population, or changes in the average age of the population. Any change has economic implications, especially when the ratio between working and non-working people is considered. At the present time children stay at school longer than they used to and people are living longer; both groups have to be sustained by the working population whose numbers are declining.

Statistics obtained in the government census which is taken every ten years are used to provide accurate information on the economic and social conditions of the population, and also as a basis for the government's social and economic policies.

Portfolio Collection of investments owned either by an individual or an institution.

Port of London Authority (PLA) An autonomous corporation set up under the Port of London Act 1908 to control the tidal reaches, docks and shipping of the Thames from the Nore to Teddington. Such corporations have legal status and personality conferred on them by Act of Parliament.

In 1968 some of the original arrangements were changed by a new Port of London Authority Act, which extended the Authority's powers.

Port rates schedule Port rates are paid by a shipper to the relevant Port Authority for handling cargo.

Ports Ports are terminals for ships, providing access for passengers and cargo. Most ports are also road and rail terminals, enabling easy transhipment, particularly of containerised cargoes.

The facilities a port provides depend largely on the type of shipping it caters for. Milford Haven (an 'outport' serving oil tankers) is vastly different from the container port at Tilbury.

There are certain requirements for a port to be successful;
it must be sheltered—either by artificial building or by the endowment of nature,
it should have the right depth of water for the type of shipping served—if necessary maintained by dredging,
it should supply everything that ships need while on a voyage—food, oil, water, electricity,
it should have labour and machinery for loading and unloading, and commercial services to deal with all the documentation

Post Office

involved with international trade,
it should provide good communications with other forms of transport—road, rail, air, etc.

A freeport is an enclosed zone within or adjacent to a seaport or airport inside which goods are treated for customs purposes as being outside the customs territory of the country.

In February 1984 freeports were designated at Belfast International Airport, Birmingham International Airport, Port of Cardiff, Port of Liverpool, Prestwick International Airport, Port of Southampton.

Post Office (Government Department) The Post Office now controls:
all inland postal services in Great Britain (letters and cards, newspapers, parcels, express services, registration and recorded delivery services),
all overseas post (air and surface mail—letters and postcards, small packets and parcels; registration, insurance and compensation),
National Girobank services,
postal orders
inland telegraph and international payments,
National Savings Bank,
government stock and securities on the National Savings Stock Register,
Savings Certificates,
premium savings bonds,
payment of pensions and allowances,

the Yearly Plan **National Savings** scheme which has replaced the National **SAYE** scheme.

Post Office Guide This is published annually by HMSO, containing complete information on all postal regulations for inland and overseas post, the services of Girobank, Post Office monetary and investment services, licences, pensions and allowances.

216

Preference shares   See **shares**

Preferential form   The **Stock Exchange** allows companies offering shares to the public to set aside up to 10% of the issue for applications from employees, or, where a parent company is floating off a subsidiary, shareholders of the parent company. Special differently coloured application forms, usually pink, (hence the nickname 'pink forms') are used for this.

Premium   The sum of money payable by the policyholder to the insurance company or **underwriters** for the protection being given. It varies according to the nature of the risk and the value of the property insured; the greater the risk and value the higher the premium.
   Premiums must be paid when due or the policy will lapse.

Premium (Stock Exchange)   Premium is the amount by which a **security** is traded above its original price. If the market price is lower, the difference is a *discount*.

Premium Bonds   See **National Savings**

Prepayments   When the payment period for business expenses such as insurance, rent and rates does not coincide with the accounting period an adjustment must be made to the books to show any amounts paid in advance as an asset to the firm. The purpose of these adjustments is to produce an accurate set of final accounts for the period under review.

Prestel   British Telecom's computer-based information service that links a specially adapted TV set to a centralised computer using the public telephone network. Subscribers to the service pay for viewing particular 'pages' of information (though much information is provided free of charge) in addition to the normal cost of the telephone call connecting them to the computer. A special key pad enables the viewer to 'page' through and select the information he needs, or to enter information interactively if he wishes to place an order or make a booking via Prestel.

Many business groups operate 'closed user groups' within the Prestel service to allow privileged access to confidential or sensitive information to selected users. Other information providers use Prestel as a 'gateway' to their own company computer databases. The Royal Bank of Scotland has recently launched its Home Banking Service to its Prestel customers, enabling them to view their personal accounts and to authorise payments or transfers of funds.

Price/earnings (p/e) ratio   The current share price divided by the last published earnings (expressed as pence per share). It is used as a measure of whether a share should be considered expensive.

Price elasticity   See **elasticity**

Price Index (of Retail Prices)   See **Retail Price Index**

Price mechanism   The mechanism by which supply and demand are balanced is referred to as the 'price mechanism' or 'pricing'. If supply increases while demand remains constant, prices will fall; if demand increases while supply remains constant, prices will rise. These movements restore the balance between supply and demand. Organisations must respond to movements in demand by a complete marketing strategy.

Price of labour   Labour is one of the factors of production, the others being capital and land. From the employer's point of view the cheaper the price at which labour can be 'bought', the better it is from the viewpoint of business costs. It enables the price of his product to be kept down on the market, and thus keeps the product competitive.

Price/pricing   Price is a way of expressing how much a good or service is worth, as measured by the quantity of goods and services that one unit of the good or service can be exchanged for.

The relationship between the prices of different goods is determined by the relative demand for the various goods, and by the amount of each good available and the ease with which the supply can be altered. For any one good the price will tend to be the level where supply equals demand; normally an increase in price will cause demand to fall, and conversely a fall in price will cause demand to rise—ie, market forces prevail. If a change in price leads to a large change in demand then the demand is described as elastic; a small change in demand is said to be inelastic.

If perfect competition exists the price for identical articles will be the same in all markets. The price of an article in such a situation will tend to equal the marginal cost of production.

Prices and consumer protection   See **Restrictive practices**

Prices and incomes policy   The aim of such a policy is to curb inflation and to avoid unemployment.

Primage   In addition to the declared freight charges shipping companies sometimes impose a supplementary charge known as 'primage', originally designed to cover the cost of handling and stowing the cargo.

Primary production   The first stage of production involves the production of goods made available by nature in mines, oilfields, and quarries (the extractive industries), and goods produced in the forestry, farming and fishing industries.

Many of these materials proceed to secondary production where they are manufactured into producer or consumer goods.

Primary research   Also known as field research; this is the process of finding out new facts directly from source. It is normally undertaken by selecting a representative sample of a population and asking carefully chosen questions. Their answers are then analysed in an effort to find a solution to the research problem.

Prime costs   Those which are essentially incurred in the purchase or preparation of an article for sale.

Principles of insurance   See **insurance**

Prior charges   Trustees are appointed to look after the interests of **debenture** holders. If the debenture holders do not receive their interest on time, the trustees can take over some or all of the company's assets and sell them off to repay the loan.

Private bills   Private Parliamentary Bills can be defined in broad terms as being for the benefit of a person or body, for example, local authorities and public utilities.
   Private members' Bills are, in fact, **public bills**.

Private corporations   All private and public limited companies are corporations in the private sector.

Private enterprise   Private enterprise is one of the three main groups of business units. In it are included **sole traders**, partnerships, **private and public limited companies**, holding companies and **multinational corporations**.
   The second group—non-profitmaking organisations—are also in the 'private' sector in so far as they are not publicly owned.
   The third group covers all publicly owned organisations.

Private investors   Private investors are individuals who use their money for investment, usually on the Stock Exchange, as opposed to institutional investors such as banks, building societies, etc, who collect the savings of many people and invest them for the good of the savings public.

Private law   See **civil law**

Private ledger   In sole trading and partnerships the private ledger may be used to contain the capital account, drawings account and the trading and profit and loss accounts and balance sheets for each period.

It is also kept for the final accounts of limited companies.

Private limited company   See **limited company**

Private sector   The private sector is that part of the British economy which covers, in general, the production of goods and commercial and personal services by privately-owned organisations. See **private enterprise.**

Private treaty   On the **Stock Exchange**, the **Baltic**, **Foreign** and Corn Exchanges, and the Insurance Markets, dealing is by 'private treaty' on a one-to-one basis, rather than by auctions, **ring trading** or **challenging**.

Privatisation   Transfer of ownership from the public to the private sector. In 1984 British Telecom was privatised by a public issue of **shares** on the **Stock Exchange**.

Probate price   The price used in valuing shares for taxation purposes. It is calculated on the *quarter up* principle.

Process costing   A method of cost accounting generally employed when a standard product is being made which passes through a number of distinct sequential processes towards completion, as in the manufacture of paper, flour, chemicals or cement. The object is to trace and record costs for each distinct stage, to obtain the average cost per unit for each accounting period.

Process inwards/outwards relief   Procedures applicable to 'inward' and 'outward' processing have been simplified by an EEC directive.

Produce exchanges

'Inward processing' implies that materials or goods which enter the Community are worked upon and then re-exported. Such goods are not subject to quota restrictions or CCT Duties (Common Customs Tariff) but it must be ensured that re-export does take place.

'Outward processing' means the goods or materials leave the Community, are worked upon and then re-imported. Both procedures need constant vigilance to ensure that no infringements of the regulations occur.

Produce exchanges   Wholesale produce markets exist in most large towns and cities. The famous London markets are at—
Billingsgate—fish (now in the West India Dock Road)
Nine Elms—flowers, fruit and vegetables (this used to be at Covent Garden)
Smithfield—meat
Spitalfields—like Nine Elms, but in the East End of London

Producer   A member of the working population who exchanges his skills or knowledge for a wage, salary, or earnings.

Producer goods   Capital goods; plant, buildings and machinery, raw materials and partly finished goods which are all necessary for the production of consumer goods.

Product   A thing produced either by nature or a natural process, or that which is produced by any action, operation or work.

Product data store (BOTB)   This is the central 'bank' of product and industry based information about markets worldwide. Material stored is classified under 3000 headings.

Product differentiation   The distinctive packaging of branded goods which enables consumers to differentiate between similar products.

Product life cycle   A marketing term to describe the life expectancy of individual branded products which has direct

222

relevance to marketing strategy. Products of all types have limited lives during which they can earn profits. This life expectancy will vary according to the nature of the product and market conditions. Fashion clothing and pop records are subject to fast changing market demands and the pattern of the life cycle will be significantly different than, for example, household furniture.

The product life cycle for all items, however, shows a typical five phase sequence—introduction, growth, maturity, saturation and decline. It is important to the marketing strategy of a firm to know at which stage in the life cycle its existing products lie, so that subsequent phases can be managed effectively, or so that new products can be introduced appropriately for the business to remain vigorous.

Production Production is achieved by combining land, labour and capital in the creation of utilities and is the economic activity which serves to satisfy human needs by creating material goods or by providing a service. No rational owner of economic resources will use them to produce a service or commodity for which there is no demand. Production includes the activities of all those occupations which are engaged, directly or indirectly, in adding utility to man's natural resources.

There are three classes of production:

The *primary stage* of production involves the production of goods made available by nature in mines, oilfields and quarries (the extractive industries), and goods produced in the forestry, farming and fishing industries.

Secondary production uses those things produced at the primary stage to manufacture more sophisticated products.

The service industries, both personal and commercial, form *tertiary production*.

Other classifications are:

Direct production — the satisfying of a person's wants without help from any other person.

Indirect production/ The manufacture of goods on a huge scale by
Mass production automation. Standardisation, simplification
and specialisation are essential to its success.

Production costs   See **costs** (of production)

Production management/production planning   Because all manufacturing organisations, large and small, depend on the sale of what they are producing to stay in business, the managers and engineers who plan the actual production lines must be allowed a large say in the deployment of the organisation's resources in order to meet the targets set.

Production management has overall responsibility and control over all aspects of physical production, including quality control.

Production unit   The plant where production takes place. Size is dictated chiefly by the technological factors involved in production.

Productivity   The production or increase in wealth or value brought about by the full utilisation of the capacity of the work force.

Professional and executive register   See **Manpower Services Commission** (Employment Service)

Profit   There are two rewards for the use of capital—interest and profit. Profit is that part of production paid to the investor for bearing the risks of losing his capital. Generally speaking, profit is an increase in the value of assets.

In economics, profit-seeking has played an important part in economic progress, particularly in free enterprise systems. Profit can only be earned where a firm produces goods which consumers both want to buy and are willing to pay for. The possibility that losses may be made is a spur to efficient low-cost production.

Abuses of the profit system can be controlled by legislation, or taxation can be used to redistribute incomes.

In accounting, the profit shown in the Profit and Loss Accounts includes elements which are, in fact, wages, rent and interest. This is especially true of the accounts of sole-ownership businesses.

Profit and loss account   This is a summary of the resources a firm has acquired and how they have been allocated during the financial period.

Examples of such resources are stocks of raw materials, wages and salaries, directors' fees, lighting and heating, rent and rates, interest on loans, hire of plant or leasing.

Profit and loss does not show the rate of flow of revenue income; delays are not apparent and do not indicate any period where cash flow problems may have been experienced.

Depreciation is a legitimate expense on the profit and loss account.

If a firm makes sufficient profit after tax then some money can be 'ploughed back' into the organisation through a reserve fund.

Every profit and loss account must give a true and fair view of the profit or loss of the company for the financial year.

Pro-forma invoice   An invoice sent to a customer who will pay cash for goods rather than being allowed credit. Payment is made on or before receipt of the goods. It is sometimes used when trading with customers who have temporarily exceeded their credit limit.

Progressing/progress chasing   The process of expediting orders to eliminate bottlenecks or production stoppages. It may involve telephoning suppliers who are behind schedule with deliveries, reorganising component production in the event of a machine breakdown, or simply chivvying the primary shops for faster production.

Projects and Export Policy Division   The PEP Division of the **BOTB** deals with large international projects. The PEP is divided into industrial sectors and offers experience in co-ordinating every aspect of government assistance.

Promissory note   Unconditional promise in writing, signed by the promiser, to pay on demand, or on a fixed or ascertainable future date, a definite sum of money to, or to the order of, a named person. It is a **negotiable instrument**.

Promoters

Promoters (of limited companies) Anyone who pleases may register a company with the Registrar of Companies, and so 'promote' it. Anyone who undertakes to form a company with a definite object in mind and who takes the necessary steps to accomplish that object is a promoter.

Property The exclusive right of possessing, enjoying and disposing of a thing, or, by extension, the subjects of such exclusive rights (the things themselves).

The non-physical properties of companies which can be bought and sold, are such things as goodwill, trademarks, patents and copyrights.

Property insurance See **accident insurance**

Proposal form See **insurance**

Prospectus (of limited company) A prospectus is an advertisement giving details of a company and inviting the public to buy shares in that company. A copy of the prospectus must be lodged with the Registrar of Companies before the public are invited to subscribe, and must always be available for inspection at the company's registry.

Protectionist policies Many devices may be used to protect a country's home trade and industries. These include:
embargoes which prohibit the import of particular goods;
quotas which limit the amounts of particular goods;
tariffs which impose a duty (customs duty) on certain goods entering a country.

Provincial stock exchanges There are provincial stock exchanges in Birmingham, Bristol, Liverpool, Manchester, Glasgow, Belfast and Dublin.

Proximate cause See **insurance**

Proxy   A person empowered by a **shareholder** to vote on his behalf at company meetings.

Proxy card   The form supplied by the company by which the **shareholder** apoints his *proxy*, the person who is to vote on his behalf.

Prudential controls   Controls designed to ensure the stability and health of the banking system. These include measures to ensure that banks have sufficient shareholders' funds (to protect depositors against losses) and sufficient liquid **assets** (to meet deposit withdrawals and other commitments).

Public Accounts Committee   This committee is empowered to scrutinise the accounts of all nationalised industries.

Public Bills   These are introduced to Parliament by a Member of Parliament (usually by a minister unless it is a private member's Bill).
   See also **private bills.**

Public borrowing   See **Public Sector Borrowing Requirement (PSBR)**

Public company   See **limited company**

Public corporations   Public corporations are independent bodies set up by statute or, as in the case of the BBC, by a charter issued under the Royal Prerogative, to carry out the duties entrusted to it by Parliament.
   Nationalised industries such as coal, gas, electricity, atomic energy, rail and steel, are run as public corporations.

Public enterprises   These cover municipal undertakings and nationalised undertakings.
   Municipal undertakings are commercial enterprises which can be operated by borough and district councils. Examples of these are swimming baths, bus services, leisure centres and theatres.

Public expenditure   Government expenditure is made up of:
Capital expenditure on new fixed assets, such as schools, hospitals, roads, etc.
Current expenditure — the 'running costs' necessary for schools, hospitals, the armed forces, etc.
Transfer payments — money contributed by taxpayers and paid out in unemployment, sickness, child and retirement benefits, and subsidies such as those on council housing.
Wages and salaries to Civil Servants and others in the public sector.

Public finance/income   The sources of public finance are:
Direct Taxes — Personal (**Income Tax**), including **National Insurance**; **Corporation Tax**, **Capital Gains Tax**, **Capital Transfer Tax**.
Indirect Taxation — VAT, Customs and Excise Duties, Motor Vehicle Duty, Rates.

Public law   This involves administrative law, constitutional law, and criminal law, details of which are to be found under their own headings.

Public limited company (plc)   See **limited company**

Public ownership   All organisations in the public sector of the economy are publicly or 'socially' owned.

Public relations (PR)   Defined by the Institute of Public Relations as the 'deliberate, planned and sustained effort to establish and maintain mutual understanding between an organisation and its public'.

In Britain, public relations have now become generally accepted. Their value is fully appreciated in industry and has become an acknowledged part of both central and local government.

Members of the Institute of Public Relations are employed by institutions; some are staff members of individual companies whose job is concerned with the interests of their employer.

228

Public sector   Mixed economies (such as that of the United Kingdom) have a mixture of public and private enterprises.

All organisations in the public sector of the economy are publicly or 'socially' owned.

Public Sector Borrowing Requirement (PSBR)   The excess of public sector spending over public sector revenue.

Publicity for exports   There is a leaflet issued by the **BOTB** entitled *Publicity for Exports* which gives information on the BOTB Publicity Unit, the Central Office of Information, BBC External Services, British-based foreign correspondents, UK publicity, and 'aiming at editorial coverage'.

Purchases (day)book   When a purchase is made from a supplier an **invoice** will be received. The amount of each invoice will be credited to the account of the supplier in the purchase ledger, or entered first in the purchases (day)book and from that into the ledger.

Purchases ledger   See **bought ledger**

Purchasing   This department is responsible for buying all the goods required by a factory or business, which will include raw materials, component parts, consumables, and often capital equipment. The job of a buyer can be summed up as purchasing the right goods, in the right quantity, at the right price at the right time.

Pure competition   In perfect or perfectly competitive markets prices are fixed in an atmosphere of 'pure competition'; in such markets the price adjusts to that level which equates demand and supply.

Put option   An option to sell **shares** at an agreed price at a future date, whatever happens to the market.

Put through

Put through (Stock Exchange) Special dealing procedure, applying usually to very large orders, by which the **broker** finds both a seller and a buyer, and the **jobber** 'puts the shares through' the market for a very small '**turn**'.

Q

Qualified privilege   A defence in an action for defamation in respect of reports published in newspapers or statements made in discharge of a legal, moral or social duty (eg, employer's references) providing that malice is not proven.

Qualitative guidance   'Requests' by the central bank asking the banks to give priority to lending to certain sectors of the economy and to restrain lending to other sectors.

Quality control   Tests to ensure that standards of quality are being maintained should take place at all stages of production.

Quango   An American word accepted as meaning 'quasi-autonomous national government organisation'.
   Examples of quangos are the British Medical Council, various tourist boards, and consumer councils.

Quantity discount   A discount allowed to a purchaser for buying in bulk.

Quarter up   The price used in valuing **shares** for taxation purposes. It is calculated on the 'quarter up' principle, that is, instead of taking the middle price in the official list, the difference between the two prices given under 'Quotations' is divided by four, and this amount added to the lower one.

Quasi-governmental bodies   Examples of such bodies are the **Advisory, Conciliation and Arbitration Service (ACAS),** the

231

Commission for Racial Equality, and the **Equal Opportunities Commission**.

Quasi-judicial bodies   Examples of such bodies are agricultural land tribunals, rent tribunals, and industrial tribunals.

Quasi-rent   If the supply of any factor is inelastic (ie, it is fixed at a certain quantity), that factor will be enabled to demand more than normal rewards. (See **economic rent**).

Queen, functions of the/Queen and Parliament   Examples of some of the most important duties of the monarch are:
appointment of the Prime Minister;
appointment of other ministers (guided by the choice of the Prime Minister);
summoning, proroguing and dissolving of Parliament.
The monarch gives the Royal Assent to all Bills passed by the House of Lords and the House of Commons, thereby converting them into Acts of Parliament.
The monarch appoints the judges, acting on the advice of the Prime Minister and the Lord Chancellor.
The Queen may grant a free pardon (on the recommendation of the Home Secretary) to those found guilty by the Courts and who have subsequently been shown to be innocent.

Quick ratio   The quick or 'liquid' ratio measures the ability of a business to meet its immediate commitments. See also **acid test ratio**.

Quorum   The minimum number of persons required to be present at a meeting in order that business may be validly transacted.

Quota licences   These allow entry into the country of a specific quantity of a certain type of good; the part of the world from which they may come is usually named.
   Quota licences restrict the import of goods by either a volume quota or a value quota.

Quota sampling A quota sample, or stratified sample is one which is controlled according to certain characteristics known about the population it represents. The market research sample is selected so that it reproduces exactly those characteristics in the same proportion as they are present in the total population.

Quotations (Stock Exchange) The double price given in the Official List indicates the range of buying and selling prices.

Quoted company Also **listed company**. A company whose shares are listed on **The Stock Exchange**. If a company wishes to have the advantages of a regulated market in its securities, it must conform with company law and must sign The Stock Exchange Listed Agreement, after which it is known as a 'listed company'.

Companies listed on the Stock Exchange undertake to provide far more information about themselves than company law alone demands.

R

Race relations The Commission for Racial Equality is empowered to investigate cases of racial discrimination, and has a duty to promote education in the field of race relations and to improve the public attitude especially where it concerns equality of opportunity.

Random sample A sample selected in such a way that every item in the population has an equal chance of being included.

Rate of return (on capital) This is the ratio between net profit and the capital employed.

Rate of turnover The number of times the average stock is sold during the trading period.

$$\text{Rate of turnover} = \frac{\text{Turnover}}{\text{Average stock}}$$

Rates Rates provide about one-third of the income of local authorities; rates are taxes based on the rateable value of a property, the amount being decided by individual local authorities.

Water authorities also obtain revenue from water rates which again are based on the rateable value of properties.

Rationalisation The application of the most efficient methods in production, distribution and transport.

Raw materials These are the essential materials and

commodities for manufacturing processes, usually taken to include all primary products such as minerals, skins and fleeces of animals, and some agricultural products such as timber, fibres, etc.

Primary production is involved with making use of the natural resources of a country — eg, the extractive industries of coal-mining and the tapping of oil and natural gas; also agriculture and fishing.

However, Britain has to import large quantities of raw materials which are brought in mostly as primary products.

Primary products are usually imported into Britain as bulk cargoes in purpose-built vessels (oil tankers, refrigerated meat carriers). They are either handled by the commodity markets in the City of London, financed, transported and warehoused until required by middlemen, or directly imported by a manufacturing firm which has built up a strong link with an overseas supplier.

Real accounts   The **ledger** contains all the accounts, whether personal, real or nominal. The real accounts represents assets, or items of property. The balance on a real account must be a debit balance—for example, when furniture or plant and machinery is purchased. Real accounts are records of property, such as the stock account, and therefore debit balances in the real accounts are always assets.

Real incomes/wages   'Money wages' refers to the actual income earned by the worker. Real wages refers to the actual 'basket of goods' (and services) which he can purchase with it.

In times of **inflation** money wages may rise, but in fact will often not enable workers to buy as many goods or services as before.

Real value   The nominal value of a share—the value named on it—is retained throughout its life, but its actual value varies with supply and demand, and the extent to which profits have been ploughed back since the share was issued.

Receipts and payments account   A receipts and payments account is a summarised cash account.

235

Capital expenditure—the cost of acquiring assets—is included in it, but not **depreciation**, together with expenses which relate entirely to the period covered by the account.

This type of account is sometimes used by small clubs and other non-trading societies as a final statement of their annual transactions.

Receiving order An order putting a receiver in temporary possession of a debtor's estate, pending bankruptcy proceedings.

Recognised banks Institutions recognised as banks by the **Bank of England**. Recognised banks and licensed deposit-taking institutions (together with a few other institutions) make up the monetary sector.

Reconciliation statement See **bank reconciliation statement**

Redeemable preference shares Provided a company is authorised by its **Articles of Association** it may issue preference **shares** which are liable, at the option of the company, to be redeemed.

Redemption date The date on which a security is due to be redeemed by the issuer at its full face value. The year is included in the title of the security; the actual redemption date is that on which the last interest payment is due.

Redundancy payments The Redundancy Payments Acts, 1965 and 1969, require employers to pay compensation to certain employees laid off or put on short time, or dismissed as redundant because the work they are doing is no longer necessary or has ceased to exist.

The amount of the payment is related to pay, length of service and age.

The Act also established a central Redundancy Payments Fund financed by surcharges on the employers' **National Insurance** contributions.

Re-export   Imported goods which are to be re-exported or are for transhipment are entered on special 'Entry' forms by the Customs authorities and must be exported within one month; no Customs duty needs to be paid. Primary products embodied into manufactured goods for export are free from Customs duties.

Regional development fund See **European Economic Community** (EEC finances)

Regional development grants   The Department of Trade and Industry (DTI) has regional development grant offices at Billingham (Cleveland), Bootle (Merseyside), Cardiff (Wales), Cornwall (including the Isles of Scilly) and Glasgow, which provide financial aid for capital expenditure on new machinery, plant, buildings and mining work.

Registrar of Companies   The Registrar of Joint-Stock Companies registers companies formed under the Companies Act 1948.

Registrar of Government Stocks   The **Bank of England** is responsible for the registration of government stocks, the stocks of nationalised industries and public boards. It also pays dividends on such stocks when they become due.

Registration of business names   If the name of a sole trader's business is other than his own name it must be registered under the Registration of Business Names Act, 1916. Partnership names and the names of limited companies must also be registered.

Reinsurance   Insurance companies limit their liability on a risk to a reasonable amount. Where a proposal in excess of that limit is made it is dealt with by reinsurance, the excess being offered to other companies.

Some companies only deal in reinsurance business offered to them by companies undertaking direct risks.

Reintermediation The unwinding of **disintermediation**. Generally this occurs when direct controls on banks are removed thus allowing lending business previously re-routed through uncontrolled channels to return to the banking system.

Renounceable documents   Temporary evidence of ownership; each includes full instructions on what the holder should do if he wishes to have the newly issued **shares** registered in his own name, or if he wishes to renounce them in favour of somebody else.

Rent   1   Money or other periodic payment made for the use of land, buildings, etc. (Part of the general expenses of a business—fixed costs—as distinct from the direct cost of producing an article).

2   The term 'rent' has a special meaning in economics—it is the payment made for the use of factors of production whose supply is inelastic (ie, cannot be increased with ease). Land is a prime example because it is a factor of production which is in inelastic supply to changes in price. But there are other examples of factors which cannot be easily reproduced even if earnings rise—natural ability, for example. A footballer who receives a differential payment based on his superlative skill may be said to be in receipt of rent for the ability.

Rent tribunals   The 1965 Rent Act set up local Rent Assessment Committees to fix 'fair rents' and made intimidation and harassment of tenants illegal. Landlords, tenants or the local authority may apply to these rent tribunals to have the rent of property fixed.

Reports   The furnishing of reports is a necessary function of management.

Special reports are called for to investigate a special field of activity; in such reports the terms of reference should be clearly stated and the reports should include recommendations or suggestions.

Resale Price Maintenance   Under the Resale Prices Act 1976 manufacturers cannot compel retailers to charge a certain price for their goods.

Research and Development (R & D)   Government assistance for R & D is provided by the **Department of Trade and Industry**, especially in the area of **Information Technology**. Through the Department's 'Support for Innovation' programme companies can receive assistance both for longer term R & D projects designed to strengthen their technological base and for development work on new and improved products and processes.

Reserve requirement   Obligation on banks (or other institutions) to invest a specified minimum percentage of their deposits in specified assets.

Reserves, capital   Reserves created by some extraordinary activity of a company, such as reserves created by revaluation of property.

Reserves, gold and foreign currency   Today gold reserves represent only part of the face value of the country's issued currency. Another part is reflected in the amount of foreign currency it holds.
   See **Exchange Equalisation Account.**

Resolution   A resolution is the acceptance of a motion that has been put to a vote and agreed by the necessary majority at a meeting.

Resources   Resources are a stock which can be drawn on to satisfy a want.
   Any attempt made to satisfy a want must make use of three classes of resources (the factors of production). These are—
land — natural resources
capital — the resources of tools and equipment
labour — or human resources

Restrictive practices   If a number of firms making or selling a particular product, or providing a commercial service, agree to fix prices, divide up the market, or restrict supplies, this agreement must be submitted beforehand to the **OFT**. It is then placed on a register, open to public inspection. The Restrictive Practices court is then asked to rule whether the agreement is against the public interest and, if so, to ban it.

Retail Price Index (RPI)   Each month a figure is calculated which is officially described as the Index of Retail Prices. This index (which replaced the old cost of living index) measures the changes in the prices paid for the goods and services which the great majority of householders spend most of their money on.

The index is widely used in discussions on wage claims, and in some industries wages vary with it automatically. Also, the government uses the index to measure the effects of its policies.

The index is compiled on the basis of recommendations made by a committee on which employers, trade unions, co-operative societies, shopkeepers, housewives and others are represented. The Index of Retail Prices is produced every month.

Retail trade   The retail trade is that part of commercial services which provides the last link in the chain of distribution, where goods are sold to the final consumer.

Retailer-wholesaler co-operatives (voluntary chains)   In order to compete with the large supermarket chains associations of small retailers have been set up—SPAR and MACE are examples. (SPAR stands for Society for the Protection of the Average Retailer). By joining forces and buying in bulk—ie, by controlling their own wholesaling and warehousing—these associations afford the opportunity to small retailers to buy at more favourable prices, and to pass the advantage on to the consumer.

Retained profits   That part of the profits of a company belonging to the holders of the **equity**, but not distributed by way of **dividend**. Also known as *retentions*.

Return on capital invested This figure is essential if a businessman is to know how his business is faring.

$$\text{Return on } \textbf{capital} \text{ invested} = \frac{\text{Net profit} \times 100}{\text{Capital at start of the year}}$$

Returns inward/returns outward When a business returns goods or, for some reason, receives an allowance on goods it has already purchased it will receive a credit note from the supplier. These credit notes may be entered into a purchase returns and allowances book and the necessary ledger postings made from that book.

If goods have been undercharged a debit note will be sent to the customer. This will be treated as an additional invoice and passed through the sales book, or will be debited direct to the customer's account.

Returns to scale When an increase in the size of a production unit results in a more than proportional increase in output there are increased returns to scale.

Revenue reserves Reserves created by ploughing back profits into the business. They may be either special reserves for particular purposes, or general reserves held back for the equalisation of dividends as between good and bad years.

Revocable credits See **letter of credit**

Revolving credit See **budget account (2).**

Rewards to factors The factors of production are land, capital and labour.

The economic rewards for each of these are—
Land—rent
Capital — Interest is paid to the investor for the postponement of his own consumption, and for allowing his capital to be used by entrepreneurs; profits are paid to the investor for the risk of losing his capital.
Labour—wages.

Rider   An addition to a motion. Unlike an amendment a rider can be put either before or after the motion is voted upon.

Rights issue   When a company whose **shares** are already listed makes a further offer of shares for sale, the **Stock Exchange** requires that these be offered to existing **shareholders** in proportion to their existing shareholdings. This is known as a rights issue (see **renounceable documents**.)

Ring trading   In some commodity markets 'ring trading' is carried on. In the **Baltic Exchange** the 'grain' ring is identified by a circular rail around which deals are struck for future grains deliveries at agreed prices.

In the **London Metal Exchange**, members sit on benches arranged in a circle (it used to be a chalk ring drawn on the floor) and there are 'rings' for various metals, each metal being traded twice a day. A dealer in the LME ring calls out his bids and offers to the 'ring' by 'open outcry' so that all can hear the price.

Road transport   This provides door-to-door delivery, offering many specialised vehicles—bulk haulage, containers, tankers for liquids, etc. Vehicles can take the best routes available and there are computerised routes for heavy vehicles made available to drivers. Though slower than rail for journeys over 200 miles, the advantages of door-to-door consignments are often allowed to outweigh this consideration.

Because the actual use of the roads is free, hauliers' capital requirements are reduced.

However, among the disadvantages of road transport are the heavy social costs borne by the congestion and pollution it generates. Running costs are heavy, as petrol costs are particularly vulnerable to international pressures and taxation.

Motorways provide the answer to many road transport problems. A further consideration is the effect of the existence of a motorway on the location of industry, and the availability of labour.

Roll-on, roll-off ferries   These ships are designed to allow intercontinental road vehicles to embark and disembark without unloading.

Round-tripping   The process whereby bank customers borrow from the banks and then redeposit the funds in the money markets at a higher rate of **interest**.

Royal Mail International Services   These offer the exporter price stability, collection from premises, simplified payment of postal charges by 'Postage Paid Impression', and delivery to consignee's address. They offer also a variety of special rates for different classes of merchandise.

For overseas parcels, once postage is paid, the charge covers: collection and transfer to port, handling throughout the journey, all documentation, Customs clearance from UK, Customs clearance into destination country, and delivery to consignee's address.

The *Argonaut* International Freighting Service offers a complete Freight Forwarding Service for exporters for goods in bags, on pallets, or in boxes or cartons, in weights of up to 1 tonne.

Royalty   Payment to an author, composer, etc, for every copy sold or every public performance.

A firm that licences an overseas company to produce its products 'under licence' abroad can earn 'royalties' on sales, which moves the licensing firm into the invisible exports field.

S

Sale and repurchase agreement   Purchase of bills by the **Bank of England** from the **discount houses** with an agreement that the discount houses will buy the bills back on an agreed day. On occasion the bank has also conducted sale and repurchase operations in gilt-edged stock with the **clearing banks**.

Sale of Goods Act, 1893   See **consumer protection**

Sale or return   Goods 'on sale or return' are those sent to a person or firm on the understanding that they may be returned to the supplier if unsold, usually by a specified time.

Sales accounting   When a sale on credit is made an **invoice** is sent to the customer. A retained copy forms the basis of bookkeeping entries relating to the transaction. The invoices are initially listed in the sales record (sales daybook), and debited to the customer's account. At the end of the month the sales book is totalled and the total credited to the sales ledger (or sales account). At the end of the year the twelve monthly totals in the sales account give the total sales for the year for transfer to the trading account.

Sales ledger   A volume of the **ledger** is set aside for the personal accounts of customers and is known as the sales ledger.

Sampling   Sampling as a part of market research can provide useful information. Large-scale sampling is expensive but it has been found that for many purposes adequate information can be obtained from carefully selected samples.

Save As You Earn (SAYE) Several organisations, including building societies, run SAYE schemes, and some employers will make automatic deductions from pay of the amount to be saved and will pay the savings organisations direct. Contributors may also pay by Standing Order or by direct payment. Note that the National Savings Index-linked SAYE scheme has been superseded by the *Yearly Plan Scheme*. Existing contracts will continue until their expiry date but no further contracts will be accepted.

Savings If people or businesses are not consuming their entire incomes, saving is taking place. If the savings are 'hoarded' they will be non-productive.

Most ordinary people save through the institutional investors (banks, building societies, insurance companies, pension funds, etc.) who pass on the savings in the way of investment to entrepreneurs.

Scrip issue The process whereby money from a company's reserves is converted into issued **capital**, which is then distributed to **shareholders** as new shares in proportion to their original holdings, in a capitalisation issue. (Also known as a **bonus share**).

Seals of approval The British Standards Institution approval mark indicates that goods have been made to their standards (Kitemark).
goods comply with British Standards for safety.

The Design Centre, London awards a label for products which have been approved for being attractive and efficient in use.

Sea transport An efficient mercantile marine force is essential to a nation which depends on international trade for survival. Though air transport almost monopolises international passenger transport, the requirements of the import trade (raw materials) and the export trade (mostly manufactured goods) demand that a large shipping force—including many 'specialist' ships—are available for specific types of cargo. Among these specialist vessels are—

Container ships which, besides carrying large and varied cargoes,

245

offer also the facility of a quick 'turn round' at container ports.

Bulk carriers which carry only one commodity.

Oil tankers — bulk carriers but of enormous size and known as Vlccs (vlcc = very large crude carriers).

In addition, to cover the day-to-day and varied requirements of the import and export trades there are—

Passenger cargo liners — cargo ships which cater for a few passengers and *tramps* (small cargo ships).

Sea waybill Documentary delays had become a serious problem when the General Council of British Shipping and SITPRO developed the sea waybill. It is not intended to replace the **bill of lading** where it is necessary for the exporter to retain clear title to the goods until security of payment is assured. Unlike the bill of lading the sea waybill is not a document of title; it provides a receipt for the goods by the carrier, and evidence of the contract of carriage for the goods as described.

Secondary production This utilises those things produced at the primary stage to manufacture more sophisticated products.

Security Financial asset which can be bought and sold by investors in organised markets.

Security (for loan) See **collateral security**

Segmentation (market) The identification and delineation of sections of buyers who might reasonably be expected to purchase a particular commodity.

Selective credit policy The use of monetary and credit controls to influence the allocation of credit between different categories of borrowers.

Semi-manufactures Among the resources which manufacturers call on to assist in the process of production are semi-manufactures—components for assembly into major installations.

They are improved primary products and are classed as producer or capital goods.

Service industries The service industries together comprise commercial and personal services and form the tertiary arm of production.

Commercial services include (a) trade—retail and wholesale, home trade and international trade; and (b) ancillary commercial services (aids to trade)—advertising, banking, communications, financial services, insurance, transport and warehousing.

Personal services are sometimes known as direct services—they are 'intangible' and given direct from the producer of the service to the consumer. Examples of producers engaged in tertiary production are doctors, teachers, entertainers, editors, and policemen.

Sex Discrimination Act 1975 This set up the Equal Opportunities Commission which makes it illegal to discriminate against employees or applicants because of their sex.

Share capital See **capital** (types of)

Share certificate The legal document issued to a **shareholder** certifying ownership of a part of the company concerned.

Shareholder The owner of a share is a part-owner of a **limited company**; the right to vote varies with the type of share held. The **board of directors** is accountable to shareholders for the running of the company.

Shareholders pay **income tax** on any profits earned.

Shares A **limited company** must issue shares according to its **Memorandum of Association**. The shares of public limited companies may be issued to the public in three ways—

by a prospectus which is an advertisement giving details of a company and inviting the public to buy shares in it;

by an offer for sale using the services of an **Issuing House**;

by a placing—a system of issuing shares by asking institutional investors to buy up the extra issue.

The *nominal value* of a share—the value named on it—is retained throughout its life, but its actual value varies with supply and demand.

TYPES OF SHARE

Deferred shares—also called *founder's shares*. These are shares issued to the original creator of a firm who sells out to a company. The owner agrees to defer any **dividend** due to him until the other shareholders have had a reasonable dividend, but he has voting rights.

Ordinary shares or *'equities'*; the ordinary shareholders own the company. These shares carry the most risk, but also the best prospects of future growth. Their price is often determined not so much by past results as the expectation of future events. It is the ordinary shareholders who have the right to speak and vote at general meetings of the company, (a right sometimes extended to the holders of (participating) preference shares, but only if the **dividend** is in arrears, and not always then) and they elect the directors to run the business for them.

Preference shares carry a fixed rate of dividend, but this need not be paid if a company's profits are too low to justify this expense. Unless the shares are 'cumulative' once a dividend has been 'passed' it is lost forever. *Cumulative preference shares* still qualify for dividends passed in previous years, and until these have been paid up to date no payment can be made to ordinary shareholders.

See also **over-the-counter market, Stock Exchange, premium, yield.**

Shipbroker A **broker** who represents a shipowner and deals in the sales and insurance of ships; he also arranges cargoes for them.

Shipowner's liability Shipowners have many liabilities, not only in regard to the cargo, passengers and crew, but also in regard to any damage which may be caused by the ship itself in collision with other vessels or port installations, etc. Pollution due to sea contamination is another eventuality which shipowners must insure against.

Shipping London is the world's shipping capital, and the commercial centre of this world is the Baltic Mercantile and Shipping Exchange ('The **Baltic**'). **Lloyds of London** was originally a market exclusively for marine insurance. An important aspect of this work was that it resulted in the development of a world-wide shipping intelligence network, as one of the functions of its agents was to send to Lloyd's shipping, aviation and other news relating to the ports and areas in which they operated.

Both the Baltic and Lloyds contribute greatly to the 'invisible exports' of the **balance of payments**.

Shipping and forwarding agents These agents carry out the handling, through-transport arrangements, and payment collection for the greater part of exports from the United Kingdom.

Shipping Conference See **Liner Conferences**

Shipping marks The identification marks put on the cargo containers or chests by the shipping company. Every consignment must bear comprehensive shipping marks, details of which must appear on the invoice. Not only the final destination but also any special handling instructions must be clearly marked. The international signs for 'Keep dry', 'This side up', 'Fragile', and 'Radioactive' are used.

Shipping note A printed form which needs to be completed when goods are shipped. It is submitted to the receiving authority at the docks and lists the ship on which the goods are to be loaded, the marks, numbers, measurements, etc.

The **SITPRO** Standard Shipping Note can be used when delivering non-hazardous export consignments to any British port, container base or other cargo reception point.

The **SITPRO** Dangerous Goods Note should be used if the delivery includes items which are classified as dangerous.

Short-notice money When bill-brokers borrow money from banks, commercial firms, institutional investors, etc, which is repayable in a few days it is said to be 'short-notice' money.

Shorts   Government and other stocks with less than five years to redemption.

Sight deposits   Deposits which can be withdrawn at any time.

Sight drafts   A 'foreign sight' Bill of Exchange used in a 'D/P transaction'. See **Bill of Exchange**.

Silver Bullion Market   The price of silver is dictated by supply and demand which at any particular time varies from one world centre to another.

The Silver Bullion Market is conducted by three merchant bankers who meet once a day to fix the price. Quotations are made in both sterling and dollars.

Simplification   The three 'S's' of mass production techniques are simplification, standardisation, and specialisation.

Simplification is the process of making a manufactured article as simple and functional as possible.

Simplification of International Trade Procedures (SITPRO) SITPRO is a **BOTB** activity which has produced a revised set of forms to simplify overseas trade procedures.

SITPRO Docspeed allows freight forwarders to produce export documents from a single typing operation or computer printout, and is an extension of the SITPRO Aligned Export Documentation Scheme.

Sinking fund   A fund created by setting aside a fixed sum of money each year to provide for the replacement of assets.

Skillcentre Training Agency See **Manpower Services Commission**

Sleeping partner   See **partners** (Limited)

Small Firms Service   Run by the DTI, this is an information and counselling service to help owners and managers of small businesses with their plans and problems. It also acts as an advisory service to those thinking of starting their own business. The service, which operates through a nationwide network of Small Firms Centres, is designed to encourage business efficiency. There is no limit to the type of business the service will help.

The Small Firms Service provides information on any business problem; from finance, diversification and industrial training to exporting, planning, technological advances, industrial relations and marketing.

The service can put enquirers in touch quickly with the right people in local authorities, government departments, the professions, libraries, chambers of commerce or any other body to help with the problem. It can also identify national and international sources of information that may be needed.

If the enquiry is beyond straightforward sources of information it can be discussed with a Small Firms Counsellor, an experienced businessman who may well have faced a similar situation. He will help by offering advice and guidance, impartially and in strict confidence.

Smithfield Market   The principal London meat market.

Social capital   See **capital** (types of)

Social costs   All organisations should have a sense of responsibility towards society. **Pollution** of the sea and rivers, air pollution, noise, congestion on the roads, or the charging of excessive prices are all anti-social activities whose costs are borne socially—that is, by the public.

Social environment   The social environment in which an organisation works places certain responsibilities upon it which it should not ignore. See **social costs**.

Social needs   Education, health, and welfare are social needs provided for by the government, though there is a 'private sector' which charges for such services. Other social needs are provided

251

by other service industries—the legal profession, insurance, banking, etc. which are also in the private sector.

Social services   Education, pensions and social security are examples of the social services provided by the government departments.

Societies and clubs   These are private organisations, usually run by a committee elected by the members. The annual accounts are normally presented as a **receipts and payments account**; any surplus cash in hand or at the bank is available for the members to dispose of as they wish.

Socio-economic groups   A method of dividing the population into groups based on income and social status. The groupings are often used by market researchers when compiling samples.

Software   A general term to describe computer programs, that is, the set of instructions given to a computer for it to perform its processing tasks.

Sole trader   The small sole trader business is simple to establish and has the advantage that the owner is entitled to all the profits. Other advantages are the freedom of action enjoyed by the owner, the personal incentive which exists, and the personal contact with employees and customers.

Disadvantages lie in the uncertain future of such businesses which can fail through no fault of the owner, who suffers the entire loss of his personal fortune if this happens. Also there may be problems of management in so far as the owner must take full responsibility for all decisions, and small businesses often find finance for expansion difficult to obtain.

Sole traders, especially small retailers, do manage to survive in spite of the many difficulties at present facing them.

Span of control   Refers to the number of subordinates a manager can effectively control. The factors that govern this number are the complexity of the work, whether duties interlock, the degree of self-discipline amongst the subordinates and the capabilities of the manager.

Special deposits   Calls by the **Bank of England** for institutions in the monetary sector to place balances with the Bank equal to a specified percentage of their eligible liabilities.

This is a monetary measure used to take money 'out' of the economy and effectively reduces the amount of money which the banks can lend.

Special Drawing Rights (SDRs)   The **International Monetary Fund** gave to all its members that agreed to accept them an allocation of units, each worth one US dollar. A country wishing to use SDR notifies the Fund that it wishes to exchange some of these units for usable foreign currency. The authorities then designate which countries will make currency available and take SDR units instead.

Specialisation   Mass production—the manufacture of goods on a large scale—is made possibly only by the division of **labour**. Each worker becomes a specialist, specialising in his own particular part of the productive process. Specialisation, together with simplification and standardisation are the basis of mass production.

Specific duties   Customs duties may be specific duties or *ad valorem* duties. *Specific duties* are based on a fixed quantity—ie, the rate is per unit of weight, volume, measure or number.

Specific guarantees   Policies issued by the Export Credit Guarantee Department of the Board of Trade for large, capital projects.

Speculator   A speculator is an investor who invests his money in a more or less risky way for the sake of unusually large profits.

Speculators are especially active on the highly-organised markets of the City of London, particularly the Stock Exchange and commodity markets.

Spitalfields Market

On the Stock Exchange there are three main kinds of speculator—**bulls, bears,** and **stags**.

Speculators on the Stock Exchange exert a moderating effect on the market; prices do not rise as high nor sink as low as they might do if they were not active.

Speculators on the commodity markets deal in 'futures', and play an important role in balancing supply and demand between the producers (miners and farmers) and the consumers (the companies which process and sell these products to the public).

Spitalfields Market   The fruit, flower and vegetable market in the East End of London. The West End was served by Covent Garden Market, now relocated at Nine Elms.

Spot dealing/spot markets   On the physical **commodity markets** materials are bought at agreed prices on either 'spot' or '**futures**' contracts. 'Spot' dealings are for goods already available which are delivered on immediate settlement (in 'spot cash').

Spread   The difference between a jobber's buying and selling price (Stock Exchange).

Stag   A speculator who applies for **shares** in a new issue with the intention of selling them at once on the **Stock Exchange** should they be over-subscribed, and therefore in strong demand. The price at which he sells will be greater than his buying price.

Stamp Duty   The general name for a group of taxes levied by the **Inland Revenue**, usually in the form of stamps which have to be affixed to certain documents. In the **Stock Exchange**, Transfer Stamp Duty is paid by the purchaser on all contracts, and Contract Stamp Duty on all contract notes. Certain securities, mainly Gilts (Government stock) and those represented by **renounceable documents**, do not attract Stamp Duty.

Standard costing   The process of determining the total cost of a product or service based on a budgeted level of output under standard conditions. It enables actual costs to be compared with the standard yardstick and any variances investigated if they exceed a permitted level.

Standard shipping note   See **shipping note**

Standardisation   **1**   The three S's of mass production techniques are standardisation, simplification and specialisation. Standardisation is the making of standard parts which can be used in many different manufactures.
2   The standards committees of the **British Standards Institution** are drawn from industry, government departments, professional, scientific and technical bodies and consumer groups; they prepare standards issued by the divisional councils in building, chemicals, engineering and textiles. British Codes of Practice are drawn up by a special council.

Standing committee   See **committees**

Standing order   An order given to a bank to pay a fixed sum of money at regular intervals to a designated payee. Payments to a building society or hire-purchase firm are often treated in this way, since it saves the repeated drawing of cheques as well as ensuring that payments are never forgotten.

Standing orders   The term applied to the rules regulating the conduct and procedure of certain official bodies.

Statement of account   All businesses make a practice of balancing their debtors' accounts at regular intervals, usually a month. At the end of each month a statement of account is made up and sent to each debtor.

Statement of affairs   In the case of a trader who has kept incomplete records of his financial dealings it is sometimes necessary to complete a statement of affairs to give a true financial picture of his business. To prepare such a statement the following figures have to be ascertained:
value of stock;

value of cash in hand and at the bank;
the total sums due from debtors and to trade creditors;
the value of any other assets;
the value of further liabilities and outstanding expenses;
the value of any payments made in advance.

A statement of affairs is also submitted by a debtor who has been served with a receiving order (a person who cannot pay his debts and who is insolvent). This lists the debtors' assets and his debts, giving the names and addresses of creditors and how much they are owed.

State Pension   All employed persons are covered by the State Pension Scheme in Great Britain.

State-owned concerns/State undertakings   All organisations in the public sector are 'publicly' or 'socially' owned.

Statistics and Market Intelligence Library   At the Statistics and Market Intelligence Library there is access to a wide and thorough collection of foreign and UK statistics, trade directories, development plans and other published information on overseas markets. The Library is at 1, Victoria Street, London SW1.

Status enquiry agent   Provides information to suppliers regarding the financial status of buyers.

Statute Law   A law expressly written by the legislature and therefore an Act of Parliament.

All Acts of Parliament contribute to the British Constitution.

Statutory declaration of compliance   This is a sworn statement drawn up on the promotion of a company confirming that the requirements of the Companies Acts relevant to registration and 'matters precedent and incidental thereto' have been completed.

It is one of the initial documents lodged with the Registrar of Companies for approval before a **Certificate of Incorporation** can be issued.

Statutory deductions   Refers to the compulsory deductions from an employee's gross pay for tax and national insurance.

Statutory instrument   Certain Acts of Parliament empower ministers of the Crown to make regulations having force of law on matters of detail. These are known as statutory instruments and must be laid before Parliament, which can annul them. This procedure is 'delegated legislation'; sometimes power is given to local authorities, public transport undertakings and other organisations to make rules such as byelaws which come under the general heading of 'delegated legislation'.

Statutory meeting   See **meetings** (of limited companies)

Statutory report   This report must, by the provisions of the Companies Acts, be sent to every member of a public **limited company** fourteen days before the *statutory meeting* and must be filed with the Registrar of Companies. The information must include the following:
total number of **shares** allotted and how payments have been made;
the amount of cash received for shares;
the receipts and payments of the company;
an account or estimate of the preliminary expenses;
names, addresses and descriptions of directors, auditors, managers and secretary;
parts of any modification of any contract which requires the approval of the statutory meeting.
   The report must be certified by two directors and the auditors.

Statutory tribunals   There are over 2000 special courts called administrative tribunals which have been set up to settle disputes in such areas as rent control and national health insurance. Industrial tribunals deal with a particularly large number of complaints concerned with disputes arising out of employment.
   These tribunals, though dealing with the laws of the land, cover many aspects of life and are less formal than ordinary law courts.
   Each tribunal specialises in one type of dispute.

Sterling   The pound sterling is the British monetary unit.

Sterling Area   Today this consists of the UK, the Channel Isles, the Isle of Man and Gilbraltar.

Stock   A set of shares put together to form one unit. A unit of stock is usually valued at £100.

Stockbroker   A broker does far more than simply carry out his clients' buying and selling orders. He is also an analyst, a researcher, and an adviser on a whole range of financial topics, for individual savers, for investing institutions and for companies seeking investment.

A broker's responsibility does not end with the bargain on the trading floor. He has a responsibility, both to his client and to the market, to see that the business is properly completed, that shares being sold are delivered to the broker acting for the new owner, and paid for, and that any benefits due to the buyer are secured on his behalf.

Brokers have research departartments which are constantly monitoring the performance of individual companies in countries all over the world, as well as the political and general economic news that may affect a sector of industry as a whole. Investment decisions may well be affected by a client's tax position, and brokers may not always advise putting money directly into stocks and shares. Brokers therefore become involved in giving guidance on taxation, life assurance, **unit trusts**, building society and money market investments.

Many brokers are also involved in corporate finance, working side by side with merchant banks, lawyers and accountants as advisers to companies and local authorities.

Stock control   The function of the stock controller is to ensure that there is always sufficient stock in hand to meet current requirements, and that the replenishment of stock is efficiently organised. The keeping of stock records is vitally important to the correct running of a stockroom.

Stock Exchange The Stock Exchange is a highly organised financial market where stocks and shares are bought and sold. Its purpose is to put those who wish to sell securities in touch with those who wish to buy them, so that investments can change hands in the quickest, cheapest and fairest way possible.

The general level of prices is decided by the investors who use the Stock Exchange; they create the supply and demand to which the jobbers react by offering prices that they hope will be attractive to an equal number of buyers and sellers.

To an investor the buying of stocks and shares is a temporary 'loan' which he may wish to cash at any time; the only way in which he can do this is to sell his shares at the best price he can get for them on the market.

On the other hand, the directors of a company regard the money received for shares as a permanent 'loan'; they spend part of it on land, buildings, plant and machinery, transport, etc. The *fixed capital* which purchased these *fixed assets* cannot be turned into cash ('liquified') and cannot be returned to the investor. The investor's reward for his investment is in the form of a **dividend**, a share of the company's profits which are divided up between the shareholders.

Types of investment The three main types of securities are **gilt-edged, debentures** and **shares**.

BUYING AND SELLING SECURITIES

Brokers buy and sell shares on behalf of the general public or may deal on their own account. Brokers buy through jobbers for their clients. Jobbers are also known as 'dealers' and are the wholesalers of stocks and shares, and specialise in one particular type. Whether he is buying or selling the broker gets two prices from the jobber—a 'bid' price and an 'offer' price; the difference in price is the jobber's reward—the 'jobber's turn'.

There are provincial Stock Exchanges at Birmingham, Bristol, Liverpool, Manchester, Glasgow, Belfast and Dublin.

See also **Option dealing, Over-The-Counter Market**.

Stock Exchange Account   See **account** (Stock Exchange)

Stock Exchange Council   Control of the Stock Exchange is vested in a Council which is elected by members.

The Council is responsible for the rules and regulations which are enforced by strict disciplinary powers and supplemented by a traditional integrity among the members. Based upon the motto *Dictum meum pactum*—'my word is my bond'—a high standard of honesty and fairness is maintained by members.

Stock Exchange quotation   In order to obtain a quotation for its securities a company must make application to The Stock Exchange Council, through a member firm, and comply with their requirements.

A quotation—the price range, fixed by the market each day, within which the market is prepared to deal on that day in that particular share—is published in *The Stock Exchange Daily Official List*.

Stock in trade   The quantity and value of the goods and merchandise which a trader has in stock at any particular time.

Stock records   Records of all stock into and out of stockrooms should be maintained so that adequate supplies can be held and undue wastage controlled.

A stock record card should be kept for each item, the cards being filed in alphabetical or code number order.

Before stock is issued to individuals or departments a Requisition Form should be filled in and authorised by a senior member of the department issuing it.

When it is received by the Stockroom the stock required should be taken out and the necessary entries made on the stock record card. Similarly stock being received from suppliers is entered on the stock card.

Stock cards should contain the following information:

A description of the item, including size, weight, etc, and code number, if any.

The maximum stock level   This figure depends on two factors—the amount of this particular item which is used, and the capacity of the stockroom.

The minimum stock level This depends on the amount used and the length of time which will elapse between placing an order for fresh supplies and their delivery period.

Re-order level This figure is larger than the minimum stock level and depends on the delivery period for the particular item. When supplies drop to re-order level an order should be placed for fresh supplies.

Stock valuation One of the purposes of stocktaking is to support the value of stock shown in the balance sheet by physical verification.

It will be seen that, at any time, the value of the balance in hand is the amount of money which has actually been paid for that amount of stock, at the price of the latest consignment. This makes it easier to calculate the value of stocks for balance-sheet purposes.

Stockjobber See **Jobber**

Stocktaking Stockrooms should be checked for stock periodically or have an annual stocktaking at the end of each year. A physical check or count of all stock is made, and the results checked against the figures shown on the stock record cards. If the stock records have been properly kept, shortages in stock through pilferage, wastage, or deterioration may be brought to light. See **perpetual inventory**.

Stockturn (of businesses) The rate of turnover; the number of times a stock is sold and replaced in the course of a year. The Stockturn can be worked out on the cost or selling price of goods, as long as cost price is related to the total *cost* of the goods sold, and the selling price is related to net turnover. See **average stock**

Store promotions When a big retail outlet overseas puts on a 'theme' production and there is a specifically British flavour to the event, with increased sales of British goods as the aim, the **British Overseas Trade Board** can often provide support to the store.

Taking part in one of these well-organised promotions can help exporters to enter a new market or expand business.

Strategic commodities   These are arms and ammunitions and are among items requiring an Export Licence before they can leave Britain.

Street markets   Some local authorities provide special facilities for conducting street markets.

Strict liability   A person is strictly liable for a tort committed by himself. (cf **vicarious liability**).

Structural unemployment   See **unemployment**

Subsidiaries   A company (the first-named) is deemed to be a subsidiary of another company (the second-named) only if—

the second-named company controls the composition of the **board of directors** or holds more than half of its **share capital**,
or
if the first-named is a subsidiary of a third company which is also a subsidiary of the second-named company.

Subsidies   Government grants to industries, commercial undertakings, etc. The best known are the food subsidies of the Second World War and after. There is still a large subsidy for housing.

Subsidies are also available to regions designated by the government as being in need of financial support. Industrial subsidies in these areas help the firms involved, but the cost in the end is borne by the taxpayer.

Succession, law of   This law deals with the ways in which the property of a dead person is transferred to the new owners. What is done depends on whether the deceased made a will. If he did, personal representatives called executors or administrators transfer the property; if there is no will a dead person's effects are distributed according to rules laid down by statute.

Supermarkets   These are cut-price, self-service chain stores, offering many different types of goods.

Supermarkets (and hypermarkets) are run by large-scale organisations from a centralised head office. They sell many 'own brand' goods and have their own large warehouses.

Supply   The supply of any commodity at any given time may mean, in general, the total existing stocks of the commodity wherever they may be (the 'potential supply') or in particular, the quantity available for a particular country or market (the 'market supply').

A more particular meaning of supply in economics is 'the supply of a commodity or service in that quantity of it which entrepreneurs are prepared to make available at a given price in a given period of time'.

Supply and demand, law of   The economic statement that the price of a commodity depends on supply and demand means that the price of commodities must be so adjusted whether consciously or unconsciously as to equalise the demand with the supply, and that, in general, the demand increases with a decrease in price, and conversely the demand decreases with an increase in price. Equilibrium price is the price which equates supply and demand.

Neither the conditions of supply nor those of demand are sufficient alone to determine the price; in all cases the two sets of conditions are required.

The equilibrium between supply and demand conditions depends essentially upon the actions of producers in anticipating the demand.

Supply of Goods (Implied Terms) Act 1973   See **consumer protection**

Support for Innovation   Innovation is not an easy option. It calls for special management skills, the co-operation of a committed workforce, and finance. The responsibility for instigating new developments is that of the company itself, while the government must create the optimum overall conditions to encourage success.

Government financial support is available to encourage all areas of industrial research and development and—reflecting the importance of this role—the **Department of Trade and Industry** has streamlined its assistance machinery to make it more responsive to the needs of industry. All the department's schemes for supporting industrial **Research and Development** and promoting the adoption of new technologies are now embraced by *Support for Innovation*. This provides assistance for any stage of R&D up to and including the launch of new or significantly improved products and processes; in certain cases it can contribute towards post-development production and marketing costs. The overall balance and direction of R&D support is overseen by industrialists and other specialists in the Requirements Boards and their advice is closely integrated into the Department's industrial programme.

To qualify for support, the DTI must be satisfied that the organisation has the technical, financial and managerial resources to undertake the project, and that government assistance is essential to ensure that the project goes ahead. Projects may be supported from the design and development stage, through market appraisal and the capital equipment needed for production, to the launch of products and processes.

Suspense account An account in which items are entered temporarily until their proper 'heading' is known.

The suspense account is also used when the two sides of a **trial balance** do not agree. If it is necessary to allow the **profit and loss account** and the **balance sheet** to be drawn up before the two sides have been reconciled, the amount of the difference must be inserted under the suspense account. The procedure is to eliminate the figure in the suspense account as errors are discovered.

Syndicate It is the modern practice for Lloyds **underwriters** to work in syndicates, sharing the risks they insure. The syndicate will normally operate through an underwriting agent (who may be a member of the syndicate). Each syndicate will normally specialise in a particular type of insurance.

Systems analysis Describes the collection, organising and evaluation of facts about a system in order to determine how the necessary operations and procedures may best be computerised.

Systems approach A system is a sequence of activities—a procedure—which is necessary to achieve an objective.

A systems approach to an organisation's activities views that organisation as a system made up of many subsystems which interact and interrelate with one another. First it must be proved that the object of each procedure is necessary for the efficiency of the organisation, and then it must be established that all the procedures in question are designed both for speed and efficiency.

T

Take-over bid   An offer addressed to the shareholders of a company by an individual or firm to buy their shares at a named price above the present market price, with a view to securing control of the company.

Take-overs and Mergers, City Code on   This has been prepared by the Council for the Securities Industry, whose Markets Committee has succeeded the *ad hoc* City Working Party in supervising the Code. This body is representative of various elements in the City interested in the Securities Industry, and was set up initially at the request of the **Bank of England**. It ensures that its general principles are understood, and that its rules and the spirit behind the rules, are observed.

Talisman   The Stock Exchange's computerised settlement system. The letters stand for Transfer Accounting, Lodging for Investors and Stock MANagement for Jobbers.

Tap stocks   Government stocks which the Government Broker will supply at a given price. The price he chooses, set in consultation with the **Bank of England**, provides a means of influencing interest rates in general.

Tare   Tare is the allowance deducted from the gross weight of the goods to allow for the weight of the box, chest, case or wrapper in which the goods are packed.

Target prices (EEC)   CAP (Common Agricultural Policy) imposes

266

levies on cheap imports to keep them up to *threshold price*. To this price is added transport costs, the resulting price being called the *target price* which is the market price the Community has agreed upon for the sale of agricultural products.

Tariffs   A list of Customs duties to be paid on imports (usually) or exports; they are imposed for protection or revenue purposes.

Taxation   The method of raising the revenue required for public services through compulsory levies.
Direct taxes   Personal (Income Tax), including National Insurance; Corporation Tax, Capital Gains Tax, Capital Transfer Tax.
Indirect Taxation   VAT, Customs and Excise Duties, Motor Vehicle Duty, rates.

Technical Help to Exporters (BOTB)   This is the name of the organisation which will give advice on foreign technical requirements.

Teletext   A system of conveying textual and pictorial information from a broadcaster to a TV screen. The Ceefax service of the BBC and ITN's Oracle are two examples of teletext services in Britain. Because it is a broadcast service, teletext is more limited in scope than computer based 'viewdata' services like Prestel.

Tenders (for contracts)   A tender, like an estimate, is an offer to undertake specified work at a given price. It is often used in connection with contracts placed annually by local authorities for the supply of uniforms, stationery, and other necessary supplies. Very large overseas contracts such as the building of hospitals, dams, roads, etc, are advertised in the press and tenders invited.

Tenders (for shares)   A way of selling shares to the highest bidder. In some new issues the interested public are invited to put in a tender for the shares they require.

Tenders (for Treasury Bills)   See **discount market**.

Term draft   A 'foreign sight' Bill of Exchange used in a 'D/A transaction' (documents against acceptance of the Bill).
See **Bill of Exchange**.

Terminal   A terminal is situated at the end of a recognised transport route; seaports, airports, bus stations, oil refineries (for pipelines) and railway terminals come into this category. Essentially terminals need to be also junctions between differing forms of transport, so that easy transfer for passengers or cargoes can be effected to complete journeys; this is particularly true of container traffic in order that road/rail/sea/air transhipments can take place speedily and efficiently.

One of the difficulties of siting new airports in remote areas where noise pollution will not affect well-established residential areas is the lack of road and rail communications. The provision of these adds greatly to the capital costs.

Terminal (Markets)   See **futures**

Terms of payment (Trade)   Before a business transaction is entered into it is necessary that the terms of payment are known and agreed by both parties.

On the large, highly-organised markets in the City of London and elsewhere the controlling authorities lay down regulations for the settlement of deals made under their control (cf **'spot'** and **'futures'** markets).

Conditions also vary in different industries, and manufacturers, wholesalers, retailers and consumers follow patterns already set.

Generally speaking, sales can be cash or credit sales, the length of credit (monthly account, etc.) being by arrangement.

Discounts (cash, trade or quantity) are agreed before sale.

Terms of trade   These are an indication of the exchange rate existing between any two countries for a particular commodity. The terms may favour either country, but a continuing unfavourable balance for one country will force that country to cease dealing in that particular commodity.

Tertiary production   See **service industries**

Test marketing   Attempts to minimise the risk of a new product launch by selling to a carefully selected localised area first. Advertising and sales promotion activity is given the same weight and intensity as they would be if the product were launched nationally. During the test period statistical data about sales, stock levels, reorder levels and reactions of customers and retailers to the product are collected. Any problems which are seen to occur can then be solved prior to a national launch.

Ticket day   In a **Stock Exchange** Account period the day on which buying brokers pass to selling brokers the names of eventual purchasers, so that transfers can be arranged.

Time charters   In maritime law a charter-party is a contract between the owner or master of a ship and the person who hires the ship for the purpose of conveying goods from one port to another. If the vessel is hired for a period of time (ie, not for a particular voyage) it is known as a time charter.

Time policies   See **hull insurance**

Tort   Tort is in law a type of civil wrong done to a private person by a private person—a civil wrong which is neither a breach of contract nor a breach of trust.
    The usual remedy for tort is the award of damages.
    In general a person is only liable for a tort committed by himself (*strict liability*) but he may be *vicariously liable* for the faults of another if that person is his servant (employee) if the tort is done in the course of carrying out his duties.

Total costs (of production) are the addition of fixed costs and variable costs.
Fixed costs are those which cover rent, rates, interest on loans, and depreciation which an organisation has to pay, even when production is not taking place.
Variable costs are those which vary with output, such as

expenditure on raw materials, fuel, lighting, heating, and the wages of those directly engaged in production.

Tourism   Despite the fact that the tourist industry in Britain makes a large contribution to the 'invisible' trade figure in the **balance of payments** this is counterbalanced by the fact that large numbers of UK residents holiday abroad.

Trade   Trade—the buying and selling of goods and services—is an important commercial service and part of tertiary production. Trade covers the home, export and import trades, and retail and wholesale trading. Further details of each can be found under their own headings.

In the study of commerce the ancillary commercial systems—the aids to trade—must also be considered. These are advertising, banking, communications, finance, insurance, transport and warehousing.

Trade and Industry, Department of (DTI)   The central aim of the department is to encourage, assist and ensure the proper regulation of British trade, industry and commerce; and to increase the growth of world trade and the national production of wealth. It lists its aims under three headings: climate (financial and fiscal), international competitiveness, and innovation.

The DTI management task is 'to use Departmental resources efficiently to pursue these aims'.

'Awareness and rapid adoption of key technologies' is an important part of the DTI approach. Under the headings **Information Technology** and **Support for Innovation** will be found many areas of activity initiated by the DTI.

The many services which the **British Overseas Trade Board** (BOTB) offers to exporters are also listed; it is also responsible for the **Export Credit Guarantee Department**.

The Department also has the responsibility for consumer and safety regulations.

The Invest in Britain Bureau co-ordinates promotional work to bring further inward investments to the UK.

Trade associations   These are formed to protect and assist members in the same industry—for instance, the Association of British Travel Agents.

Trade bills   See **Bill of Exchange**

Trade credit   Trade credit is usually given by a firm to other firms or persons who are regular customers. The length of credit can vary, but usually accounts are made up monthly.

Trade Descriptions Act 1968   See **consumer protection**

Trade discount   The term given to a percentage discount allowed to trade buyers on the list price of goods. It is deducted from the invoice before calculation of VAT.

Trade fairs overseas   The BOTB can provide an exhibition stand and display aids at reduced rates for exhibiting abroad. There are also travel grants for fairs outside Europe.

Trade gap   The difference between the value of imported goods and the value of exported goods is known as the 'trade gap'. There is an adverse trade gap if the import figure is greater than the export figure.

Trade mark   A trade mark is any word or distinctive device warranting goods for sale as the production of any individual or firm; packaging and labels can be trade marks.

Trade promotions guide   This is a quarterly supplement of *British Business* which gives details of forthcoming BOTB-supported events including overseas trade fairs, store promotions, inward missions and outward missions; information about major UK fairs and exhibitions is also given. Copies are available at BOTB Regional Offices.

Trade Union and Labour Relations Act 1974   This protects employees from unfair dismissal.

Trade unions   A trade union is an organisation of work-people formed primarily for the purpose of collective bargaining about wages and working conditions, and the provision of educational, recreational and social amenities. Trade unions form an influential pressure group.

Traded options   See **options trading**

Trades Union Congress   Most trade unions are affiliated to the TUC, whose main objective is to act as a pressure group to influence government and business decisions.

It also promotes research and publicity on behalf of organised labour.

Trading account   This is constructed from:
Stock of goods (finished articles, raw materials, etc) held at the commencement of the trading period;
total purchases made during the trading period less any goods which have been returned;
total sales made during the trading period less any goods which have been returned;
the value of stock held at the end of the trading period.

It is desirable that the trading account should present in summarised form the total value of all transactions in goods for the period under review.

Trading bloc(k)   Examples of such trading bloc(k)s are the **EEC, EFTA,** the British Commonwealth, and **Comecon.**

Trading capital   See **capital** (types of)

Trading Certificate   See **floating a company**

Trading stamps   Vouchers in the form of stamps issued by retailers to their customers in accordance with the amount of their purchases, and which can be exchanged for gifts or money.

The Trading Stamps Act 1964, provides that stamps should carry their cash value stamped upon them, and that where the customer has accumulated more than 25p worth, they should be redeemable in cash if so desired.

Trading Standards Office/Consumer Protection Department
Offices run by local authorities where, among other services
offered, consumer advisers help with people's complaints about
such things as faulty goods, or goods or services which are
misdescribed. Informative literature published by the **Office of
Fair Trading** is available at these offices.

Training The human resources of an organisation are most
important and it is in the organisation's own interests to develop
employee skills and knowledge. Skills in team-work and co-
operation are necessary in a changing technological environment.

In a large firm a training officer will be a responsible member of
the personnel department. He will provide induction courses for
new members of staff, and technical and supervisory training in
all departments and at all levels.

Training for adults   See **Manpower Services Commission**

Training Services Agency   See **Manpower Services Commission**
for details of all MSC training services.

Tramp   This is a small cargo ship which will travel anywhere in
the world to make a living. Tramps can be chartered for a voyage
(voyage charter) or for a specified time (time charter).

Transaction   The word 'transaction' implies a transfer of goods
or services from one person to another. Where the transaction
involves immediate payment for goods or services it is a cash
transaction. Where payment is delayed until a later date it is a
credit transaction.

Transfer payments   A transfer payment occurs when taxes are
used by the government to pay unemployment benefit, sickness
benefit, child benefits and state pensions, or when it uses the
money to subsidise council rents. Most transfer payments are
made for social reasons.

Transhipment

Transhipment To transfer from one ship to another ship, or to another conveyance or vice versa.

In practice goods landed in Britain for re-export and for transhipment (transfer to another vessel for delivery to an overseas port) must be exported within one month.

Transmission mechanism The way in which the effects of changes in monetary policy are transmitted through the economy.

Transport Transport is a part of tertiary production and an aid to trade; its function is to move goods and passengers geographically.

It enables fuller use to be made of the division of labour by increasing the size of the production force and of the market. If the scale of production increases it increases the wealth of the nation.

The extractive industries and service industries have little choice in the matter of location, but the cost of transport is an important factor in the location of manufacturing industry.

Besides the four main transport systems—air, rail, road and sea—the use of pipelines should also be considered. Their use in the movement of oil and gas has considerably simplified what could present a difficult transportation problem.

Treasury The central department of State which manages the financial resources of the UK and controls public expenditure. The First Lord of the Treasury is the Prime Minister, the Chancellor of the Exchequer as the Second Lord of the Treasury is the effective head.

The main tasks of the Treasury are to collect taxes (in fact effected by the **Inland Revenue** and **Customs and Excise** Departments), to regulate spending in other government departments, and to a certain extent to control the national economy.

The Chancellor of the Exchequer is responsible for the planning of the **Budget** and the passing of the annual Finance Bill into law as an Act.

The Department of National Savings is responsible to the Treasury.

Treasury Bills   Treasury Bills are the means by which the British Government borrows money for short periods. The Bill itself is a promise to pay a stated sum within a period not exceeding one year, though normally the period is three months. Bills are issued in multiples of £5000 by the **Bank of England**, and form the largest part of the government's floating debt; they are offered for tender (sale) on Friday of each week.

Treasury Bills are bought almost exclusively by the **discount houses** which put in weekly tenders for the Bills, the sum total each week being decided by the Bank of England in the light of government needs. The Bank allots the Bills to the highest bidders (ie, those requiring the lowest interest) and the houses 'buy' them at the discounted rate. When the Bills become due (mostly in three months' time) the Bank 'honours' them (buys them back) at the full value of the Bill, so that the discount houses gain considerable amounts of money on their loans. Treasury Bills are negotiable and sometimes pass through several banks before being finally honoured.

Treaty of Rome   The Treaty of Rome was signed in 1957 and brought into being the **EEC** of which Great Britain became a member in 1972. In that year the European Communities Act was passed by the Parliament of the UK to make the provisions of the Treaty part of the law of the UK as from 1 January 1973.

In a referendum in 1975 the electorate decided by a majority to remain in the EEC.

See **European Economic Community.**

Trial balance   A trial balance is taken in order to see that all the accounts in the **ledger** have been posted properly. It is made before the accounts have been closed for the month or the quarter of the year, and generally is a preliminary for getting out a **balance sheet**. The total of the debit balance of all the accounts must equal the total of the credit balances, including the cash and bank balances from the cash book.

If the totals of these two columns balance the account is arithmetically correct.

Tribunals   There are now many laws and regulations covering aspects of life such as rent and industrial relations. Sometimes disputes occur in these areas which need to be resolved, and administrative tribunals have been set up to deal with such problems. Each type of tribunal specialises in one type of dispute—eg, industrial, immigration, transport.

Trustee Savings Bank   Today the TSB offers a comprehensive range of money transmission and deposit-taking services, and has many branches all over the country.

The Central Trustee Savings Bank (CTSB) was set up in 1973 (members are the regional TSBs) with offices in the City of London and is a functional member of the Committee of the London Clearing Bankers. It provides the TSBs with banking and clearing services, though the CTSB takes no part in its administration.

In 1976 the TSB Act allowed TSBs to pay trustees and to widen their investment spread; it also gave them permission to carry on business as bankers. Cheque accounts have been introduced; the TSB also launched unit trusts which have since become a unit-linked life assurance operation.

The group will be publicly floated in 1986. Had the TSB been owned by the government—or even its depositors—this would have been relatively simple. As it is, nobody knows who 'owns' the company that is being sold. The proceeds of the flotation will stay within the TSB and give it a capital boost.

The TSB has the largest personal banking base of any banking group in the UK, though its branch network and total deposits are smaller than those of the big **clearing banks**. It has interests in **credit cards, insurance, hire-purchase**, and car rentals, and is now an all-round financial services group.

Trustee status   Used with reference to ordinary shares of those companies which meet the requirements of the 'wider range' investments defined by the Trustee Investments Act 1961. Briefly, trustee status means that the company is UK registered, has paid-up **capital** of at least £1 million, and has paid a **dividend** for at least the last five years.

Trusts   A commercial trust is a large financial and industrial combination of firms 'federated' for common policies on price, output, etc, but otherwise independent in domestic matters. The aim of trusts is partly monopolistic. The firms involved in a trust are all in the same or similar industries or industrial chains and are often vertically integrated. Trusts can be distinguished from conglomerates which are combinations of firms covering many diverse industries.

Trusts can be investigated under British anti-monopoly legislation if they control 25% or more of the output or supply of a monopoly.

See also **investment trusts, unit trusts.**

'Turn'   The difference between a buying and selling price where business done has resulted in a profit. To 'make a turn' means to buy and sell at a profit. See **jobber.**

Turnover (of a business)   The total net sales during a trading period—ie, the total gross sales less returns inwards.

U

uberrima fides   See **utmost good faith**

ultra vires (Latin) 'Beyond one's power of authority'. Legal phrase used particularly with regard to the limitation of the legal or constitutional powers of a person, court, company or corporation.

In company law anything done by a company outside the powers given in the **Memorandum of Association** is *ultra vires* and void; nor can the company make it valid even if every member assents to it, because the rule is framed for the protection of future shareholders and the public at large, who may have dealings with the company.

Acts, however, beyond the powers of the *directors* only may be ratified by the shareholders. Acts *ultra vires* the **Articles of Association** can be indirectly cured by altering the Articles in the proper manner.

Unconfirmed credits   See **letter of credit**

Underwriters   Underwriters are members of **Lloyds**; there are 18,500 members in 430 *syndicates*. Most of the members are private individuals who accept unlimited liability. They guarantee that the required amount of money will be available for an insurance risk.

Underwriting of share issue   An arrangement by which a company is guaranteed that an issue of shares will raise a given amount of cash, because the underwriters, for a small commission, undertake to subscribe for any of the issue not take up by the public. (See **Issuing Houses**).

Unemployment Term applied officially to the condition of those capable of, and available for, remunerative work and registered for, but unable to secure, employment.

The demand for labour is directly associated with economic activity, but a state of 'full employment' does not necessarily mean there is no unemployment.

Frictional unemployment is the result of temporary readjustments between the supply of and demand for labour, and may be met by increasing the mobility of workers or by ensuring that the supply of workers in any one place has the qualifications required.

Structural unemployment is the result of the demands on an industry slackening. Structural unemployment tends to be regionally restricted.

The government employment policy lies in retraining the unemployed (see MSC) and the designation of certain areas as 'Enterprise Zones' where employment is encouraged through tax and rates relief.

Unfair Contract Terms Act 1977 This Act makes restrictive clauses in a contract inoperable, while others can apply only if they are adjudged to be fair and reasonable. Guarantees can never exclude or restrict liability for loss or damage caused by goods which are defective.

Unincorporated associations A body which has not been authorised by law to act as one individual—ie, not made into a **corporation** or **limited company**, and not enjoying limited liability. Examples of unincorporated associations are partnerships, trade unions and social clubs.

Unit costs See **costs**

United Nations Commission for Trade and Development (UNCTAD)/United Nations Food and Agriculture Organisation

UNESCO

(FAO) All **EEC** states are members of these organisations, and also of other UN subsidiary bodies. At the general assemblies of these organisations they combine in their efforts to try to arrive at a common policy—on development aid, trade preferences for developing countries, special measures in favour of the least-developed countries, and similar issues.

United Nations Educational, Scientific and Cultural Organisation (UNESCO) The purpose of this organisation is to 'contribute to peace and security by promoting collaboration among the nations through education, science and culture in order to further universal respect for justice, for the rule of law, and for the human rights and fundamental freedoms which are affirmed for the peoples of the world, without distinction of race, sex, language or religion, by the Charter of the United Nations'.

United Nations Organisation The UK became an original member of the UN and subscribes to the Charter which, as its constitution, sets out the rules. The chief of these are—
all members are equal;
international disputes must be settled by peaceful means;
force will not be used in any way not allowed by the Charter;
they will assist the UN in any action it takes.

The General Assembly which meets in New York every September resembles an international Parliament, and every member state is represented equally, having one vote each.

The Security Council is primarily responsible for keeping international peace.

An important achievement of the UN was the Universal Declaration of Human Rights, proclaimed in 1948.

UNICEF (United Nations International Children's Emergency Fund) and the judicial arm of the International Courts of Justice are associated with the UN.

USA initiative (British Overseas Trade Board) As part of the BOTB Export USA campaign, eight market sectors have been identified in which British companies are well placed to succeed. Reports are available on them all, and are available from the BOTB.

Unit costing A system of costing used where production is continuous and the unit of cost identical throughout, eg in coal mining where the unit of cost is a tonne of coal.

Unit shop/unit trader See **sole trader**

Unit trusts Unit trusts are those where groups of small investors pool their resources to buy shares through a professionally managed company. Each unit is spread over a large number of investments, thereby reducing the risk of loss to the small investor.

A unit trust is a legal trust and so an investor only holds units and does not become a **shareholder**.

Unlimited liability Some corporations choose not to have the advantages of **limited liability**. Usually these concerns are very small and their liability in the event of failure would not be considerable.

Sole traders and partnerships always have unlimited liability and in the event of failure are liable to the limits of the personal wealth of one or all owners of the business.

Unlisted security One which has not been admitted to the *Official List*. Usually, the issuer will be an unlisted company, but not always. It is not uncommon for a company to apply to the **Stock Exchange** for its ordinary shares to be listed but not its loan stocks, or vice versa.

Special provisions are made for newer and smaller companies admitted to the Unlisted Securities Market. Though not given the status of a listed company, these companies sign a 'general undertaking' to obey the Stock Exchange rules.

Unsecured loan stock (ULS) A type of **debenture.**

Unsolicited Goods and Services Act 1971 Goods sent by a supplier to anyone who has not requested them are 'unsolicited' and under this Act it is illegal to demand money from those who receive such goods. If the recipient asks for the goods to be removed and no action is taken to do so, the goods become the property of the recipient. If no action is taken by the recipient and the goods are not collected by the sender within six months they automatically become the property of the recipient.

Utilities   The basic concept connected with demand is that before there is a demand for any kind of good or service it must possess utility for those who want to buy it; it must have a capacity to satisfy a desire or serve a purpose. As long as a commodity or service gives satisfaction in some form to those who demand it, it possesses utility in the economic sense.

Total utility is the total satisfaction which is derived from the possession of a commodity though there might come a point where total utility has reached a maximum and a further supply would not be wanted.

Marginal utility is the satisfaction of possessing one more unit of any commodity, or the satisfaction lost by giving up one unit. Choice is fundamental to economic life, but only when an item's marginal utility to the consumer exceeds the marginal utility of the income that must be given up to buy it, is that item actually bought.

Utmost good faith (uberrima fides)   A contract of **insurance** is voidable if any fact is withheld by either party which may affect the judgment of the other.

   At the time of completing the proposal form, it is expected that the person taking out the insurance, or assurance, will acquaint the insurer with all the true facts, and any risk the insurer accepts is based on what he believes to be the true facts. The would-be policy holder also has a right to be provided by the insurer with complete information regarding the proposed contract.

V

Valuation of assets   The valuation of assets shown on a **balance sheet**, which has regard to **depreciation** and outstanding debts, is necessarily an estimate only of the assets of the business as a going concern. It is impossible to make an actual test unless the business is wound up, its assets converted into cash and its liabilities paid off. Only then could it be said that the valuations were fair estimates and the balance sheet a true picture of the financial position. The only action possible without this is to ensure there are no overstatements of value, and all precautions taken to present a true and honest statement.

Valuation of stock account   It is unusual to value stock at cost price, but if there is a current fall in prices the value should be at the current market price. On the other hand, if the current price is rising, there should be no marking-up of stock values. The rise may be temporary and it is always unwise to overstate profits and allow inflated values to appear on the **balance sheet**.

Value added tax (VAT)   This is a tax levied by the government on goods and services by way of business; it is therefore a commercial tax. A standard rate of tax is payable on any goods and services which fall within the scope of the tax; it is collected by HM **Customs and Excise**.

Zero-rated goods and services carry no Value Added Tax.

Whenever a trader buys goods or services to which VAT applies, he receives from the supplier a tax invoice indicating the cost of the goods and the tax charged on them. When, in turn, the trader supplies taxable goods and services to his customers he charges them tax at the same rate. At regular intervals, normally every quarter, the trader makes a tax return to the Customs and Excise, showing the tax charged to him (input tax) and the tax he has charged his customers (output tax) and will pay the difference.

Tax point is the time when VAT becomes chargeable and is usually the date when goods or services are delivered or invoiced.

VAT is an *indirect* tax.

Value analysis/value engineering   The critical examination of a product, its functions and component parts, with the objective of producing a product to equally high standards at the least total cost. The exercise is carried out by a team of investigators drawn from a cross-section of functional managers. These may include representatives from marketing, costing, purchasing and work study as well as production or engineering staff, whose specialist knowledge may bring new ideas to augment those of the designer.

Value quotas   See **quota licences**

Variable costs   See **costs** (of production)

Variable pricing   The price of one commodity, produced by the same supplier, may vary in price. Two reasons are—
the granting of cash, quantity or trade discounts;
'off-peak' or 'out-of-season' pricing—cf the cheap day-returns of BR which put an embargo on the use of rush-hour trains, and hotel prices which escalate during school holidays when they are most popular.

Variable proportions, law of   This is also called the law of non-proportional returns. It is commonly known as the **law of diminishing returns**.

Variety chain stores   The chain store is a multiple which sells a variety of goods; it is one of a large number of branch shops, each of which usually exhibits the same appearance, especially in the shop front and window design.

Velocity of circulation See **income velocity of circulation of money**

Vending machines A slot-machine which can provide a large range of goods, including cigarettes, drinks, packaged meals, etc. They are useful out of shop hours or on premises away from a normal retail outlet.

Vertical integration (of businesses) occurs where a holding company controls all the stages of a particular product by taking over the companies which supply components.

Vicarious liability (Law of tort) In general a person is only liable for a **tort** committed by himself (strict liability) but he may be *vicariously liable* for the faults of another if that person is his servant (employee) if the tort is done while carrying out his duties.

Viewdata The name for a class of information services by which a specially adapted television set or a computer terminal is linked via the public telephone network to a host computer. The public service in this country is called Prestel but a number of large companies and institutions operate their own private viewdata systems, allowing information retrieval to staff and paying subscribers.

Visible balance/visible trade (International trade) The excess of imports over exports, or exports over imports is called the **balance of trade**,—this is the figure for 'visibles'—ie, trade in *goods*.
   It is an unfavourable balance if imports are greater than exports.

volenti non fit injuria (Law of tort) 'No wrong is done to one who consents'. An occupier may limit his liability by requiring a visitor to accept the risk of coming onto the premises by placing a warning notice—provided the visitor is reasonably safe.

Volume quotas See **quota licences**

Voluntary liquidation/voluntary winding-up (of businesses)   In the case of a voluntary winding-up either a member or a creditor petitions the Court which makes a winding-up order. A liquidator is appointed who proceeds to wind up the affairs of the company by realising the assets and paying off the creditors. When this is done the company is dissolved and ceases to exist.

Voluntary Projects Programme   See **Manpower Services Commission**

Voyage charters   In maritime law a charter-party is a contract between the owner or master of a ship and the person who hires the ship for the purpose of conveying goods from one port to another. If the vessel is hired for a particular voyage it is covered by a *voyage charter*.

Voyage policy (Marine insurance)   See **hull insurance**

W

Wages Wages are the price of labour or that part of wealth (the produce of the earth) which is paid to the worker for the use of his labour.

Waiver The act of refraining from claiming, demanding, taking or enforcing.

Wants The *needs* of mankind are for food (and water), clothing and shelter.

Wants are not needed for survival, but production is undertaken in order to supply people's wants. The goods and services produced are called 'utilities'—'things which have the power to satisfy wants'.

Warehousing Warehousing is the method used to store manufactured goods until they are required, and is an essential part of the production process—the commercial service which enables consumers to obtain their goods at the right time, at the right place, in the right quantity and the right condition. 'Condition' is particularly important—it is the warehouseman's obligation to keep the goods in saleable condition (eg, frozen foods which might go bad, metal objects which might rust, etc.), and make seasonal goods like Christmas crackers and beach toys available at the right time.

The traditional warehouse has been eliminated by the large supermarket chains who provide their own warehousing services, and this is an area where the wholesaler as a warehouseman has been affected. The **cash and carry warehouses** and the **retailer-**

wholesaler co-operatives, both of which cater for the small retailer, have also affected traditional warehousing.

Traditionally warehouses have been owned by wholesalers whose function must be performed by someone in the chain of production even if his traditional role is disappearing. It is impossible to consider warehousing without considering the position of the wholesaler whose role and function is discussed fully under its own heading.

See **bonded warehouse.**

Warrant A special kind of option, given by a company to holders of a particular security, giving them the right to subscribe for future issues, either of the same or some other security.

Wealth The wealth of a country is determined by its resources. A nation's wealth consists of its lands, minerals, forests, crops, railways, canals, factories, warehouses, dwelling-houses and the great mass of consumable goods lying in warehouses, shops, etc.

Economic growth means an increase in the national income (or national wealth) in real terms—it means there are more goods and services about and the country is wealthier.

Welfare The welfare of the work force, both physically and socially, is the responsibility of the personnel department, as also is the implementation of all Acts regarding the health and safety of staff. See also **employment legislation.**

Which? The magazine of the **Consumers' Association.**

White Paper Before a government bill is introduced the government may issue to the press and public a 'Green Paper' explaining the proposals with a view to creating public discussion. This is followed by a 'White Paper' outlining the proposals more fully; after further consultation and discussion with interested bodies the Bill is submitted to the **Cabinet**, put into proper legal wording by lawyers who specialise in such work; it is then introduced into **Parliament**.

Whole-life policies These provide for a sum to be payable on the death of the insured.

Wholesaler Whatever commodity he may deal in, the wholesaler is a middleman, an intermediary in the chain of distribution, and the profit he makes must necessarily add to the cost of the goods to the final consumer.

If he deals in raw materials the wholesaler may act as a link between the different branches of an industry, or he may be a source of supply to the retailer.

The wholesaler has an important function in the chain of distribution and even if he is 'eliminated'—such as when a large retailing group buys direct from a manufacturer and delivers to its own outlets—the work he would have performed must still be done by somebody in the organisation.

These functions include buying in bulk and breaking bulk; taking on the risk that demand for the goods may cease, the price drop, stock deteriorate or become out of date; the wholesaler is also responsible for the safeguarding of goods when in transit or in a warehouse.

The traditional wholesaler buys from the manufacturer and sells to the retailer. To the manufacturer his services enable the production lines to be cleared, and often the whole marketing function (advertising, packaging, branding, etc.) is performed by the wholesaler. His position in the chain gives him the opportunity to mediate between the manufacturer and retailer and also, through the retailer, to learn the views of the consumer.

Very importantly the 'time gap' between manufacturing and retailing is covered by the wholesaler.

To the retailer the wholesaler is a constant source of supply, allowing him to stock up to suit his own requirements. For the retailer the wholesaler breaks bulk, gives credit, offers a choice of wares, and will transport the goods if required.

The consumer is usually unaware of the services he receives from the wholesaler, but is is through him that a steady flow of goods is maintained in the shops and he is the one who, through information obtained from retailers, provides 'feedback' to the manufacturer of consumer preferences. An efficient wholesaling transport system is also effective in helping to keep down the price of goods.

A modern wholesaling venture is the **cash and carry warehouse**. Large **mail order** firms which sell from catalogues are wholesalers operating from warehouses.

See **physical distribution.**

Winding-up (of companies)   A company may cease to exist by winding up (**liquidation**). There are two principal ways in which a company may be wound up: one is by voluntary liquidation, the other is by a compulsory winding-up order by the Court.

A liquidator is appointed who proceeds to wind up the affairs of the company by realizing the assets and paying off the creditors. When this is done the company is dissolved and ceases to exist.

With particular average (WPA)   This is an 'against all risks' (aar) policy. It covers not only complete loss, but any particular loss or injury which may be suffered in marine transit. ('Average' in **marine insurance** means expense or loss at sea).

Woolsack   Seat of the Lord High Chancellor in the House of Lords, where as a politician he is speaker of that House.

Work legislation   See **employment legislation**

Work measurement   The analysis and timing of a work task over a period of time in order to arrive at a correct time to do that job. Tasks are broken down into small elements and each element is watched and timed several times. The observer must decide how quickly or slowly the job is being carried out in relation to a standard—this is called 'rating'. The times for each element are added together and an allowance added to the total for fatigue, rest or contingencies. The result becomes the standard time for the job.

Work study   The scientific study of work tasks to establish standards against which individual performance may be compared for planning and control purposes. There are two major components to work study: method study and work measurement which are explained under their separate headings.

Worker directors (of companies)   An employee of a **limited company** who is appointed to the **board of directors.**

Working capital (of businesses)   Amount of capital needed to carry on a business from day to day. It is calculated by deducting current liabilities from current assets.

A firm should never allow itself to run short of working capital. The buying of too many fixed assets is called over-capitalisation and produces this situation. The minimum working capital ratio (the ratio between current assets and current liabilities) should ideally be 1:1.

Working party   A committee of experts appointed to investigate and advise on a particular issue.

World Aid Section   Finance for projects and programmes totalling billions of pounds every year as arranged through international aid agencies such as the World Bank. As Britain contributes, UK companies are eligible to tender for the resulting contracts.

Advance information covering the full range of agencies is brought together by the **BOTB** and is available to UK firms.

World Bank   See **International Bank for Reconstruction and Development**

Worldscale   An international standard rate of charges for the chartering of bulk carriers.

XYZ

Yearly plan See **National Savings**.

Yield on shares The yield on a share is the profit gained by the investment. This is worked out, not on the face value of the security, but on the market price.

$$\text{Yield} = \frac{\text{par value}}{\text{market value}} \times \text{rate of dividend percentage}$$

Youth Training Scheme See **Manpower Services Commission**

Zero-rated (VAT) Zero-rated goods are those on which the purchaser pays no Value Added Tax.

ABBREVIATIONS

A1   first-class, first rate (at Lloyds)
aar   Against all risks
ACAS   Advisory, Conciliation and Arbitration Service
a/d   after date
ad hoc (Latin)   for a particular purpose
ad val   *ad valorem* (Latin); according to value
AGM   Annual General Meeting
agt   agent
AMD   Aggregate Monetary Demand
APR   Annual Percentage Rate
av   average
a.v.   *ad valorem* (Latin); according to value

b/d   brought down
B/D   bank draft
B/E   Bill of Exchange
b/f   brought forward
bkpt   bankrupt
B/L   bill of lading
B/N   banknote
BNEC   British National Export Council
BNOC   British National Oil Corporation

BOTB   British Overseas Trade Board
BR   British Rail
BRB   British Railways Board
BREL   British Rail Engineering Ltd
BRS   British Road Services
BSI   British Standards Institution
BTG   British Technology Group

CAA   Civil Aviation Authority
CAB   Citizen's Advice Bureau
CACM   Central American Common Market (South America)
CADCAM   Computer-aided design/computer-aided manufacture (Info. Tech.)
CADMAT   Computer-aided design, manufacture and test
c & f   cost and freight
cap   capital
CAP   Common Agricultural Policy
CARICOM   Caribbean Community and Common Market
CB   Cash book
CBA   Cost benefit analysis
CBI   Confederation of British Industry

CC   County Council
CCT   Common Customs Tariff (EEC)
C/D   Certificate of Deposit
CDA   Co-operative Development Agency
c.div.   *cum dividend*; with dividend
CET   Common External Tariff
CH   Clearing House (Banking), Customs House
cif, c, i & f   cost, insurance and freight (sometimes cfi)
C/N   credit note
co   company
COD   cash on delivery
COI   Central Office of Information
Comecon   Communist Economic Community (Council for Mutual Economic Assistance)
comm   commission
Consols   Consolidated Funds
cont   contract
COREPER   (French abbreviation) Committee of Permanent Representatives (EEC)
CPU   central processing unit
cr   credit, creditor
C/R   company's risk
CRS   Co-operative Retail Society
CSI   Council for the Securities Industry
CSO   Central Selling Organisation
CT   Community Transit
cum.div.   *cum dividend*; with dividend
cum pref   cumulative preference
CWS   Co-operative Wholesale Society

D/A   documents against acceptance
DAS   Disablement Advisory Service (MSC)
DCE   Domestic Credit Expansion
DCF   discounted cash flow
D/D   days after date
deb   debenture
def   deferred
DES   Department of Education and Science
dft   draft
DHSS   Department of Health and Social Security
disc   discount
div   dividend, division
DNS   Department of National Savings
DOE   Department of the Environment
D/P   documents against payment
dr   debit, debtor, doctor
DSO   Defence Sales Organisation
DTI   Department of Trade and Industry

ECGD   Export Credit Guarantee Department
ECOWAS   Economic Community of West African States
ECS   *échantillons commerciaux* (commercial samples)
ECSC   European Coal and Steel Community
ECU   European Currency Unit
EDC   Economic Development Committee
EEC   European Economic Community
EFTA   European Free Trade Association
EFTS   Electronic Funds Transfer System

EGM   Extraordinary General Meeting
EIB   European Investment Bank
EMS   European Monetary System
enc   enclosure
E & OE   errors and omissions excepted
ERC   Employment Rehabilitation Centre (MSC)
EURATOM   European Atomic Energy Community
EXBO   Export Buying Offices Association
ex div   ex dividend

faa   free of all average (marine insurance)
fac   facsimile
FAO   (United Nations) Food and Agriculture Organisation
faq   fair average quality
fas   free alongside ship
FEOGA   (French initial letters) European Agricultural Guidance and Guarantee Fund
FFI   Finance for Industry (now replaced by Investment in Industry—3i)
fga   free of general average (marine insurance)
FHA   Finance Houses Association
FIFO   first in, first out (of stock)
fo, fol   folio
fob   free on board
for   free on rail
fpa   free of particular average (marine insurance)
FT   *Financial Times*
fwd   forward

g/a   general average (marine insurance)
GAFTA   Grain and Feed Trade Association
GATT   General Agreement on Tariffs and Trade
GDP   Gross Domestic Product
GNP   Gross National Product
grn   goods received note

HC   House of Commons
HL   House of Lords
HMC   Her Majesty's Customs
HMSO   Her Majesty's Stationery Office
HO   Home Office
HP   hire-purchase

3i   Investors in Industry
IBELS   Interest-Bearing Eligible Liabilities
IBRD   International Bank for Reconstruction and Development
ic   in charge
ICS   International Chamber of Shipping
ICCH   International Commodities Clearing House
ILO   International Labour Organisation
IMF   International Monetary Fund
ISO   International Organisation for Standardisation
IT   Information Technology
ITUSA   Information Technology Users' Standards Association

JET   Joint European Torus (EEC)

Abbreviations

LAFTA   Latin American Free Trade Association
L/C   letter of credit
LDC   Less developed country
LDMA   London Discount Market Association
LIFFE   London International Financial Futures Exchange
LOCH   London Options Clearing House
LS   *locus sigilli* (Latin); the place of the seal
LIFO   last in, first out

MAP   Microelectronics Application Project (IT)
MBO   management by objectives
MD   managing director
MEP   Member of the European Parliament
mfr   manufacturer
MICR   magnetic ink character recognition
MIDA   Maritime Industrial Development Area
MIP   marine insurance policy
MISP   Microelectronics Industry Support Programme (IT)
MLR   Minimum Lending Rate
MOD   Ministry of Defence
MSC   Manpower Services Commission
MTFS   medium-term financial strategy (of government)

NATO   North Atlantic Treaty Organisation
NBFI   Non-Bank Financial Intermediaries
NCB   National Coal Board
NEB   National Enterprise Board (replaced by BTG)

nem con   No-one contradicting
nem diss   No-one dissenting
NEDC   National Economic Development Council
NEDO   National Economic Development Office
NFC   National Freight Consortium
NI   National Insurance
nom   nominal
NPV   no par value (Stock Exchange); net present value
NRDC   National Research Development Corporation (replaced by BTG)

o/a   on account
O & M   Organisation and Method
o/c   overcharge; out of charge (Customs)
OCR   optical character recognition
o/d   on demand; overdraft; overdrawn
OECD   Organisation for European Co-operation and Development
OFT   Office of Fair Trading
OFTEL   Office of Telecommunications
OPEC   Organisation of Petroleum Exporting Countries
OR   Official Receiver; Operational Reserach; Owner's Risk
o/s   outstanding
OTC   Over-The-Counter (market in unlisted securities)

P and L   profit and loss
PAYE   pay as you earn
PC   Privy Councillor

P/E (Ratio)   price/earnings (ratio)
PEP   Projects and Export Policy Division (BOTB)
PER   Professional and Executive Recruitment
PESC   Public Expenditure Survey Committee
pft   profit
PLA   Port of London Authority
plc   public limited company
PO   Post Office, Postal Order
PR   Public Relations
PSBR   Public Sector Borrowing Requirement
PSL   Private Sector Liquidity
PSO   Public Services Obligation (British Rail)
PTE   Public Transport Executive (British Rail)

QB   Queen's Bench
QC   Queen's Counsel

R & D   Research and Development
ROI   Return on investment
RO-RO   Roll-on, roll-off (ferries)
RPI   Retail Price Index

SAYE   save as you earn
SDR   Special Drawing Rights
SERPS   State Earnings-Related Pension Scheme
SITPRO   Simplification of International Trade Procedures
S/N   shipping note
STA   Skill Training Agency (MSC)
std   standard
STD   Subscriber Trunk Dialling

stg   sterling

TSB   Trustee Savings Bank
TUC   Trades Union Congress
TVEI   Technical and Vocational Education Initiative (MSC)
TWI   Training within industry

ULS   unsecured loan stock
UNCTAD   United Nations Commission for Trade and Development
UNEP   United Nations Environment Programme
UNESCO   United Nations Educational, Scientific and Cultural Organisation
UNFAO   United Nations Food and Agriculture Organisation
UNO   United Nations Organisation
USM   Unlisted Securities Market
U/W   underwriter

v   *versus* (Latin); against
V.D.U.   visual display unit
VLCC   very large crude carrier
VLSI   very large scale integration

WB   Waybill
whf   wharf
WHO   World Health Organisation
w.i.p.   work in progress

xc, xcp   ex (without) coupon
xd; ex. div.   ex (without) dividend
x.int   ex (without) interest
YTS   Youth Training Scheme